THE EDGES OF THE EARTH IN ANCIENT THOUGHT

THE EDGES OF THE EARTH IN ANCIENT THOUGHT

GEOGRAPHY, EXPLORATION, AND FICTION

James S. Romm

PRINCETON UNIVERSITY PRESS PRINCETON, NEW JERSEY

Published by Princeton University Press, 41 William Street,
Princeton, New Jersey 08540
In the United Kingdom: Princeton University Press,
Chichester, West Sussex

Library of Congress Cataloging-in-Publication Data

Romm, James S.
The edges of the earth in ancient thought : geography,
exploration, and fiction / James S. Romm.
p. cm.
Includes bibliographical references and index.
ISBN 0-691-06933-6
ISBN 0-691-03788-4 (pbk.)
1. Classical literature–History and criticism.
2. Geography in literature. I. Title
PA3015.G44R65 1992
809'.93591—dc20 91-25748 CIP

This book has been composed in Linotron Galliard

Princeton University Press books are printed
on acid-free paper and meet the guidelines
for permanence and durability of the Committee
on Production Guidelines for Book Longevity
of the Council on Library Resources

First Princeton paperback printing, 1994

Printed in the United States of America

10 9 8 7 6 5 4 3 2

For Isabel, Eva, and Esther

If one is disturbed by the evidence that speculation played so large a role in the beginnings of history and geography, which, like most of the sciences, were founded by the Greeks, one may be comforted by the reflection that in all things the factor of greatest importance is the idea; once that is put forward, positive and negative evidence is bound to be discovered, and upon the data thus brought to light a structure can gradually arise that may rightly demand the assent of a schooled intelligence.

—William Arthur Heidel, "A Suggestion Concerning Plato's Atlantis," 228

The business of the philosopher, as I believe, includes geography as much as any other science; and it is geography we have now chosen to examine.

—opening sentence of Strabo's *Geographies*

Contents

Acknowledgments xi

Works Frequently Cited xiii

Introduction
Geography as a Literary Tradition 3

One
The Boundaries of Earth 9

Boundaries and the Boundless 11
Ocean and Cosmic Disorder 20
Roads around the World 26
Herodotus and the Changing World Picture 32
Aristotle and After 41

Two
Ethiopian and Hyperborean 45

The Blameless Ethiopians 49
The Fortunate Hyperboreans 60
Arimaspians and Scythians 67
The Kunokephaloi 77

Three
Wonders of the East 82

Before Alexander 83
Marvel-Collectors and Critics 94
The Late Romance Tradition 109

Four
Ultima Thule and Beyond 121

Antipodal Ambitions 124
The North Sea Coast 140
The Headwaters of the Nile 149
The Atlantic Horizon 156

Five
Geography and Fiction 172

Ocean and Poetry 176
The Voyage of Odysseus 183
Pytheas, Euhemerus, and Others 196
The Fictions of Exploration 202

Epilogue
After Columbus 215

Index 223

Acknowledgments

SINCE THIS BOOK has taken shape at three different institutions it has benefited from my consultations with a great number of people. Among the members of the Princeton Comparative Literature and Classics Departments who saw its genesis, I would especially like to thank the following for their advice and support: Froma Zeitlin, Charles Segal, Alban Forcione, Richard Martin, Bill Levitan, David Quint, and Tony Grafton. The anonymous readers of Princeton University Press helped to reveal the problems of this original version, while Joanna Hitchcock generously encouraged me to revise; my colleagues at Cornell then contributed to the process of revision, in particular Jeff Rusten, Fred Ahl, Piero Pucci, Bill Kennedy, Phil Mitsis, and Jim Tyler of the Olin Rare Book Room. Most recently Bill Mullen of Bard College and Rob Brown of Vassar have given advice and have lent much-needed computer equipment, while Valerie Jablow and Bill Laznovsky of Princeton University Press have aided in the final preparation of the manuscript.

My parents, my family, and friends have helped in ways that I cannot even begin to acknowledge; and my grandmothers, to whom the book is dedicated, made the task worthwhile simply by being interested.

As a final note I would like to thank those who taught me at Yale and at Princeton, without whose guidance I might never have discovered the *alii orbes* lying beyond my own horizons of expectation. Among those from whom I, and many others, have gained much, let me mention four: Jack Winkler, Art Hanson, John Herington, and Bob Fagles. It is a source of great sadness to me that neither Jack nor Art lived to see the completion of this book; I can only hope they would have been pleased to see how much they contributed to it.

Works Frequently Cited

AJP = *American Journal of Philology*

Aly = W. Aly, "Die Entdeckung des Westens," *Hermes* 62 (1927): 299–341.

Aujac (1966) = Germaine Aujac, *Strabon et la science de son temps* (Paris 1966).

Ballabriga = Alain Ballabriga, *Le soleil et le Tartare: L'image mythique du monde en Grèce archaique* (Recherches d'histoire et de sciences sociales 20, Paris 1986).

Berger (1880) = Hugo Berger, *Die Geographischen Fragmente des Eratosthenes* (Leipzig 1880).

Berger (1898) = Hugo Berger, "Die Grundlagen des Marinisch-Ptolemäischen Erdbildes," *Berichte über die Verhandlungen der königlich-sächsischen Gesellschaft der Wissenschaft zu Leipzig* (Philol.-Hist. Classe) 5 (1898): 87–143.

Berger (1903) = Hugo Berger, *Geschichte der wissenschaftlichen Erdkunde der Griechen*[2] (Leipzig 1903).

Berger (1904) = Hugo Berger, *Mythische Kosmographie der Griechen* (Leipzig 1904).

Bolton = James P. Bolton, *Aristeas of Proconnesus* (Oxford 1964).

Bunbury = E. H. Bunbury, *A History of Ancient Geography*, 2 vols. (London 1879; repr. Amsterdam 1979).

CP = *Classical Philology*

CQ = *Classical Quarterly*

CR = *Classical Review*

Carpenter = Rhys Carpenter, *Beyond the Pillars of Heracles* (Great Explorers Series, n.p., 1966).

Cary and Warmington = M. Cary and E. H. Warmington, *The Ancient Explorers* (N.Y. 1929; rev. ed. Baltimore 1963).

Casson (1974) = Lionel Casson, *Travel in the Ancient World* (London 1974).

Céard = Jean Céard, *La Nature et les Prodiges: L'Insolite aux XVIe siècle, en France* (Travaux d'Humanisme et Renaissance 158, Geneva 1977).

Diels-Kranz = H. Diels, *Die Fragmente der Vorsokratiker*[7] with additions by W. Kranz (Berlin 1954).

Dilke (1985) = O.A.W. Dilke, *Greek and Roman Maps* (Ithaca 1985).

Fiore = Lanfranco Fiore, *Le Esplorazioni Geografiche dei Greci* (Le Piccole Storie Illustrate 41, Florence n.d.).

G&R = *Greece and Rome*

Gisinger (1929) = F. Gisinger, "Geographie," *RE* sup. 4 (1929) cols. 521–685.

Gisinger (1937) = F. Gisinger, "*Oikoumenē*," *RE* bd. 34 (1937) cols. 2123–74.

Güngerich = R. Güngerich, *Die Küstenbeschreibung in der griechischen Literatur* (Orbis Antiquus 4, Münster 1950).

HSCP = *Harvard Studies in Classical Philology*

Hartog = François Hartog, *Le Miroir d'Hérodote: Essai sur la representation de l'autre* (Paris 1980); translated as *The Mirror of Herodotus*, trans. J. Lloyd (Berkeley and Los Angeles 1988).

Heidel (1933) = William Arthur Heidel, "A Suggestion Concerning Plato's Atlantis," *Proceedings of the American Academy of Arts and Sciences* 68 (1933): 206–39.

Heidel (1937) = William Arthur Heidel, *The Frame of the Ancient Greek Maps* (American Geographical Soc. Research Series 20, N.Y., 1937).

Hennig (1936) = Richard Hennig, *Terrae Incognitae: Eine Zusammenstellung und kritische Bewertung der wichtigsten vorko-*

lumbischen Entdeckungsreisen an Hand der darüber vorliegenden Originalberichte, vol. 1 (Leiden 1936).

How and Wells = W. W. How and H. J. Wells, *A Commentary on Herodotus*, vol. 1 (Oxford 1912).

Immerwahr = Henry Immerwahr, *Form and Thought in Herodotus* (Oxford 1963).

JHS = *Journal of Hellenic Studies*

Jacoby, or *Fr. Gr. H* = Felix Jacoby, *Die Fragmente der griechischen Historiker*, 3 pts. (Leiden 1957).

Kirk and Raven = G. S. Kirk and J. E. Raven, *The Presocratic Philosophers* (Cambridge 1957).

Kretschmer = Konrad Kretschmer, *Die Entdeckung Amerikas in ihrer Bedeutung für die Geschichte des Weltbildes*, chap. 1 (Berlin 1892).

Lovejoy and Boas = Arthur O. Lovejoy and George Boas, *Primitivism and Related Ideas in Antiquity* (A Documentary History of Primitivism, vol. 1, Baltimore 1935).

Mette (1936) = H. J. Mette, *Sphairopoiia* (Munich 1936).

Müller, *GGM* = Karl Müller, *Geographi Graeci Minores*, 2 vols. (Paris 1855–1861).

Müller (1972) = Karl Müller, *Geschichte der Antike Ethnographie und Ethnologische Theoriebildung von den Anfängen bis auf die byzantinischen Historiographen*, 2 vols. (Studien zur Kulturkunde 25, Wiesbaden 1972–1980).

Nicolet = Claude Nicolet, *Space, Geography and Politics in the Early Roman Empire* (Ann Arbor, Mich. 1990).

Ninck = Martin Ninck, *Die Entdeckung von Europa durch die Griechen* (Basel 1945).

van Paassen = Christiaan van Paassen, *The Classical Tradition of Geography* (Groningen 1957).

Pédech 1976 = Paul Pédech, *La géographie des Grecs* (Collection SUP 5, Paris 1976).

RE = Paully-Wissowa, *Realencyclopedie der Klassischen Altertumswissenschaft*

REG = *Revue des Études Grecques*

Ramin = J. Ramin, *Mythologie et Géographie* (Paris 1979).

Rh. Mus. = *Rheinisches Museum*

Rohde (1914) = Erwin Rohde, *Der griechische Roman und seine Vorläufer*[3] (Leipzig 1914).

Seel = Otto Seel, *Antike Entdeckerfahrten: Zwei Reiseberichte* (Zurich 1961).

TAPA = *Transactions of the American Philological Association*

Tandoi (1964) = Vincenzo Tandoi, "Albinovano Pedone e la Retorica Giulio-Claudia della Conquiste," *Studi Italiani di Filologia Classica* 36 (1964): 129–68.

Tandoi (1967) = ibid., part 2, *Studi Italiani di Filologia Classica* 39 (1967): 5–66.

Thomson = J. Oliver Thomson, *History of Ancient Geography* (Cambridge 1948).

Tozer = H. F. Tozer, *A History of Ancient Geography*[2] (Cambridge 1935).

Trüdinger = K. Trüdinger, *Studien zur Geschichte der griechisch-römischen Ethnographie* (Basel 1918).

Wright = John Kirtland Wright, *The Geographical Lore at the Time of the Crusades* (American Geographical Soc. Research Series 15, N.Y. 1925; repr. N.Y. 1965).

YCS = *Yale Classical Studies*

THE EDGES OF THE EARTH IN ANCIENT THOUGHT

Introduction

Geography as a Literary Tradition

FEW OF TODAY'S leading essayists, philosophers, or statesmen would think it necessary to undertake, as part of their development and training, a treatise on geography. Yet that is exactly what Cicero was instructed to do, during a brief retreat to his country house in Antium, by his friend and adviser Titus Pomponius Atticus. Cicero approached the task with some apprehension, as he tells Atticus in a letter dated to April of 59 B.C. (2.4.3).[1] Indeed after a few days he writes again to tell Atticus that he has almost abandoned the task (2.6.1), complaining that geography is too difficult a subject to explain and offers too few opportunities for literary embellishment; and above all, he adds, any sort of writing seems laborious to him in his current state of idleness. However, Atticus seems to have continued to urge the project even after this point, since in a further letter (2.7.1) Cicero grudgingly concedes that "we will continue to give thought to the 'Geography.' "

Whether anything further came of Cicero's planned *Geography* we do not know, and certainly nothing survives of such a work. But his exchange with Atticus on the idea reveals how important this pursuit could be for men of letters in antiquity, especially for those like Atticus whose tastes inclined toward the Hellenic end of the Mediterranean. For the ancient Greeks, and to a lesser degree for Romans as well, *geōgraphia* represented a literary genre more than a branch of physical science.[2]

[1] Nicolet 66; F. W. Walbank, "The Geography of Polybius," *Classica et Mediaevalia* 9 (1948): 155.

[2] See Francesco Prontera's lengthy development of this idea in "Prima di Strabone: Materiali per uno studio della geografia antica come genere letterario," in *Strabone: Contributi allo studio della personalità e dell'opera*, vol. 1, ed. F.Prontera (Perugia 1984) 187–256. Much the same point is made about Renaissance geographic writings by L. Olschki, *Storia letteraria delle scoperte geografiche* (Florence 1937).

It belonged far more to the cultural mainstream than to the specialized backwaters to which we, today, have assigned it. It was a tradition to which a student of *litterae humaniores* like Cicero might feel obliged to contribute (even while protesting that its dry subject matter did not lend itself to stylistic flourishes). And it made its impact felt on other literary genres to an extraordinary degree.

Of course, this attempt to see geography as a branch of popular literature in antiquity must not be carried too far; some geographers, certainly, wrote only for a highly specialized audience,[3] and their names are seldom mentioned by readers who are not themselves geographers. Moreover, the cognitive gap which separated these specialists from the public at large could at times be surprisingly large. An oft-quoted passage of Aristophanes' *Clouds* (206–17), for example, depicts an Athenian citizen who cannot make heads or tails of a map; but since the character in question is portrayed as comically ignorant throughout the play, we should not take his cartographic naïveté as being at all true to life.[4] More conclusive evidence comes from the Roman world, where both Vergil and Tacitus, remarkably, seem to have believed the earth to be flat[5]—a notion that even Pliny the Elder knew better than to accept. Nevertheless, what stands out in both authors is not so much the errors in their image of the globe as the fact that they sought to articulate that image in the first place, even in works where it was not strictly required. In a backhanded way they too attest to the literary status of geographic lore in antiquity, and to the

[3] Prontera has constructed an interesting table ("Prima di Strabone" 198–99), aligning all the ancient writers concerned with geography along a spectrum ranging from "geography" to "history." It would be a worthy task to construct a similar chart to illustrate the breadth of audience these writers were seeking to reach: Ptolemy would stand at one extreme, perhaps Dionysius Periegetes at the other.

[4] The point has been made recently by E. M. Hall, "The Geography of Euripides' *Iphigeneia Among the Taurians*," *AJP* 108 (1987): 431.

[5] Vergil *Georgics* 1.242–51; Tacitus *Agricola* 12.4, with the note by Furneaux (*Cornelii Taciti Vita Agricolae* [Oxford 1898] 96). Vergil commits another famous blunder at *Georgics* 4.211 by locating the river Hydaspes on the wrong continent.

relish with which even the nonspecialized reader must have received it.

If ancient geography can be considered a literary genre, moreover, it should also be seen as largely a narrative rather than a merely descriptive genre. It relied on narratives as a source of information: All that was known about distant lands had to be derived from someone's report of them, and the information tended to remain embedded in these reports far longer than we might expect. Not until Ptolemy's landmark *Geography*, in the second century A.D., did the record of the earth take on the objective detachment which typifies our own approach to the sciences. Earlier geographers, such as Hecataeus, Herodotus, and Strabo, went about their task chiefly by way of narratives: They sifted through a vast storehouse of traveler's tales in order to separate fact from fiction, then retold those which they thought credible enough to claim a reader's attention. More important, they often retold even those they deemed *in*credible—revealing that the geographer's science and storyteller's art, in many periods of antiquity, could not be fully detached from each other.

These connections between geography and narrative literature, unfortunately, have become all but invisible to modern-day students of the classics. Readers of Herodotus, for example, are routinely directed to skip over geographic "digressions" in the history of the Persian Wars; and the delicate vocabulary of lands, winds, rivers, and peoples, used to such striking effect by writers like Seneca and Horace,[6] has fallen into far greater disuse than the Latin language in which they wrote. Indeed our current disregard for geographical themes in classical literature can be measured by the paucity of relevant texts and translations: Poems like Manilius's *Astronomicon*, Dionysius's *Periēgēsis*, or Aratus's *Phaenomena*, though once widely read and imitated in the ancient world, have rarely appeared in print in their original languages, and English-language versions are often nonexistent. In our current taxonomy of the classics such

[6] These and other authors are discussed in Ronald Syme's brief survey "Exotic Names, Notably in Seneca's Tragedies," *Acta Classica* 30 (1987): 49–64.

texts seem the property of historians of science rather than literary critics, and are rarely allowed to impinge on or distract from our readings of more canonical works.

If modernity offers a comparatively small niche for what might be termed geographic literature, however, there is ample redress to be gained from looking to the fifteenth and sixteenth centuries. The era in which the Greek and Roman classics were first being widely published and studied was also the heyday of New-World exploration, and the cross-breeding of the two movements produced an exotic array of hybrids: On the one side, cosmographic treatises written in imitation of Plutarchan dialogues,[7] maps showing terrestrial landmasses in the shapes of mythologic figures,[8] and an atlas which bore the remarkable title *Theatrum Orbis*, "Theater of the World"; on the other, countless fictions and fantasies which portray themselves as journeys of exploration, including, most prominently, More's *Utopia* and Rabelais' *Quart Livre*. The "humanist geography"[9] which flourished in this period still has much that captivates us, even in an era when geography and humanism have increasingly little in common. In fact it was my own fascination with such curious crossovers between the realms of myth and science, and my belief that they were not original to the Renaissance but were rooted in a particular branch of classical literature, that first led me to undertake the study that went on to become this book.

It is to be regretted that "geographic literature" is not a topic that has appealed to classicists as it has to students of the Renaissance, or for that matter of the Middle Ages; but there are signs that this circumstance may now be changing rapidly. The last few years have seen increasing attention paid to issues of space, topography, and geographic structure in ancient literature, in particular among French scholars and critics. Claude

[7] Francisco Maurolico, *Cosmographia* (Venice 1543).

[8] E.g., Heinrich Bunting's map of Asia (Magdeburg c. 1585), now in the British Library. Reproduced in Mary Campbell's *The Witness and the Other World: Exotic European Travel Writing, 400–1600* (Ithaca, N.Y. 1988) 12.

[9] A rough translation of the title of de Dainville's famous study, *La Géographie des humanistes*.

Nicolet's excellent study *L'Inventaire du Monde*, now published in English as *Space, Geography and Politics in the Early Roman Empire*, reached me just as my own book was going to press, and upon opening to its introduction I was immediately encouraged to find the following sentences: "There is . . . a geography of Virgil, of Horace, and of Ovid. Indeed nearly all literature is open to a geographic reading" (8). To this striking assertion I would add a converse, that is, that nearly all geography, in antiquity, can be read as a form of literature. And it is this reading that my book has tried to achieve.

A word or two should be said about the structure I have used to present this reading. In each of the book's chapters I have dealt with a single geographical issue, or set of related issues, which emerged during a particular period of ancient culture. The result is not by any means a complete or synoptic literary survey; the topic seemed too diffuse for any attempt at an exhaustive treatment. Each chapter is meant to stand on its own, but each tries to connect with those that either precede or follow it, so as to establish at least some loose sense of historical continuity. Thus, chapter 1 is centered on Homeric and archaic literature, but ends with a section that looks ahead to the whole range of history encompassed by the book. Chapter 2 concentrates on literature of the Greek classical age, chapter 3 on Hellenistic science and scholarship, chapter 4 on Rome. The fifth chapter is the most theoretical and least grounded in history, but to the extent that it includes several Greek authors of the second century A.D. it can be said to form a capstone to the temporal progression of the whole. An epilogue then briefly traces the revival of ancient geographic literature in the Age of Exploration.

Out of consideration for the nonspecialized reader I have tried to focus my discussions on texts and authors that are widely known or, at the least, widely available in English translation. It was my wish to avoid spending much time on obscure texts or collections of fragments, which have little appeal for students of the humanities outside the discipline of classics itself. At times, however, I have been forced to deal at some length with fragmentary works, such as Ctesias's *Indika* and Aristeas's *Arimaspeia*, or to stray rather far from the beaten path of the "great books" tradition. In such cases I have sought to provide enough background information that no reader need feel left by the wayside.

Also in consideration of nonspecialists, I have translated all quotations into English, and transliterated what few Greek words I have chosen to retain. Quoted passages are taken from the editions identified as standard in the *Canon of Greek Literature* or in the *Oxford Latin Dictionary*, except where some other edition offered particular advantages (such as cross-references to a published English translation). I have appended notes or discussion where there are significant disputes over the reading of a text. All translations are my own. Greek verse passages have been rendered into prose, so that linguistic accuracy would not be sacrificed to meter; with Latin this seemed to be less of a concern, and I have retained the verse format of the originals.

One

The Boundaries of Earth

WE WHO HAVE SEEN the whole earth, either as represented on maps and globes or as reproduced in satellite photographs, find it difficult to adopt the perspective of those who have not. The image of a floating blue and green sphere, with sharply defined oceans and continents, has been so thoroughly assimilated into our mind's eye as to become intuitive. However, the great majority of mankind has lived and died without ever glimpsing this image, and even today, many isolated races remain innocent of it. For such peoples, mind must take the place of maps in giving shape and structure to the inhabited earth; where empirical data give out they employ any other means available—theory, myth, and fantasy—to define and depict the space in which they dwell.[1] To us these processes are foreign, as attested by the fact that we have no word to represent them accurately: "Geography" will not do unless modified by some adjective like "conceptual," "imaginative," "mythic," or the self-congratulatory "early."

The Greeks of the archaic and classical periods, conversely, had no word corresponding to our "geography"; neither the noun *geōgraphia* nor the verb from which it derives occur before Eratosthenes of Cyrene, that is, before the third century B.C.[2] By that time the study of the earth had already become an

[1] The process by which such images are created is discussed in several essays in *Geographies of the Mind: Essays in Honor of Historical Geosophy*, D. Lowenthal and M. J. Bowden eds. (Oxford 1976). For the Greek tradition in particular, see Christian Jacob, "The Greek Traveler's Areas of Knowledge: Myths and Other Discourses in Pausanias' *Description of Greece*," *Yale French Studies* 59 (1980): 65–85, and Berger (1904).

[2] See van Paassen 34 and n. 3, 44–45; Nicolet 60. Eratosthenes evidently used some form of the word as the title of his major treatise on geography, which is variously reported as *Geōgraphika*, *Geōgraphoumena*, and *Geōgraphia* (see Berger [1880] 17–18 and frs. III B 76, III B 112, Strabo 1.2.21).

exact science, capable, for example, of measuring the circumference of the globe to a high degree of accuracy. What the philosopher Anaximander did four centuries earlier in drawing the first known world-map would have been considered a branch of *phusiologia* or natural science by his contemporaries; similarly the great travelogue of places and peoples composed by Hecataeus, and the logs of seafarers like Scylax and Euthymenes, were considered offshoots of *historia*, as Herodotus's use of them attests. And the legends of far-off lands enshrined in the works of Homer and Hesiod, whatever their factual or scientific content, could only be characterized as *muthoi*, a word which in this context encompasses the meanings "myth," "fable," and "fiction."

It was from a mixture of these diverse sources—cosmography and natural philosophy, travelogue and traveler's tale, and above all epic poetry—that the archaic Greeks formed their notions about the structure of the earth. For this reason we may fairly lump these various sources together in the investigation that follows, even if under an artificial and anachronistic heading like "geography."

Perhaps the most fundamental act by which the archaic Greeks defined their world was to give it boundaries, marking off a finite stretch of earth from the otherwise formless expanse surrounding it. Without such boundaries both land and sea would become *apeirōn*, "boundless," and in fact they are sometimes so called in the poems of Homer and Hesiod.[3] The epithet attests to the cognitive discomfort which an unlimited extent of space could inspire, in that it is only an adjectival form of *to apeiron*, the name chosen by Anaximander for the "bound-

[3] For the connection see Hermann Fränkel, *Early Greek Poetry and Philosophy* (Oxford 1975) 262n. 22. The root meaning of the adjective *apeirōn* may be closer to "uncrossable" than "boundless" (see Charles E. Kahn, *Anaximander and the Origins of Greek Cosmology* [Columbia 1960] 231–32), which would explain how a space so designated can also be said to have *peirata* (a scholium of Porphyry on *Il.* 14.200 discusses this paradox at length; cf. *Porphyrii quaestionum Homericarum ad Iliadem pertinentium reliquiae*, ed. H. Schrader [Leipzig 1880] 189–93). However, in an era when geographic distance is measured only in terms of travel (see n. 60 below), the distinction between an unbounded land and one whose boundaries can never be reached was undoubtedly slight.

less" welter of elements from which the universe had been formed.[4] Whether Anaximander thought of this *apeiron* as "boundless" in terms of its spatial extension or internal non-differentiation, or both at once,[5] is unclear; but in either case the word implies a formlessness and diffusion that are the enemies of order and hierarchy.[6] The "boundless" earth, therefore, had to be given boundaries before it could be made intelligible. And for the archaic Greeks, who did not yet know the true extent of any of the three continents within their ken, this separation of earth from infinite space was achieved simply by deciding that, in whatever direction one traveled, the land must eventually end and water begin.

Boundaries and the Boundless

If an *apeiron* is, in linguistic terms, a space which lacks *peirata* or "boundaries," then the epic poets effectively supplied these boundaries by way of the formulaic phrase *epi peirasi gaiēs*, "at the borders of the earth." These *peirata* or "borders" are purely an imaginative construct and are conceived in only the vaguest

[4] On the nature of Anaximander's *apeiron* see Kirk and Raven 104–21; Kahn, *Anaximander* 231–9; and Uvo Hölscher, "Anaximander und die Anfänge der Philosophie," *Hermes* 81 (1953): 257–77, 385–418.

[5] On the dispute between these two positions see Kirk and Raven 109–10 and Kahn, *Anaximander*, 41–42, 236 n. 5. David Furley has recently suggested a sensible synthesis of these positions (*The Greek Cosmologists*, vol. 1 [Cambridge 1987] 28–30).

[6] Just as, in a doctrine formulated later by the Pythagoreans and by Plato, "all the fair and seasonable things that we experience arise out of the intermixture of the boundless with that which has bounds" (*Philebus* 26a12-b2). W. A. Heidel's article, "*Peras* and *apeiron* in the Pythagorean Philosophy" (*Archiv für Geschichte der Philosophie* 14 [1901]: 384–99; repr. in *Selected Papers*) contains valuable remarks on the opposition of these two concepts, and the "emotional connotations" (see 388–89) of the latter; see also C. J. de Vogel, "La théorie de l'*apeiron* chez Platon et la tradition platonicienne," *Revue de Philosophie* (1959): 21–39. A more far-reaching and comprehensive study has been undertaken by Rodolfo Mondolfo, *L'Infinito nel pensiero dell'antichità classica* (Il Pensiero Classico 5, Florence 1956); see 275–85 for remarks on the role of Ocean in this tradition.

terms; as defined by Ann Bergren in an extensive study of *peirar* and its archaic usages, they represent "the physical extremities of the earth . . . the limit of the human world."[7] At times the word *peirata* is modified by *makra*, "great," which, in this context, might refer either to their remoteness ("greatly distant") or to their extent ("encompassing the entire earth"), or, more probably, to both at once. These "borders," moreover, have no particular location, but are found at every point of the compass. Hesiod even refers to the underworld as one of the *peirata gaiēs* (*Theog*. 622), presumably because it also lies at an extreme distance from his own point of reference, although in this case as measured along a vertical rather than a horizontal axis.[8] Once, in the *Odyssey*, Odysseus uses the phrase to describe the shoreline of Polyphemus's island (9.284)—a "boundary of earth" in a less global but equally final sense.[9]

This last conception of *peirar*, as the shoreline or coast surrounding an island, is represented on the macrocosmic scale by Ocean,[10] the vast "river" thought to surround the landmass formed by Europe, Africa, and Asia. The river Ocean limits the extent of earth in all directions, acting essentially as a physical embodiment of the phrase *peirata gaiēs*; in fact the name "Ocean" is often linked with this phrase in epic poetry, and once we even find a variant *peirata Ōkeanoio*, "boundaries of

[7] *The Etymology and Uses of "Peirar" in Early Greek Poetry* (American Classical Studies 2, n.p. 1975) 22–23, 102–15; see also R. B. Onians, *Origins of European Thought* (Cambridge 1951) 310–13.

[8] Xenophanes shows a similar concern with the vertical boundaries of earth's extent (fr. 28 Diels-Kranz, Kirk and Raven p. 11); cf. Homer *Il*. 8.13–17, *Od*. 11.157.

[9] Bergren uses this passage to advance a parallel between the Cyclops' island and "the other side of the world" (*Etymology and Uses* 27–28), but this seems somewhat strained; although the island reveals certain golden-age features (see Lovejoy and Boas 303–4), it is far from "other-worldly" by comparison with other paradisical landscapes.

[10] On Ocean's role in archaic myth and cosmology, see Albin Lesky, "Okeanos," the third chapter of *Thalatta* (Vienna 1947); F. Gisinger, "Okeanos," *RE* bd. 34 (1937) cols. 2308–10; Berger (1904) 1–3; Kretschmer 35–42; and Ramin 17–26. Other sources are cited below, where the subject is explored in greater detail.

Ocean," used as an equivalent (*Od.* 11.13).[11] Even the non-Greek name of this mythical river may well bespeak its limiting function, for two plausible etymologies, deriving *Ōkeanos* from Phoenician *ma'uk* or from Sanskrit *a-çayana*, would both give it the original meaning "that which encircles" the island of earth.[12]

This scheme of an island earth surrounded by a circular Ocean became a pervasive feature of the archaic Greek world-view, dominating both literary and visual representations of the *peirata gaiēs*. For evidence of its literary impact we may turn to the two great shield ecphrases of early epic, the Shield of Achilles in *Iliad* 18 and the Shield of Heracles in the Hesiodic poem *Shield*.[13] Each of these passages envisions the world in the shape of a shield (that is, round) and girt by Ocean at the outermost rim:

[11] Similar collocations elsewhere in archaic poetry: *Cypria* fr. 7 (Athenaeus 334b), *Homeric Hymn to Aphrodite* 227.

[12] The derivation of the name *Ōkeanos* is still an open question; the first theory I have here cited is supported by A. Schulten, "Die Säulen des Herakles," in *Die Strasse von Gibraltar* by O. Jessep (Berlin 1927) 177; the second, by Berger (1904) 1-2, and Onians (above, n. 7) 249. Both theories, however, are rejected by Albin Lesky (*Thalatta* 65); see his notes for further discussion, as well as G. Germain, *Genèse de l'Odyssée* (Paris 1954) 548–50. Diodorus Siculus refers to "Ocean" as a Phoenician name (5.20.1), perhaps supporting the first theory above. Ancient etymologists usually derived the name from *ókus*, "swift," and *anuein*, "to rise," from the seeming emergence of the constellations out of its waters (see Schol. *Il.* 5.6).

[13] On the Homeric passage see Oliver Taplin, "The Shield of Achilles within the *Iliad*," *G&R* 27 (1980) and E. Vanderlinden, "Le Bouclier d'Achille," *Études Classiques* 48 (1980): 97–126; and on both Homer and Hesiod, Daremberg-Saglio's *Dictionnaire des Antiquités* s.v. "Astronomia." The importance of the shield schema in the *Iliad*, as well as the larger concept of a circumambient Ocean in archaic thought, have been assaulted in a pair of tendentious articles by L. G. Pocock, "The Nature of Ocean in Early Epic," *Proc. African Class. Assoc.* 5 (1962): 1–17, and "Note on *apsorrou Ōkeanou*," *Hermes* 88 (1960): 371–74; these have done little to change the traditional view, however. For an interesting parallel in Aristides' *Panathenaicus*, in which the earth is again compared to a shield, with Athens at its hub, see Laurent Perrot, "Topique et topographie," in *Arts et légends d'espace*, ed. C. Jacob (Paris 1981) 104–7.

And thereon Hephaestus set the great strength of river Ocean, beside the outermost rim of the shield so cleverly made. (*Iliad* 18.607–8)

Around the rim Ocean flowed, seeming as if in flood, and surrounded the entire much-embellished shield. (*Shield* 314–15)

This shared image of a circular, water-bound earth, moreover, is paralleled on a visual level in the first Greek maps of the world, which similarly portrayed the earth as a disk of land surrounded by Ocean.[14] In fact the similarity between these visual and verbal images was remarked as early as the second century A.D. by Crates of Mallos,[15] who called Achilles' shield a ***kosmou mimēma*** or "image of the world"; the parallel thereafter became a commonplace among Stoic geographers and critics.[16] (More recently scholars like J. P. Vernant[17] have gone yet further and found other, similarly circular structures attached to archaic views of the city-state, whose round perimeter walls could also

[14] Our best evidence surrounds the *pinax* of Anaximander in the sixth century, cf. Agathemerus (1.1, in Müller *GGM* 2.471); see also Herodotus 4.36, Aristotle *Meteor.* 362b15, and Geminus *Elem. Astr.* 16.4–5 for evidence of round earth-maps in the archaic age. Good discussions of early cartography in Greece can be found in Dilke chap. 2, Kubitschek in *RE* bd. 10.2 (1919) *s.v.* "Karten" (cols. 2046–51), and the authoritative *History of Cartography* by Leo Bagrow (trans. D. L. Paisey, rev. R. A. Skelton, London 1964); also Heidel (1933) 206–7. J. L. Myres's inquiry into the subject ("An Attempt to Reconstruct the Maps Used by Herodotus," *Geographical Journal* 8 [1896]: 606–31) seems to me to be highly speculative.

[15] Following the attribution to Crates of the doctrine recorded in a scholium to Aratus (*Phaen.* 26); see chap. 5, pp. 179–80, below, and Mette (1936); K. Pfeiffer, *History of Classical Scholarship*, vol. 1 (Oxford 1968) 240; and F. Buffière, *Les Mythes d'Homère et la pensée grecque* (Paris 1956) chap. 6.1.

[16] E.g., in Strabo's *Geographies* (1.1.7). See also Eustathius's comment ad loc., and, more recently, Berger (1904) 5; Aujac (1966) 21; Ballabriga 66–67; and Taplin, "The Shield of Achilles" (above, n. 13) 11.

[17] In *The Origins of Greek Thought* (Ithaca, N.Y. 1982); see, in particular, chaps. 6 and 8, "The Structure of the Human Cosmos" and "The New Image of the World." Also, by the same author, *Mythe et pensée chez les Grecs* (Paris 1966), esp. pt. 3, "L'Organisation de l'espace." For the importance of circular constructs within the realm of presocratic philosophy, see O. J. Brendel, *The Symbolism of the Sphere* (Leiden 1977).

be referred to as *peirata* or as a *periodos*; but we shall not have occasion here to pursue this line of inquiry.)

If Ocean supplied definitive *peirata* to the circle of lands, the boundaries which in turn contained Ocean were a more problematic issue. The phrase *potamos Ōkeanoio*, "river of Ocean," in Homer and Hesiod implies no clear conception of another "bank" on the farther side; in fact, early writers seem to have assumed, for lack of evidence to the contrary, that Ocean's waters stretched unbounded toward a distant horizon. Thus, the many passages in epic poetry which describe the sun and stars as arising from or setting into Ocean, and in particular Homer's assertion that Ursa Major lacks a "share of the baths of Ocean" (*Od.* 5.275, *Il.* 18.489), were taken to mean that Ocean's waters extended to the edge of the celestial dome.[18] Moreover, it is doubtful whether Homer or Hesiod had any concept of a "new world" beyond Ocean,[19] although such a concept was later attributed to them (as we shall see in chapter 4 below) by Crates and others.[20] In one intriguing passage of the *Odyssey* Circe instructs Odysseus to "cross through Ocean" (*di'Ōkeanoio perēsēis*) on his way to the underworld (10.508), but this probably means only that he should "coast" along the shore from which he embarked, not that he should seek a new land beyond Ocean.[21]

In spite of its traditional epithet "river," then, the Ocean of

[18] See Berger (1904) 2–4; E. Buchholz, *Die Homerischen Realien*, vol. 1 (Leipzig 1871) 27–33; and Gisinger (1937) col. 2313.

[19] Hesiod, for one, envisions places like the Isles of the Blessed which lie *perēn klutou Ōkeanoio*, "beyond glorious Ocean" (*Theog.* 215, 274, 294), but these are islands and not continents; see Jean Rudhardt, *La Thème de l'eau primordiale dans la mythologie grècque* (Bern 1971) 75. A curious couplet of hexameter verses quoted by Strabo (2.3.5), of unknown authorship but possibly of archaic provenance, claim of Ocean that "No bond of continental land surrounds it, but it pours forth into infinity; nothing corrupts it."

[20] See Mette (1936) on Crates' discussion of Homer's double Ethiopians, 69–74.

[21] Weiszäcker argues strongly for this interpretation in his article on "Okeanos" in Roscher's *Lexikon der Mythologie* (811). For the opposing point of view, however, see Germain, *Genèse de l'Odyssée* (above, n. 12) 529, and Lesky, *Thalatta* 69–70.

the archaic era simply stretches out into unimaginable distance, forming a region beyond the boundaries of earth which was every bit as vast and formless as Anaximander's *apeiron*. As a result of this vastitude, in fact, Ocean presents itself to the early Greeks as a terrifying and unapproachable entity. Just as a mouse placed in the center of an empty room will immediately dash toward one of the walls, so Greek sailors and seamen felt ill at ease when surrounded by large stretches of open water; they were accustomed, even when sailing the comparatively placid Aegean, to hug the coasts and stay within sight of land at all times. The prospect of sailing in waters so wide that no land could be seen was regarded with great apprehension, and open-sea voyages were attempted only under extreme duress.[22]

Two incidents recorded by Herodotus may be taken as cases in point. First, Herodotus records that Sataspes, a Persian nobleman of the early fifth century, was ordered by King Xerxes to sail around the southern coast of Africa, but fear of the distances involved made him abandon the mission:[23]

> Sataspes, son of Teaspis, an Achaemenid, did not succeed in circling Libya, though he had been sent on that mission; for, fearing the length and emptiness of the journey, he turned back. . . . After sailing out [of the Mediterranean] and rounding the promontory of Libya called Solois, he proceeded south; but, after crossing a great stretch of sea, over many months, he remained terrified of the expanse ahead, and turned back toward Egypt. (4.43)

Sataspes experienced this dread even during a coasting voyage, moreover—so that we can imagine how much greater such

[22] The point is made quite forcefully by Seel 38–49, and by Cary and Warmington 43. The Greeks experienced a similar sense of trepidation in their travels to the Black Sea, according to E. H. Minns (*Scythians and Greeks* [Cambridge 1913] 9). The much-touted Hellenic fondness for the sea has probably been over-emphasized; Benveniste reminds us that, although the Greek word for "open sea" (*pontos*) is derived from a root meaning "path," the particular implication is that of "a path in a region off-limits to normal travel" (*Problèmes de linguistique générale* [Paris 1966] 296–98). One factor influencing the tendency toward "coasting" voyages, we note, was the Greek seaman's dread of having to sleep or take his meals while still on shipboard.

[23] Heidel (1933) 207–8, in discussing this passage, notes that Africa was still considered too large to be circumnavigated in Strabo's day (see Strabo 1.2.26).

fears would become in midocean with no land in sight. The same point is illustrated by a later incident described by Herodotus, in which a Greek crew refuses to transport a group of political exiles back to their native Samos and instead drops them off at Delos (about halfway):

> That which lay beyond inspired dread in the Hellenes, who were unfamiliar with those parts; they thought the whole region was occupied by the enemy, and imagined that Samos stood as far off as the Pillars of Heracles. (8.132)

In this case, although the voyage in question is contained within the Mediterranean, the vast distance involved seems to the crew to be reminiscent of Ocean; at least, it is identified with the remote and terrifying Pillars of Heracles, which stood at Ocean's threshhold.[24]

Indeed, since the Pillars or Columns of Heracles—the name usually associated with the twin rocks standing astride the Straits of Gibraltar[25]—afforded the only known connection between the familiar Mediterranean and alien Ocean, they became a vivid symbol of the gateway or barrier between inner and outer worlds. For the most part they stood in the Greek imagination as a forbidding *non plus ultra*, a warning to mariners not to proceed any further. Pindar, for example, adopts this landmark as a paradigm of the limits to human daring, in his celebrations of victorious athletes:[26]

> Now Theron, approaching the outer limit in his feats of strength, touches the Pillars of Heracles. What lies beyond cannot be approached by wise men or unwise. I shall not try, or I would be a fool. (*Ol.* 3.43–45)

[24] In later literature see Apollonius Rhodius, *Argonautica* 4. 637–44, where the Argonauts are prevented from sailing into Ocean on the grounds that this would spell certain death (see chap. 5, pp. 194–96, below); and Seneca's first *Suasoria* (chap. 4, pp. 138–39).

[25] The location of the Pillars later had to be moved to accord with the fact that the Straits themselves had become penetrable (see Strabo 3.5.5). For modern discussions see Carpenter chap. 1; A. Schulten, "Die Säulen des Herakles" (above, n. 12).

[26] Discussed by Heidel (1933) 203–6, and Thomas Hubbard, *The Pindaric Mind: A Study of Logical Structure in Early Greek Poetry* (Leiden 1985) 11–27.

> As a man of beauty, who accomplishes feats beautiful as himself, the son of Aristophanes may set forth on supreme, manly endeavors; but not easily across the untrodden sea, beyond the Pillars of Heracles, which that hero-god set in place, as a famed witness of the furthest limit of seafaring. (*Nem.* 3.20–23)

> By the uttermost deeds of strength did these men touch the Pillars of Heracles, an achievement all their own; let none pursue valor any farther than that. (*Isthm.* 4.11–14)

In these passages Pindar measures the prowess of his athlete-patrons in geographic terms, seeing their victories as journeys into distant space; but these journeys must end, he insists, before they enter the forbidden realm of Ocean. The Pillars have here come to stand for the boundary of the human condition itself: To pass beyond them is the prerogative of god alone, or of mythic figures like Heracles who manage to bridge the human and divine.[27] (Significantly, the only human being who was thought capable of such transgression was the latter-day Heracles, Alexander the Great—as we shall see in chapter 4.)

To some extent, of course, the Pillars really were a *non plus ultra* to the early Greeks, since Phoenician naval operations, designed to protect the rich silver trade on the Atlantic coast of Spain, closed them to all non-Punic ships from the late sixth century to around 300 B.C.[28] Furthermore, there is speculation that the Phoenicians deliberately exaggerated reports of dire perils beyond the Straits in order to scare away competitors (the legend behind the proverbial expression "Phoenician lie").

[27] Even Heracles himself, moreover, crossed through this space only with the special permission of the gods (as related by Stesichorus, fr. 7). See also Diodorus Siculus 4.18.5–6, and Strabo 3.5.5, for two later accounts of the tradition behind the Pillars. Paul Fabre conducts a lengthy discussion of these in *Les Grecs et la connaissance de l'Occident* (Lille 1971) 274–94 and n. 479. See also Ramin 105–13; Leon Lacroix, "Herakles, heros voyageur et civilisateur," *Bull. de la Classe des Lettres (Acad. Royale de Belge)* 60 (1974) 34–59.

[28] Attested by Eratosthenes *apud* Strabo (17.1.19 = Berger fr. I B 9); see Schulten, "Die Säulen des Herakles" (above n. 12), esp. 181–83. Schulten's theory that the Pillars originally represented an open-door passage to the Greeks, but that their mythology changed to reflect the historical fact of the Phoenician blockade, is not well supported by the evidence.

We must be cautious, however, in using historical evidence of this kind to explain the largely mythic images which the Greeks attached to the Pillars, and to other distant-world locales as well. Even when such evidence can be accurately recovered—a tricky issue to begin with—it can at best be used to explain the genesis of a particular legend, not its subsequent development and elaboration. Thus, whatever recollection of the original Punic blockade may be contained within the Pillars myth, this landmark soon took on an independent life in the Greek imagination, and more importantly continued to loom large there long after the Phoenicians had been dislodged from the Straits.[29]

Even the Phoenicians themselves, moreover, seem to have felt uneasy and fearful when sailing in the waters outside the Pillars, as attested by what is apparently a Carthaginian explorer's log preserved from the early fifth century B.C. Hanno's *Periplous*[30] or "Coasting Voyage" describes the journey of a colonizing expedition which sailed out of the Pillars and south along the coast of Africa, perhaps as far as modern-day Sierra Leone. It reveals that Hanno, despite his willingness to tackle such a mission, was not impervious to the terrors of Ocean's expanse. As he moves farther down the African coast Hanno reports increasingly eerie phenomena: phantom music heard in the dark (14), rivers of flame (15), and a mountain named "Chariot of the Gods" that seemed to catch fire after nightfall (16). Twice in this final section (14, 16) the explorer matter-of-factly reports that his crew was becoming frightened. At his point of furthest progress Hanno encounters "hairy wild men"

[29] Furthermore, the Greeks located a second pair of forbidding rocks, the Symplegades, at the eastern end of the Mediterranean, where the Phoenicians offered no such impediment. Other such terminal pillars are cited by Heidel (1933) 204 n. 54, 219–20; for Alexander's erection of pillars in the East see the introduction to chapter 4 below. The "Phoenician lie" idea has been put forward not only by Schulten but by How and Wells in their commentary on Herodotus 3.107, and by Hennig (1936) 1.53.

[30] Edited by L. del Turco, *Annone: Il Periplo* (Florence n.d.); for discussion and translation see Carpenter 81–103; Seel 5–8, 49–55; Cary and Warmington 63–68; Fiore 41–43; Aly 317–30; and Carl Kaeppel, *Off the Beaten Track in Classics* (Melbourne 1936) chap. 2.

whom his native guides call *gorillas* (a name subsequently revived by the nineteenth-century naturalists who discovered Africa's great apes);[31] he tries to bring some of the intractable creatures back alive, but in the end must settle for killing them and taking their skins. After this encounter his fleet runs short of provisions and makes for home.

Safely returned to Carthage, Hanno apparently ordered an account of his journey to be inscribed on a votive tablet,[32] and from this inscription the *Periplous* was later—probably in Hellenistic times—translated into Greek. In this new form, as a literary text rather than as a historical document, the *Periplous* circulated widely in the Hellenic world, and was later read and discussed by Roman geographers.[33] No doubt it represented to the ancient readers who thus transmitted it a vivid, firsthand confirmation of the vastness and mystery of the realm beyond the Pillars.

Ocean and Cosmic Disorder

If the seeming infinitude of Ocean was not daunting enough to scare away mariners, moreover, other dangers were thought to render its waters unnavigable once the Pillars of Heracles had been passed. Ocean's stream was said to be thick or sluggish, holding back the progress of ships sailing on it; dense fogs and mists enveloped it; and giant sea creatures menaced passing vessels from its depths. Himilco, another Carthaginian explorer roughly contemporary with Hanno, seems to have experienced all these phenomena in the course of his voyage northward from the Straits.[34] Unfortunately the only account we possess

[31] Although it is doubtful that the *anthrōpoi agrioi* described by Hanno were true apes, since no such creatures resided in the regions he visited; see Kaeppel, *Off the Beaten Track*. The identity of these "wild men" is one of many hotly debated problems in the *Periplous*.

[32] As attested by Aelius Aristides, *Orat.* 48 Dindorf 356.2–5, 12–13.

[33] Cited by Pliny *Hist. Nat.* 2.67.169, Mela 3.90; also Arrian *Indika* 43.

[34] For Himilco see Carpenter 212–14, Hennig (1936) 79–82, Cary and Warmington 45–47, and Berger (1903) 231–32. Pliny the Elder makes brief

of the journey dates from nearly a millennium later, but its author, Avienus, may well have adapted his version directly from the explorer's own log:[35]

> Himilco the Carthaginian claimed that this space can barely be crossed in four months, as he reported he had proved himself by sailing there. For no breeze pushes the craft onward, and a torpid flow of heavy water dulls the ship's progress. He adds this as well, that there is a mass of seaweed among the waves, and, like a hedge, it impedes the prow; notwithstanding, he says, the surface of the sea does not extend into the deep, but the soil is barely covered by a little bit of water. Wild sea-creatures stand in the way on all sides, and sea-monsters swim among the sluggish and lazily crawling ships. (*Ora Maritima* 118–29)

> A dark fog enshrouds the air as if in a kind of cloak, and clouds hide the face of the deep always, and this veil remains throughout the whole of the darkened day. (*Ora Maritima* 386–89)

Though some have seen in Himilco's experience nothing more than an exaggerated account of the Sargasso Sea, where rafts of seaweed and dense fogs create very real obstacles to navigation,[36] his account is also colored by widely held mythic and folkloric notions. A formulaic phrase in epic poetry, for example, labels the open sea (or *ponton*) *ēeroeidea*, "misty" or "airy,"[37] suggesting a "cloak of fog" like that described in Avienus's

---

mention of the voyage (*Hist. Nat.* 2.67.169), the only ancient attestation besides that of Avienus.

[35] Avienus claims to have consulted Himilco's writings himself (*Ora Maritima* 412–15), though Schulten rejects the passage as an interpolation (*Avieni Ora Maritima* [Berlin 1922] 103). The claim is rejected by Bunbury as spurious (2.686–87, n. 5), but apparently accepted by Hennig (1936) 80. Detailed discussion by Aly 312–17.

[36] See Bunbury 2.703, Note A; Cary and Warmington 46; Hennig (1936) 81.

[37] The intermingling of sea and sky is also illustrated by a classical usage according to which a ship sailing the high seas was said to be *meteōra* or "in midair." In addition Aristotle, in an attempt to rationalize the mythic traditions concerning Ocean, suggests that the early poets used this name to designate the stream of water vapor circulating through the earth's atmosphere (*Meteor.* 346b16–347a7; see chap. 5, pp. 178–79, below).

poem. As regards the shallowness and torpidity of Ocean's waters, numerous ancient writers from Plato to Plutarch entertained similar ideas.[38]

In the tendency for Ocean to be seen as foggy, muddy, or both, we sense, once again, a link between this entity and the *apeiron* of Anaximander's cosmology, seen this time in terms of physical rather than spatial disorganization. That is, the "boundaries" separating earth and water, or water and air, seem to break down within the infinitude of Ocean, rendering it a murky and undifferentiated welter of elements like the *apeiron*.[39] The most dramatic illustration of this internal boundlessness comes from another explorer's log, set down somewhat later than the era we are concerned with here but revealing much the same pattern of imagery. Sometime around 300 B.C. the explorer Pytheas of Massilia became the first Greek (as far as we know) to follow Himilco's route to the North Atlantic, eventually reaching the British Isles and possibly Scandinavia.[40] His log, significantly entitled *Peri Ōkeanou* or *Concerning the Ocean*, included the following bizarre account of Ocean's northernmost extent, according to a report by Polybius (34.5.3–4 = Strabo 2.4.1 = Pytheas fr. 7a Mette):

> In these regions obtained neither earth as such, nor sea, nor air, but a kind of mixture of these, similar to the sea-lung, in which . . . earth, sea, and everything else is held in suspension; this substance is like a fusion of them all, and can neither be trod upon nor sailed upon.

As with Himilco's log we cannot be sure what pelagic phenomena (if any) lie behind this strange description, but clearly it is

[38] Plato *Timaeus* 25a, Plutarch *De Facie* 941b; see also Strabo 1.4.2, Seneca Rhetor *Suasoria* 1.1–4, and Tacitus *Agricola* 10. Commentary by Heidel (1933), esp. 203–6, and Tandoi (1964) 131–35.

[39] Jean Rudhardt discusses ancient etymologies deriving *chaŏs* from *cheō*, the verb meaning "to pour," and other attempts to associate the qualities of disorder and confusion with liquidity (*Eau primordiale* [above, n. 19] 18–20, 117).

[40] Hennig (1936) 120–37, Cary and Warmington 47–56, Carpenter chap. 5, Seel 59–61, Thomson 143–51. More specialized sources for Pytheas can be found in chap. 4 nn.82, 84, below.

steeped in earlier conceptions like Anixamander's *apeiron* and other kinds of primeval murk. In particular Pytheas's reference to the sea-lung—probably a kind of jellyfish[41]—seems designed to illustrate the intermixture of all matter into a single, homogenous gel, thick enough to impede the seafarer yet too soft for travel by foot.

This physiologic aspect of Ocean's boundlessness becomes more intelligible when seen in temporal terms, as a vestige of a primary stage in cosmic evolution. Ocean, after all, was acknowledged in Greek myth and literature to be immensely old, even to date back to the very beginning of the universe.[42] In two cryptic lines of Homer's *Iliad*, for example, Ocean is described as "the origin of the gods" (14.201) and "he who was framed begetter of all" (14.246),[43] and a similar (possibly derivative) characterization pervades the Orphic hymn to Ocean (no. 83).[44] We shall return to examine these lines at greater length in a later chapter, but for now let us simply note their implication that Ocean, like the *apeiron*, antedates or even gives rise to the rest of the physical universe. The parallel is in fact

[41] The *pleumōn thalattios* is identified as a mollusk by Plato (*Philebus* 21c) and Aristotle (*Hist. Animal.* 5.15.21), but its Latin equivalent *pulmo marinus* evidently signified a jellyfish to Pliny the Elder (*Hist. Nat.* 9.154, 18.85.359). It is hard to imagine given the context that Polybius meant the former rather than the latter creature.

[42] Germain (*Genèse de l'Odyssée* 548) connects the root of the name *Ōkeanos* with Ogygos, an ancient and pre-Hellenic divinity. For the coincidence of temporal and spatial boundaries in antiquity, see the remarks made by Malcolm Baldry in *Grecs et Barbares* (Entretiens Hardt tome 8, Geneva 1961) 27, in response to H. Schwabl's paper on "Das Bild der fremden Welt bei den frühen Griechen." On Greek notions of cosmic prehistory in general, see W.K.C. Guthrie, *In the Beginning* (Ithaca, N.Y. 1957) chaps. 1–2, and Kirk and Raven chap. 1.

[43] There has been dispute over whether these lines represent a truly cosmogonic conception of Ocean; some have thought them to be an intrusion of an irrelevant and non-Homeric idea. The case for a cosmogonic Ocean, the counterpart of Hesiod's Ouranos/Gaia pairing, is convincingly argued by Rudhardt, *Eau primordiale* (above, n. 19) 47–52. See also Berger (1904) 2–3, Kirk and Raven 15–16.

[44] See G. Quandt, *Orphei Hymni* (Berlin 1955) 55. The *terminus ante quem* of the hymn is fixed by Plato's use of it in the *Cratylus* (402b).

drawn explicitly by Plato: In the great cosmogonic speech of the *Theaetetus* he has Socrates suggest that Homer and the other early poets used Ocean as a metaphor for the Heraclitean idea of a universal flux, "the begetter of all flow and motion" (152e; cf. 180d), and in the *Cratylus* (402b) he does the same with the above-mentioned Orphic hymn. While it is unclear whether Plato himself took this interpretation seriously,[45] the fact that it was already current in his day reveals a close link in the Greek mind between the physiologic disorganization of Ocean and its temporal primacy.

It is also worth noting in this context that Ocean, or what Jean Rudhardt has more generally termed "primordial water," is associated in many cosmogonic myths with the primeval monsters or giants that must be overcome before the universe can be properly ordered. Of course this version of Ocean is easier to illustrate in Near Eastern myths than in Hellenic ones,[46] but both Rudhardt and M. L. West claim to have uncovered instances of it in archaic Greek poetry as well.[47] Their conclusions, if accepted, would forge an even stronger link between Ocean's temporal primacy and its physical disorganization: Ocean could in that case be seen as a repository for the cosmic confusion that prevailed before the Olympian era, in just the same way that Zeus (according to Hesiod's *Theogony*) uses the *peirata gaiēs* to imprison the Giants, Titans, and other primordial rebels who had challenged his reign.[48] This pre-Olympian/

[45] Kirk and Raven, for instance, think not (17–18).

[46] The Babylonian Tiamat in the poem *Enuma Elish* is the most familiar example; for other instances cf. Germain, *Genèse de l'Odyssée* (above, n. 12) 529–32; W.J.F. Knight, *Cumaean Gates* (Oxford 1936) 44–45, and Onians, *The Origins of European Thought* (above, n. 7) 248–50, 315.

[47] Rudhardt, for example, points to the cosmogonies of Hieronymus and Hellanicus, in both of which a dragon named Chronos was the first offspring of the primal waters that existed before the creation of the earth (above, n. 19, pp. 12–18, 21). West turns to the fragmentary cosmogonic poem of Pherecydes for his evidence ("Three Presocratic Cosmologies," *CQ* 13 [1963]: 154–76).

[48] Cf. *Theog*. 333–36, 517–19, 621–23, 736–43, 807–13. In the *Works and Days* Hesiod also places the generation of heroes at the *peirasi gaiēs*, although in a much more pleasant and well-ordered landscape (166–69). For the con-

anti-Olympian dimension of Ocean is borne out by the fragmentary remains of Pherecydes' cosmologic poem *Heptamuchos*, in which Ophioneus ("Serpent") is cast into the deep waters of Ogēnos or Ocean after trying to overthrow Zeus; the animus of the monster seems thereby to have become merged with that of the world-encircling river.[49] Similarly in Aeschylus's *Prometheus Bound*, Ocean, represented this time in personified form, befriends Prometheus, the rebellious Titan who has defied the authority of Zeus. Although in this particular case Ocean has himself reached an accommodation with Zeus, nevertheless the bonds of kinship which tie him to Prometheus bespeak the common pre-Olympian heritage of the two.[50]

The entire nexus of associations outlined above—connecting Ocean's role as boundary of earth with its vast extent, impassibility, atavism, and monstrous disorder—is neatly embodied in a set of Greek epigrams, probably Hellenistic in provenance but dependent (like so many of the texts we shall examine below) on much earlier strata of geographic thought. These epigrams were collected in the first century A.D. by Seneca the Elder, as part of his *Suasoriae*, a set of rhetorical exercises extrapolated from historical situations. In this particular *suasoria* (the main argument of which we shall return to in chapter 4), Alexander the Great contemplates crossing Ocean in order to conquer new worlds, while his horror-struck counselors urge him to desist:

---

ception of Ocean as a primal murk, similar in nature to Erebos or Tartaros, see Norman Austin, *Archery at the Dark of the Moon* (Bloomington 1984) 92–98; Bernard Moreux, "La nuit, l'ombre, et la mort," *Phoenix* 21 (1967): 237–72. Gregory Nagy describes Ocean as one of several "symbolic boundaries delimiting light and darkness, life and death, wakefulness and sleep, consciousness and unconsciousness" ("Phaethon, Sappho's Phaon, and the White Rock of Leukas," *HSCP* 77 [1973]: 150).

[49] M. L. West, "Three Presocratic Cosmologies," 163–64.

[50] Similarly in *Iliad* 20 Ocean alone ignores Zeus's express command to come to an assembly of the gods (7–9), while in the next book, Achilles compares his concessions to Agamemnon with Ocean's grudging respect for Zeus's thunderbolt (21.194–99). In both cases, Ocean exemplifies the kind of lawlessness which must be overcome by the Olympian order if the cosmos is to remain at peace. See Lesky, *Thalatta* (above, n. 10) 80–81; Berger (1904) 2–3.

> This is not the river Simois, nor the Granicus [scenes of Alexander's earlier victories]; if it were not an evil thing, it would not lie here at the world's edge. (Glycon)

> It is greatest because of this: It is beyond all things, but beyond it is nothing. (Plution)

> This is not the Euphrates nor Indus, but whether it is the endpoint of the land, or the boundary of nature, or the most ancient of elements, or the origin of the gods, its water is too holy to be crossed by ships. (Artemon)

These epigrams, though coined with a view toward rhetorical effect rather than geographic accuracy, nevertheless give a good sense of the numinous awe which surrounded the mythic river Ocean. The last example in particular, with its striking juxtaposition of the phrases "boundary of nature" and the *Iliad*-inspired "origin of the gods," illustrates how Ocean could represent the outer limits of both geographic space and historical time at once, a combination which inspired equal measures of fear, fascination, and reverence.

Roads around the World

We have looked thus far at two forms of circumscription which the archaic age imposed on its model of the earth, the phrase *peirata gaiēs* and the element which was in a sense the physical embodiment of these "boundaries," the river Ocean. Let us turn now to another phrase which also lies deeply rooted in archaic distant-world lore: *periodos gēs* or "round-the-earth journey."

This phrase, it should be noted, takes us onto somewhat different turf than that which we have thus far explored, as indicated by its lack of meter. Whereas the dactylic formula *peirata gaiēs* clearly derives from epic poetry and the body of myth associated with it, *periodos gēs* instead belongs to early prose; in fact its earliest known use is as the title of a scientific treatise written by the Ionian philosopher Anaximander.[51] However, it is interesting to note that verse narratives too could be referred to as *periodoi gēs*, including, as we shall see below, an important fragment of the pseudo-Hesiodic *Catalogue of Women*. In fact the remarkable range of ancient writers who were credited with a *Periodos Gēs*—including not only Hesiod and Anaximander but Hecataeus, Democritus, Ctesias, and various Hellenistic poets—helps illustrate the ease with which geographic writing crossed the boundaries between poetry and prose, between fact and fiction (a point that will become central in the final chapter of this study).

Just as *peirata*, as we saw above, can denote "boundaries" of various types, so the Greek word *periodos* suggests a whole array of meanings, all derived from the basic idea of encirclement or enclosure: the orbit of a planet, the circumference of a lake, or the tactic by which an army outflanks and surrounds its adversary. In a geographic context the phrase *periodos gēs*[52] embodies this notion of encirclement on a number of levels. In its earliest uses the phrase can be translated "map of the earth," as in Herodotus's scoffing critique of "those who draw (*grapsantes*) *gēs periodous* in a perfect circle, rounder than that made with a compass" (4.36; cf. 5.49, 51). However since the verb *graphō* can mean "write" as well as "draw" it is not entirely clear whether Herodotus here refers to literary or cartographic portraits of the earth; after all the most famous text of the former type, that of Hecataeus of Miletus, was known (by at least some later writers) as *Periodos Gēs*.[53] In fact Aristotle does not bother to

[51] This title is attributed to Anaximander by Suidas (Diels-Kranz 1.14.23, Kirk and Raven fr. 97); see Kahn, *Anaximander*, 81–84, and W. A. Heidel, "Anaximander's Book, the Earliest Known Geographical Treatise," *Proc. Amer. Acad. of Arts and Sci.* 56 (1921): 239–87 (repr. in *Selected Papers*, N.Y. 1980), esp. 240–42 and n. 9.

[52] It is odd that this generic label has not been investigated nearly as thoroughly as its marine equivalent, *periplous*; the Pauly-Wissowa encyclopedia, for example, carries an article on the latter but not the former. However, see the introduction to Gisinger (1929) cols. 522–24 and Berger (1903) 249–52.

[53] On the variant titles, see Jacoby's commentary in *Fr. Gr. H* 1.1 p. 328; idem, "Hekataios," *RE* bd. 7 (1912) col. 2672; and G. Pasquali, "Die Schriftstellerische Form des Pausanias," *Hermes* 48 (1913): 187. Unfortunately only

distinguish between the two meanings, classifying both world maps and literary world tours under the same rubric.[54] It seems, then, that *periodos gēs* initially denotes a genre of geography defined by its all-encompassing scope rather than its medium of representation; it stands for "depiction of the earth's perimeter" in either visual or verbal terms, or perhaps in both at once.[55]

Periodos gēs can also refer, in a more literal sense, to an individual's "journey around the world," so that the orator Demosthenes can speak contemptuously of the *periodos gēs* conducted by a prostitute in search of new clients (59.108). In fact the notion of a "journey" or "route" (*hodos*) present in the word *periodos* seems at least partly active in all early uses of this phrase, even in cases where no such trip had ever been undertaken.[56] Thus Strabo, looking back over the early history of Greek geographic writing from the standpoint of the first century B.C., speaks of these archaic texts as " 'Harbors' and 'Coastal Voyages' and 'Circuits of the Earth' and that sort of thing" (8.1.1), implying that the group classified as *periodoi*, like its marine brethren *limenes* and *periploi*,[57] typically took the form of trav-

late sources, Suidas (Hecataeus fr. 1) and Strabo (fr. 217), attest to the title *Periodos Gēs*, but Herodotus's critique of the existing *gēs periodous* at 4.36 may well be a direct reference to Hecataeus. Pasquali's presumption that only works with maps in them could be titled *Periodos Gēs* is clearly refuted by the passage of Aristotle cited below.

[54] Cp. *Meteor.* 362b12, where he clearly means a visual "map," with *Pol.* 1262a18 and *Rhet.* 1360a34, where the same term is used in a very different context: "It is clear that *gēs periodoi* are useful for lawmakers, since they can there learn of the customs of peoples." See Nicolet 4.

[55] See Berger (1903) 249–50. Diogenes Laertius uses the term *perimetron*, "perimeter," as an equivalent for the cartographic sense of *periodos* (2.2); the other available term seems to have been *pinax*, "tablet," since maps of the earth were regularly inscribed on these (Herodotus 5.49, 51; Agathemerus 1.1; Diog. Laert. 2.2). See Dilke 23–25. In the second century A.D. Lucian uses *periodoi gēs*, in the plural, to stand for "the perimeter of the earth" (*Icaromen.* 6), a sense which Herodotus anticipates when speaking of the *perimetron periodou*, "perimeter of the circuit," of a body of water.

[56] On this whole topic see Christian Jacob, "The Greek Traveler's Areas of Knowledge" (above, n. 1).

[57] On this latter genre, see the *RE* article by Gisinger, "Periplus" (bd. 19.1 [1937] cols. 839–50) and the study by Güngerich.

eler's guides describing daily journeys and stopping-places. Certainly the fragments of Hecataeus's *Periodos Gēs*, from what little can be deduced regarding their original form, suggest this kind of arrangement (although it is unclear to what extent the author portrayed himself actually visiting the "stops" he describes).[58] When describing the whole earth one has to organize one's material in some manner or other, and the orderly, peripatetic sequence of the *periodos gēs* provides an effective scheme:[59] The narrative effectively "leads us around" the perimeter of the earth, as suggested by the alternate title of Hecataeus's work and of others like it, *Periēgēsis* or "guided tour."[60]

Nowhere does the holistic dimension of *periodos* writing emerge more clearly than in the Hesiodic *Periodos Gēs*, a segment of the lost *Catalogue of Women* (its "subtitle" first attested by Ephorus in the fourth century B.C.).[61] This bizarre episode, partly recovered recently in a lucky papyrus find, describes a fantastic midair chase in which the sons of the North Wind fly three times around the earth in pursuit of the foul, birdlike Harpies. In describing this whirlwind flight the poem

[58] The structure of the *Periodos Gēs* is of course conjectural, since its fragments have been recovered almost entirely from a lexicon where they are alphabetically arranged. Aly (308) notes that Hecataeus started his "tour" from the Pillars of Heracles and also ended there, suggesting a circular arrangement.

[59] This is the procedure adopted by later writers, for example Mela (*De Situ Orbis* 3), Dionysius Periegetes (see esp. 62–63).

[60] The idea that early Greek conceptions of the earth were defined by "roads," "guided tours," "voyages," and other routes of travel has been developed extensively by Pietro Janni, *La mappa e il periplo: Cartografia antica e spazio odologico* (Università di Macerata Publicazioni Facoltà di Lettere e Filosofia 19, Rome 1984). To take one prominent example, we find that distances from one place to another are expressed in early Greek texts in travel times: A day's sail, or a day's march, are the first standard units of measurement (see O.A.W. Dilke, *Mathematics and Measurement* [Reading the Past, Berkeley and London 1988] chap. 4). Later, however, such measures are replaced by other, mathematically determined units, like the stade and the mile; that is, earth measurement progresses from a system based on individual experience to one that abstracts and objectifies its data. See Bunbury 1.230–31 and 1.481 note N; Nicolet 4.

[61] Strabo 7.3.9. On the title see Nilsson, "*Kataploi*," *Rh. Mus.* 60 (1905): 178–80. The fragment is discussed at some length by F. Gisinger, "Zur Geographie bei Hesiod," *Rh. Mus.* 78 (1913): 319–28; see also Müller (1972) 66.

conducts an aerial survey of the exotica of the distant world, including Ethiopians in the farthest South, mare-milking Scythians and Hyperboreans in the far North, the Eridanos River and Mt. Aetna in the far West, and the bestial *Hemikunes* or "Half-dogs," perhaps in the East. The episode thus imaginatively takes its audience aloft to gain a bird's-eye view of the earth's perimeter, encompassing in a single glance all four corners of the globe. Unfortunately the fragmentary remains of the *Catalogue of Women* are not complete enough to allow us to say how this visionary episode figured into the larger whole. But we can well imagine that part of its effect, at least, was to expand the poem's dimensions to global scale, surrounding it with a suitably vast and all-encompassing framework. (A similar desire for global scope, we note, lies behind the great travelogues of Io and Heracles in Aeschylus's *Prometheus* trilogy, which, though not specifically identified as *periodoi*, certainly provide a worldwide panorama as backdrop for the Prometheus story).[62]

The term *periodos*, then, as applied to both Hecataeus and Hesiod, implies an encyclopedic comprehensiveness, a turning of the earth's circle through its full 360 degrees. This encyclopedic impulse, in fact, gives rise to one final, late-emerging meaning of the phrase *periodos gēs*: "study of panglobal geography." It was thus that Strabo, for example, defined his monumental survey of world geography in the early first century A.D. (1.3.21, 6.1.2), a work which he also characterizes as a "colossal project . . . concerned with vast things and with wholes" (1.1.23). In a similar fashion Hellenistic geographers like Eudoxus and Dicaearchus took *Periodos Gēs* as a title for

[62] On the geography of the Io speech, see J. L. Myres, "The Wanderings of Io, *Prometheus Bound* 707–869," *CR* 60 (1946): 2–4; J. Duchemin, "La Justice de Zeus et le Destin d'Io," *REG* 92 (1979): 1–54; E. A. Havelock, *The Crucifixion of Intellectual Man* (Boston 1951) 59–63; and Bolton 45–64. The long littany of Io's travels also has a dramatic purpose, that is, to emphasize the suffering of one of Zeus's enemies, as noted by Mark Griffith (*Prometheus Bound* [Cambridge 1983] 12). But for its appeal as a geographic "set piece" see H. C. Baldry, *The Unity of Mankind in Greek Thought* (Cambridge 1965) 18–19.

their treatises on geography, presumably to distinguish their abstract and conceptualized approach from the place-by-place descriptions of earlier writers.[63] Likewise Eratosthenes, the first and greatest member of this Hellenistic school, is praised by Arrian as the most accurate of the Greek writers on India since "he was concerned with the *periodos gēs*" (*Indika* 3.1), that is, with universal principles of measurement rather than with the particulars of individual regions.

"Whole-earth" literature of the *periodos* type, whether framed as poetry, descriptive geography, or natural science, seems to have held a unique fascination for Greek and Roman readers, to judge by the number and variety of works which fall under this rubric. The Hellenistic period in particular saw an outpouring of *periplous* and *periodos* poetry, including the works attributed to Scymnus of Chios, Apollodorus of Athens, Pseudo-Scylax, and Simmias. Even the *Argonautica* of Apollonius of Rhodes, despite its vastly higher narrative ambitions, reveals a certain independent interest in round-the-world geographical description.[64] Later, perhaps in the second century A.D., a versified "world tour" or *Periēgēsis* attributed to Dionysius (subsequently surnamed Periegetes) enshrined the Greek view of the whole earth for late antique and (in Avienus's Latin translation) medieval readers and students. These later examples lie beyond the scope of the present discussion and cannot be presented in detail; but their wide proliferation does serve to illustrate the powerful appeal of the *periodos gēs*, whether in a visual or a verbal medium. They offered their audience a pleasingly synoptic view of the earth's circuit, embellished with curious details of its most exotic phenomena.

[63] For Eudoxus see F. Lasserre, *Die Fragmente des Eudoxos von Knidos* (Texte und Kommentare 4, Berlin 1966) 239–40; for Dicaearchus, Joannes Lydus *De Mens.* 147.1 in Wünsch's Teubner edition.

[64] On the idea of Apollonius's catalogue of heroes as a *periplous*, see J. F. Carspecken, "Apollonius and Homer," *YCS* 13 (1952): 45–46, and Charles Beye, *Epic and Romance in the "Argonautica" of Apollonius* (Carbondale and Edwardsville, Ill. 1982) 22. On Hellenistic love of geographical catalogues see Nita Krevans, "Geography and the Literary Tradition in Theocritus 7," *TAPA* 113 (1983): 208.

Herodotus and the Changing World Picture

By imposing boundaries of these various kinds, then—linguistic, cosmologic, cartographic, and mythic—the archaic age succeeded in carving an intelligible chunk of earth out of the surrounding void. The terrifying *apeiron* of primal chaos was banished to the outermost edge of the globe, where flowed the stream of Ocean, so as to permit a more formal ordering of its central spaces; and this outer region was decisively fenced off from the rest of the world, both by natural impediments and by divine sanction. A two-part earth thus emerged, as defined by the Greek names for the Mediterranean and the Atlantic—"inner" and "outer" seas[65]—or by the frequent use of the phrase *exō tōn stēlōn*, "beyond the Pillars," to denote the entire circle of Ocean and the fabulous lands associated with it.[66] This outer realm, though terrifying in the extreme when actually confronted by sailors and navigators, served as an extremely rich backdrop for imaginative literature (as we shall see in more detail in the following chapters); and in the most panoramic genre of geographic writing, the *periodos* or *periplous*, its enormous span could be glimpsed or even traversed in its entirety.

As the horizon of Hellenic culture advanced, however, and as the myth-based worldview of the archaic era yielded to a more empirical and exacting mode of geographic inquiry, the validity of this imaginative world-map came increasingly into question. By the middle of the fifth century, for instance, the Greeks had begun to peer into the obscurity of the far West from their thriving new settlements in Sicily and Marseille,[67]

[65] Although Ocean's modern name was also in use as early as Herodotus's time: ". . . the sea outside the Pillars, named Atlantic" (1.202). Other common names for the western portion of Ocean include "Great Sea" (*megalē thalassa*), "Western Ocean" (*Hesperios* or *dutikos Ōkeanos*), and "Atlantic sea" (*Atlantikos pelagos*). On the variations see Smith's *Dictionary of Greek and Roman Geography* (London 1878) s.v. "Atlanticum Mare," and Kretschmer 41–42.

[66] See the interesting study of this structural phenomenon, with a survey of relevant texts, by Erik Wistrand, "Nach Innen oder nach Aussen?" in *Göteborgs Högskolas Arsskrift* 52 (1946): 3–54, and the comments by Nicolet (5).

[67] See the comprehensive but poorly organized survey of relevant material

and to a lesser degree into the far East through their contact with the vast and highly organized Persian empire. More important, however, the spirit in which the earth sciences were pursued was rapidly changing. Like philosophy, geography was coming down from the skies and putting its feet on the ground, which is to say severing an original link with theoretical cosmology in favor of real information concerning the distant world—derived either from firsthand investigation or from secondhand reports.[68] At the same time a new medium of scientific discourse, prose, was coming to the fore, and a new generation of prose writers had begun to suspect that the poets, especially Homer and Hesiod, could no longer be trusted as geographic authorities. As a result the question of the *peirata gaiēs* underwent a thorough reexamination in the later fifth century, as is apparent in the writings of the era's greatest revisionist geographer, Herodotus of Halicarnassus.

The main tenet of Herodotus's critique of archaic geography, and the one on which all the others in some sense depend, is his rejection of the legendary river Ocean. He dismisses this mythical entity on three separate occasions, each time in slightly different terms:

> The man who brings up the story of Ocean [in a discussion of the sources of the Nile] moves the debate into the realm of the obscure, and thus avoids refutation. For my part, though, I know of no river

---

by Paul Fabre, *Les Grecs et la connaissance* (above, n. 27). Also Chester G. Starr, *The Awakening of the Greek Historical Spirit* (N.Y. 1968) 41–49; Casson 58–64; Cary and Warmington 21–42; Kretschmer 11–19.

[68] As I have argued elsewhere ("Herodotus and Mythic Geography: The Case of the Hyperboreans," *TAPA* 119 [1989]: 97–117), the idea of a "rise of empiricism" in fifth-century earth science is only one element of a more complex evolution; we must not overlook the fact that the same era saw the beginnings of theoretical and mathematical geography, seemingly an extension of the abstractions of Ionian science (the "double trend" described by Nicolet 58–59). The paradox reveals itself in a note of Paul Friedländer suggesting that the traditional view (see Güngerich 12) of the development of cartography, from general *mappae mundi* to specific lists of harbors and coasts, should in fact be reversed (*Plato: An Introduction*[2] [Princeton 1969] 387 n. 9). In fact geography was developing in several directions at once during this period, but all of its branches were clearly interested in making use of new traveler's reports.

called Ocean, and I think that Homer, or some other of the early poets, invented the name and inserted it into his poetry. (2.23)

They *say* that Ocean runs around the whole earth, starting from the eastern horizon; but they don't *show* any evidence for it. (4.8)

I laugh when I see the many men who draw maps of the world without using their heads; they make the earth a perfect circle, better even than one drawn with a compass, with Ocean running around it, and Asia and Europe of equal size. (4.36)

Given that Ocean, as we have seen, had been a vital and ubiquitous feature of world geography since the *Iliad*, Herodotus's three-part refutation creates quite a dramatic shift in geographic priorities. He first points out (2.21, 2.23) that there is no direct evidence to support such a construct, except for the unreliable testimony of the poets. He then repeats this idea (4.8), this time stressing the circularity of Ocean as his main objection; the earth's perimeter was known to be girt by sea in *some* directions but not *all*. In fact Herodotus had in Book 1 erased the water boundary of the East, by asserting that the Caspian, which had traditionally been considered an inlet of Ocean, was in fact only a landlocked sea (1.203). Since land extends beyond the Caspian, then, "no one knows for certain whether Europe is bounded by sea, either at its eastern or northern extremes" (4.45).[69]

Finally, in his most decisive dismissal of Ocean (4.36), Herodotus moves this critique of circularity to a new level: He associates Ocean with artificial and overly schematic maps of the earth, probably meaning those of Ionians like Anaximander and Hecataeus, which seemed to him much too neatly geometrical and abstract to represent the true earth.[70] In thus turning

[69] On the implications of this change see Kretschmer 17–18, and Berger (1903) 56–57.

[70] See the comments on this sequence of passages by Truesdell S. Brown, "Herodotus Speculates about Egypt," *AJP* 86 (1965): 60–76, esp. 75–76; van Paassen 138–42. For the idea that Hecataeus is Herodotus's main target here see Heidel (1933) 206–7. Herodotus's argument has been misunderstood by commentators who claim that he rejects Ocean simply for lack of evidence (see,

away from the conceptual and geometric solution to the problem of the *peirata gaiēs*, Herodotus makes room for a new kind of distant-world geography, based not on geometry but on what can be learned from reliable informants.[71] Indeed, his own updated version of the world-map, which is introduced by this critique of the old "compass-drawn" model, is closely interwoven with his accounts of the voyages of exploration on which it is based: Scylax's tour of the Indian Ocean under Darius (4.44), and the alleged circumnavigation of Africa by the Persians and Phoenicians (4.42–43). In contrast to the *periodos gēs*, a purely theoretical "journey around the earth," Herodotus attempts wherever possible to follow the tracks of known travelers and to avoid what he calls *aphanes* or "unseen" territory (2.21).

By following these routes of travel outward, like the spokes of a wheel, Herodotus eventually discovers *erēmoi* or "empty spaces" at the edges of the earth, in all directions except the West.[72] We find the word *erēmos* (or its equivalent *erēmiē*), in fact, used at many crucial points in Herodotus's explorations of the distant world:

> Of the peoples we know about, or those about whom we have reliable reports, the Indians dwell furthest east and closest to the sunrise; the region eastward of India is empty (*erēmiē*) on account of the sand. (3.98)

---

for example, How and Wells 170 and Bunbury 165). The matter has been thoroughly explored in my "Herodotus and Mythic Geography" (above, n. 68).

[71] On the Herodotean empirical revolution, see especially van Paassen 117–51 (where the case is somewhat overstated); Kretschmer 17–19, 36–39; Dietram Müller, "Herodot—Vater des Empirismus? Mensch und Erkenntnis im Denken Herodots," in *Gnomosyne: Menschliches Denken und Handeln in der frühgriechischen Literatur*, ed. G. Kurz, D. Müller and W. Nicolai (Munich, 1981), 299–319; and Guido Schepens, *L'Autopsie dans la méthode des historiens grecs du Ve siècle avant J.-C.* (Brussels 1980). The contrast between *opsis*, "eyewitnessing," and *akoē*, "report," is important in this regard, as has been demonstrated in a number of recent studies, particularly in the fascinating book by Hartog, *Le Miroir d'Hérodote* (271–82).

[72] See Hannelore Edelmann, "*Erēmiē* und *erēmos* bei Herodot," *Klio* 52 (1970): 79–86; and Guy Lachenaud, "Connaissance du monde et représentations de l'espace dans Hérodote," *Hellenica* 32 (1980): 42–60.

> North of the Alazones dwell Scythian farmers, who raise grain not for food, but for sale; north of these dwell the Neuri; and the region northward of the Neuri is empty (*erēmon*) of men, so far as we know. (4.17)

> Beyond the [central African] ridge, toward the southern and inland portion of Libya, the land is empty (*erēmos*) and unirrigated, with no beasts, nor shade, nor trees; there's not even any moisture in it. (4.185)

> As to what lies north of the [Thracian] country, no one can say with any certainty what men dwell there; rather, beyond the Ister the territory seems to be empty (*erēmos*) and unbounded (*apeiros*). (5.9)

If terms like *peirata* and *periodos* imply a solid line around the borders of earth, like the shoreline of an island, then Herodotus's *erēmoi* remain diffuse and open-ended, as suggested by the pairing of *erēmos* and *apeiros* in the final passage above. This version of the world is surrounded by an expanse not of sea, but of uninhabited waste. Whether or not there are other inhabited lands lying beyond that waste is an issue that Herodotus leaves unexplored; it would come back to trouble the geographers who followed him, as we shall see in chapter 4.

We also note that in each of the passages quoted above the "emptiness" at the edge of the earth is defined both as a lack of inhabitants, especially when *erēmos* is expanded to *erēmos anthrōpōn* or "empty of men" (as in 4.17), and as a lack of information, in that it separates Herodotus from the region about which "no one knows anything clearly." In fact, the two forms of privation are closely interrelated, since news about distant territories can only travel as far as there are human beings to transmit it; for Herodotus, all contact with these realms is severed if a large, uninhabited tract breaks the chain of communication. Some deserts, of course, can be traversed, but Herodotus distinguishes these limited *erēmoi* from an *erēmos alēthōs*, a "true desert," which has never been crossed (4.19). That is to say, the *erēmos* properly speaking is a terminal space, blocking all inquiry into the regions beyond. In fact, he twice refers to these termini as *makrotata* (2.32, 4.31), the "greatest" or furthest regions, in a way which perfectly combines notions of geographic and empirical limitation: "Those are the furthest things (*ta makrotata*) that can be mentioned."

This close connection between habitation, communication, and secure knowledge helps explain the emergence of yet another geographical term which is first found in Herodotus (and in other fifth-century writers), but which thereafter becomes a standard and ubiquitous usage: *oikoumenē*, or, in its fully expanded form, *hē oikoumenē gē*.[73] Literally this phrase translates to "inhabited earth" but implies more than this, since lands which were thought to contain men (like the Antipodes) were not necessarily included within its scope, while other, uninhabited spaces might well be so included. Rather, the *oikoumenē*, in its most essential meaning, can be defined as a region made coherent by the intercommunication of its inhabitants, such that, within the radius of this region, no tribe or race is completely cut off from the peoples beyond it. Understood in this way, the term *oikoumenē* can be better translated as "known world" or "familiar world," or even (if we take account of the qualifying phrase *huph'hēmōn* or *kath'hēmas* which sometimes accompanies it) "our world." It constitutes the space within which empirical investigation, like that championed by Herodotus, can take place, since all of its regions fall within the compass either of travel or of informed report.

Herodotus, then, divides his conceptual map into an inner and an outer space based not on the physical boundary between earth and sea, as was the case with his predecessors, but on the presence of human inhabitants and the resulting availability of eyewitness information. The terminology Herodotus introduces into the study of world structure, therefore—*aphanes, erēmos, makrotata*, and above all *oikoumenē*—represent a fundamental shift in Greek conceptions of the earth from those implied by *peirar* and *peras*—words Herodotus never uses—

[73] For the history of this term, see the excellent article by Gisinger (1937), and van Paassen 16–24. The brief study by J. Kaerst, *Die Antike Idee der "Oikoumenē" in ihrer politischen und kulturellen Bedeutung* (Leipzig 1903) presents a useful history of the political, but not the geographical, applications of the term.

and *periodos*. The older, more abstract lines of demarcation are, in his era, being displaced by the rapidly increasing body of traveler's reports. Indeed, Herodotus might today be hailed as a pioneer in the development of empirical geography, were it not for the fact that in a number of important cases he shows himself still partially attached to the old abstract model.[74] In one particularly noteworthy passage, to which we now turn, Herodotus introduces into his world-map a circle of *eschatiai* or "most distant lands," a construct which is in part reliant on the mythic tradition of *peirata gaiēs*.

Herodotus's discussion of these lands[75] digresses rather freely from his central narrative, in that it does not concern any of the lands which play a role in the main story of Greece's conflict with Persia. Rather it seems to have been introduced as a purely theoretical conspectus of world structure, perhaps in answer to the passages on either side of it in which Herodotus dispenses with the myth of Ocean. The point of departure for the digression is the wealth of India, a topic which leads Herodotus to the general observation that all distant lands are richer than those close to home:

> The *eschatiai* of the inhabited world have been given all the finest things, whereas Greece has received by far the best mixture of seasons. (3.106)

Herodotus returns to this observation at the end of the digression, closing with a kind of reprise:

> At any rate the *eschatiai*, which surround the rest of the world and enclose it within, seem to possess the things we consider most lovely and rarest. (3.116)

[74] See Immerwahr 315–16, Lachenaud, "Connaissance du monde"; and my "Herodotus and Mythic Geography" (above, n. 68).

[75] On this passage see Immerwahr 49–50, 102–3; R. Falus, "Hérodote III. 108–9," *Acta Antiqua* 25 (1977): 371–76; Lachenaud, "Connaissance du monde"; James Redfield, "Herodotus the Tourist," *CP* 80 (1985): 97–118, esp. 110–12; Seth Benardete, *Herodotean Inquiries* (The Hague 1969) 87–90; and chap. 1 of Marcel Détienne's *Les Jardins d'Adonis* (Paris 1972), esp. 20–21, 36–37.

The material that falls between these two statements describes how the inhabitants of this distant realm harvest its wealth; because of its primarily ethnographic character we shall reserve discussion of it until the next chapter. For the moment let us look more closely at the term *eschatiai*, which like *oikoumenē* becomes standard geographic usage from this time forward,[76] and at the larger picture of the world that it implies. Herodotus here uses the feminine form of the adjective *eschatios*, "final" or "uttermost," so as to agree with an implied noun *gē*, "land"; later authors generally prefer a substantival neuter form, *ta eschata*, sometimes qualified by *tēs gēs*, "of the earth." In either case the word is declined in the plural yet functions as a collective noun, essentially singular in meaning. Thus, in the passage above, the furthest reaches of the earth, in all directions, form a continuous belt of lands, closely joined by common characteristics just as they are set apart from the rest of the world. Moreover, although these lands are attached to the known world (as implied by the partitive genitive in the phrase *eschatiai tēs oikoumenēs*) they are also distinct from it, much as the frame of a painting is distinct from the canvas.[77] The frame-like structure of the *eschatiai* reveals itself quite clearly, in fact, in the final sentence of the digression, in which Herodotus describes these lands as "surrounding" and "enclosing" the rest of the world.

Having dispensed with the aquatic boundary of Ocean, then, Herodotus here establishes a surrogate boundary made up of land;[78] but since this realm is conceived as part of the *oikou-*

[76] Heidel (1933) considers *eschatiai tēs oikoumenēs* to be "the technical term for the limits of the world," but without considering whether Herodotus here coins it (198 n. 29).

[77] Cf. Heidel, ibid.: "The known world is a rather drab affair, but like the death's-head in *The Merchant of Venice*, it is enclosed in a golden casket."

[78] In fact, the adjective *eschatos* or *eschatios* certainly implies—although perhaps not as vividly as the earlier term, *peirata*—a threshhold between two distinct regions, like that at the boundary of earth and ocean. In Homer the places which are described as "outermost," in almost every instance, border on the sea; similarly the *eschatoi anthrōpoi* of Homer's world, the Ethiopians, dwell by the banks of Ocean (a usage echoed by Herodotus, in his account of the Cynetae [4.49], who also dwell beside the Atlantic). Pindar, in a poem we have

menē, it can be empirically verified in a way that Ocean could not be. Thus, if Herodotus partly relies on the mythic tradition he claims to have discarded, he also reorients that tradition so as to place it within the purview of the new science. In fact it is within this digression that Herodotus again (as in 4.45) expresses doubts about the idea that Europe is surrounded by sea (3.115), and rejects outright several other features of mythic geography: the amber-bearing river Eridanus, the Tin Islands, and the race of one-eyed Arimaspians (ibid.). Because the *eschatiai* lie within the realm of informed report, that is, Herodotus is able to bring his investigative and reasoning skills to bear on them, rather than leaving them in an *aphanes* which admits no discussion.

But how should these *eschatiai* be reconciled with the *erēmoi* with which, as we have seen, Herodotus elsewhere surrounds his map of the world? It is curious that we find no mention of *erēmoi* within the above digression, just as in other sections of the *Histories* we find only one brief reference to the *eschatiai* which are so prominent here. Indeed, the two schemes seem to be at odds with one another, and it may well be the case that the *eschatiai* passage (which bears all the marks of a separately composed "set piece") was added later at a time when Herodotus's knowledge of or interest in the distant world had grown.[79] However that may be, it seems clear that the old geometric model of the world, based on the poets' Ocean and the Ionians' world-map, has been quite deliberately revised and reformulated by Herodotus in the Book 3 digression, so as to answer to the concerns of the new empiricism. While accepting the general notion of "boundaries of the earth," and even the

already looked at, compares the athlete striving for the *eschatian* of glory to a traveler approaching the Pillars of Heracles (*Ol.* 3.43).

[79] Thus Trüdinger 16. On the incongruities in Herodotus's geography see Immerwahr 163–64; Lionel Pearson, "Credulity and Skepticism in Herodotus," *TAPA* 72 (1941): 335–55; and Kurt von Fritz, "Herodotus and the Growth of Greek Historiography," *TAPA* 67 (1936): 315–40. Pearson overemphasizes the lack of consistency in Herodotus's world picture, so as to make it appear entirely unstructured. Von Fritz posits a developmental scheme in which the incongruities represent different periods in Herodotus's intellectual growth.

approximate circularity of those boundaries, Herodotus contests the mythic grounds on which they had been drawn and raises the possibility of a new system founded on traveler's reports.[80]

Aristotle and After

If Herodotus succeeded in questioning the *peirata gaiēs* established by myth and poetry, however, he was one of few in the ancient world with the courage to attempt this. In the centuries to come many changes were rung on the world-map, but these were the concern of specialists; the general public remained tenaciously committed to the original circular construct. In fact the *peirata gaiēs* idea serves as an illustrative example of one of the most striking features of ancient distant-world lore: its longevity.[81] Despite continuing advances in science and exploration the average citizens of Greece and Rome clung to the conceptions of the earth's edges that best suited their imaginative needs. Even the revisionist authors who tried to set the geographic record straight sometimes ended up endorsing its most extravagant fictions, as we shall see in chapter 3.

A few points of reference will suffice to illustrate the course of the world-map's later development. The first of Herodotus's critiques of this map, his rejection of its strict circularity, did indeed make some headway among later geographers: Agathemerus informs us that in the late fifth century Democritus mapped the earth as an oblong shape, half again as long as wide, and that in the next century Dicaearchus concurred with

[80] Ironically enough, the next revolution in descriptive geography, wrought by the mathematical geographers of Hellenistic Alexandria, discarded the evidence of the traveler's report in order to update the map of the earth (Nicolet 70–72). See, for example, Book 2 of Strabo's *Geographies*, where the fallacious reports of Indian Ocean navigators are said to have impeded attempts to chart the southern extension of the *oikoumenē*.

[81] See chap. 11 of Heidel (1937).

these proportions.[82] Yet at the same time we find Aristotle, a near contemporary of Dicaearchus, complaining in words very close to those of Herodotus about the prevalence of the circular world-map (*Meteor.* 362b11):[83]

> They draw maps of the earth (*tas periodous tēs gēs*) in a laughable manner; for they draw the *oikoumenē* in a very round form, which is impossible on the basis of both logic and observed facts.

Aristotle follows this critique with his own estimate of the length:breadth ratio of the inhabited world, revising Democritus's 3:2 figure to 5:3; but what is surprising is that Aristotle aims his polemic not at his fellow scientists but at the common run of cartographers, who have not yet put aside the "compass-drawn" model Herodotus had scorned.[84] Centuries later Geminus, the obscure author of a brief *Introduction to Astronomy*, is still pleading for an end to round maps: "[In them] the length of the earth is equal to its breadth, which is not so in nature."[85]

The second prong of Herodotus's attack on myth, moreover—his rejection of the circumambient Ocean—found similarly mixed favor in later centuries. One of the chief premises on which this rejection rested was quickly abandoned, as Greek geographers after Aristotle went back to considering the Caspian an inlet of Ocean rather than a landlocked sea. In the Hellenistic period a false report filed by Patrocles, one of the admirals appointed by Alexander the Great, claiming that the Caspian and the Indian Ocean were indeed connected by water, seemed to give irrefutable credence to this idea; it was accepted, for example, by the otherwise discriminating geographer Eratosthenes of Cyrene, who therefore concurred in the idea of a circumambient Ocean (even while rejecting Homer as a useful

[82] Agathemerus 1.1.2, in Müller *GGM* 2.471 (= Diels-Kranz fr. 15); cf. Dilke 25. Heidel (1933) 201 n. 38 believes that the 3:2 ratio is older than Democritus, but does not cite his evidence.

[83] See Heidel (1937) 89–90 and (1933) 201.

[84] Cf. Kretschmer, 13: "Thus we can see how long a time the Ionian maps must have held sway."

[85] Geminus 16.4; see the note by C. Manitius in the Teubner edition (*Elementa Astronomiae* [Leipzig 1898] 275 n. 28).

source).[86] A few Hellenistic geographers, among them Hipparchus and Polybius,[87] joined Herodotus in expressing skepticism about Homer's Ocean; but Strabo takes a giant step backward at the beginning of the Roman era, when he opens his massive *Geographies* with a long excursus (1.1–10) on how Homer's vision of the island earth had essentially been proven correct. (It is at this point that we shall again take up the theme of circumscription, in chapter 4.)

Only in Ptolemy's *Geography*, some six centuries after Herodotus and five after Aristotle, do we find an open-ended scheme of the world again put forward in a systematic way. Like these predecessors Ptolemy understands the Caspian to be a landlocked sea, and therefore claims that the East (as well as the North) is bounded not by water but by "unknown land" (*gē agnōstos*, *Geography* 3.5.1; 6.14.1, 15.1, 16.1; 7.5.2).[88] More important, he gives an explicit endorsement to his predecessors' attacks on Ocean, in the concluding sentence of his excursus on cartography:

> The known portion of the earth should be set out so that it does not have Ocean flowing everywhere around it, but only where the boundaries of Libya and Europe are marked out, in the direction of the winds Iapyx and Thrascia [i.e., West-northwest and North-northwest], in accordance with the ancient historians. (7.5.2)

In this reference to "ancient historians" we should probably see a tip of the hat to Herodotus, who had similarly acknowledged that only certain portions of the *oikoumenē* were bounded by

[86] See Strabo 1.3.14; Thomson 163, Bunbury 1.459, 574.

[87] On Hipparchus see Strabo 1.1.9, and commentary by D. R. Dicks, *The Geographical Fragments of Hipparchus* (London 1960) 114; poorly understood by Aujac (1966) 20–22 and 21 n. 2. For Polybius's view see 3.38 and Heidel (1933) 208.

[88] Gisinger believes this concept may have partly derived from Plato's myth of Atlantis ("Zur geographischen Grundlage von Platons Atlantis," *Klio* 26 [1932]: 38; seconded by J. Bidez, *Eos ou Platon et l'Orient* [Brussels 1945] 38). On Ptolemy's world-map and that of his predecessor Marinus see Berger (1898) 135–41; Kretschmer 42–48; Richard Uhden, "Das Erdbild in der Tetrabiblos des Ptolemaios," *Philologus* 88 (1933): 302–25; and Kubitschek, "Karten" (above, n. 14) cols. 2058–99.

water. But what impresses us most is, again, the fact that this idea had to be restated so stridently more than half a millennium after it was proposed. The last word in our extant record of Greek empirical geography is essentially the same as the first, a refutation of the old, Homeric boundaries of earth.

Two

Ethiopian and Hyperborean

IN THE FOURTH CENTURY B.C. the historian Ephorus published a work of descriptive geography entitled *Europe*, since lost, but known to us in part through the *Geographies* of Strabo of Amaseia. The work, to judge by Strabo's account, seems to have been a rather daring attempt at revisionist ethnography. Ephorus, it seems, had noted a duality in previous Greek accounts of the Scythians—some writers had made them out to be cannibals, others, a race who opposed all taking of life and therefore subsisted exclusively on milk[1]—and decided to emphasize the latter version over the former:[2]

> Previous writers, Ephorus says, only tell about the savagery of the Scythians, knowing that terrible and strange phenomena produce a vivid effect; but he, for his part, says that one must do the opposite of this, and depict exemplary models of humanity (*paradeigmata*). Thus he resolves to write about those Scythians who practice the most righteous customs, like the Nomad Scythians, who are fed on

[1] The significance of the adjective *hippēmolgoi*, "mare-milking," as applied to the Scythians, was variously understood by ancient writers, but certainly the desire to avoid killing fellow creatures was one of its chief components (cf. Pseudo-Scymnus 852–55, Lovejoy and Boas 324). The comic playwright Antiphanes spoofs the tradition by suggesting that drinking milk spares the Scythians from harsh wet-nurses (Athenaeus *Deipn.* 226d). John Ferguson (*Utopias in the Classical World* [Ithaca, N.Y. 1975] 17) supposes that "the scorn of the effect of meat on the mind" may play a role.

[2] The passage is discussed by van Paassen 256–58; Lovejoy and Boas 289–90; B. L. Ullman, "History and Tragedy," *TAPA* 73 (1942): 31; and M. Rostovtzeff, *Skythien und der Bosporus* vol. 1 (Berlin 1931) 80–86. Cf. also A. Riese, *Die Idealisierung der Naturvölker des Nordens in der griechischen und römischen Literatur* (Frankfurt 1875) 11 n. 1. Pierre Vidal-Naquet sees in the shift from cannibalism to vegetarianism here an instance of *coincidentia oppositorum*; see "Valeurs réligieux et mythique de la terre et du sacrifice dans *l'Odyssée*," *Annales* 25 (1970): 1281.

> the milk of horses, and who surpass all men in justice. (Strabo 7.3.9 = Ephorus fr. 42 Jacoby)

Strabo goes on to note that there is good precedent for Ephorus's idealizing brand of ethnography, since Homer and other early writers had likewise ennobled the Scythians, especially "those dwelling furthest away from the rest of mankind." It seems then that this early idealizing tradition had been eclipsed before Ephorus's time by an opposite one, which made distant peoples seem barbaric and crude; and that Ephorus attempted to redress this change by causing the pendulum of bias to swing back the other way.

The two opposing tendencies between which the Greek image of the Nomad Scythians here seems to oscillate can be described, for the sake of the discussion which follows, as an ethnocentric impulse and its inverse. Ethnocentrism, in the most literal sense of the word, denotes a construct of space which sees the center of the world as the best or most advanced location,[3] and therefore demotes distant peoples to the status of unworthy savages. An inversion of this scheme, by contrast, privileges the edges of the earth over the center: In the passage above, for example, Strabo specifies that the Scythians dwelling *furthest* from that center, the Nomads, were often idealized by early writers, and later he himself agrees with this assessment. In fact in a stinging indictment of his own culture Strabo suggests it is the Greeks who are largely to blame for the moral decay of the peoples around them:

[3] For examples from other cultures besides ancient Greece, see W. G. Sumner, *Folkways* (Boston 1907) 14, and L. Bagrow, *Die Geschichte der Kartographie* (Berlin 1931) 16. John Friedman illustrates how the late antique Christians moved Jerusalem into the center of their maps, even though this skewed the relative dimensions of East and West (*The Monstrous Races in Medieval Art and Thought* [Harvard 1981] 37, 43–44). For discussion of ethnocentrism as a universal cultural phenomenon, see the introduction to vol. 1 of Müller (1972); László Vajda, "Traditionelle Konzeption und Realität in der Ethnologie," *Festschrift für Ad. E. Jensen* vol. 2, ed. E. Haberland (Munich 1964) 759–85; and Jonathan Z. Smith, "Adde Parvum Parvo, Magnus Acervus Erit," *History of Religions* 11 (1971): 67–90.

> Our way of life has seeped out to nearly everyone, bringing a change for the worse: luxury, pleasure-seeking, guile, and a thousand forms of greed on top of these. In this way a great part of this corruption has fallen on the barbarians—even on the Nomads, in addition to the rest. (7.3.7)

This inverse or negative ethnocentric scheme envisions foreigners growing not less but more virtuous in proportion to their distance from the Greek center, which is here depicted as the most morally degenerate spot on earth.[4]

In such negative schemes, we note, it is the peoples of the *eschatiai*, in this case the Nomad Scythians, who become most prominent as ethical *paradeigmata* for the Greeks, since they are assumed to differ most widely from the rest of humankind. In other words, just as the Greeks tended to correlate historic time with geographic space (as we saw in the previous chapter), thereby locating the earliest stratum of cosmic evolution beyond the edges of the earth, so they also envisioned rings of progressively more primitive social development surrounding a Mediterranean hearth;[5] in the furthest ring, at the banks of Ocean, social primitivism becomes absolute. Moreover, whether these outermost tribes—among them the Ethiopians, Hyperboreans, Arimaspians, Scythians, and *Kunokephaloi*—were imagined in terms of "soft" or "hard" versions of primitive life, their extreme distance seemed to the Greeks to confer on them a unique ethical prerogative, licensing them to mock,

[4] On Strabo's ethnocentrism see Aujac (1966) 196–97, Müller (1972) 120–21. That this geographer tends to structure the world into concentric orbits is amply demonstrated by a cosmologic discussion at 17.1.36, in which *phusis* itself is defined as the force which keeps things centered.

[5] Müller has actually drawn an "ethnographic map" to illustrate how this principle operates in Herodotus, showing four different levels of social evolution extending concentrically outward (1972 1.121; cf. 1.5). Both Hartog (*Le Miroir d'Hérodote* 33) and Rossellini and Saïd ("Usages des femmes et autres *nomoi* chez les 'sauvages' d'Hérodote," *PSNA* 8 [1978]: 961) posit a scheme in which humankind becomes gradually more bestial as one moves outward in space, ultimately even taking on the anatomical features of beasts (cf. Tacitus *Germania* 46).

preach to, or simply ignore the peoples of the interior. In their eyes "normal" human values, as defined by those who imagine themselves at the privileged center, can appear arbitrary and even laughably absurd.

It is the early Greek texts concerning these distant races, and especially those which actually adopt their point of view, which will concern us in what follows. Scholars have usually focused attention only on the later stages of this tradition, which were dominated by the tendentious urgings of moral philosophy: The utopian voyages recounted by Iambulus and Euhemerus, for example, use eastern races to teach the Greeks about their own shortcomings,[6] and later Cynic texts like the dialogues between Alexander the Great and the Indian wise men (Pseudo-Callisthenes 3.5–6) do likewise.[7] Later still, the tradition of inverse ethnocentrism has been perceived at work in More's *Utopia* and in images of the "noble savage" created by Montaigne, Rousseau, and Montesquieu.[8] However, it has been less fre-

[6] On this tradition see John Ferguson, *Utopias* (above, n. 1) chaps. 12, 14; David Winston, "Iambulus's *Islands of the Sun* and Hellenistic Literary Utopias," *Science Fiction Studies* 3 (1976): 219–27; and C. Mossé, "Les Utopies égalitaires à l'époque hellénistique," *Revue Historique* 241 (1969): 297–308.

[7] The best survey of the relevant Greek texts (mostly fragmentary) can be found, like so much of the material that concerns the study of ancient travel lore, in Rohde (1914) section 2, "Ethnographische Utopie, Fabeln, und Romane"; also on the "noble savage" tradition see Lovejoy and Boas chap. 11, and Ferguson, *Utopias* chap. 2. Recent studies on the attitude toward barbarians in Greek literature and ethnography include William Blake Tyrrell, *Amazons: A Study in Athenian Mythmaking* (Baltimore and London 1984); Arnaldo Momigliano, *Alien Wisdom: The Limits of Hellenization* (Cambridge 1975); and Timothy Long, *Barbarians in Greek Comedy* (Carbondale and Edwardsville, Ill. 1986). Mention should also be made of Martin Bernal's multivolume study, *Black Athena: The Afroasiatic Roots of Classical Civilization*, as yet in its first volume (New Brunswick, N.J. 1987), which collects an impressive range of Greek texts dealing with Egyptian, African, and Semitic peoples but which frequently offers questionable interpretations. For the Roman contributions to the tradition see Richard Thomas, *Lands and Peoples in Roman Poetry: The Ethnographic Tradition* (Cambridge Philological Society suppl. 7, Cambridge 1982).

[8] The medieval and early modern history of the ethno-satiric tradition can be usefully studied in R. Bernheimer, *Wild Men in the Middle Ages* (Cambridge, Mass. 1952); Margaret T. Hodgen, *Early Anthropology in the Sixteenth and Seventeenth Centuries* (Philadelphia 1964), esp. 17–107; and Harry Levin, *The*

quently noted that this type of "ethnologic satire" can already be found in Greek literature as early as the Homeric and archaic periods, as Strabo indicates above in his discussion of the Nomad Scythians. In fact these early examples of the genre are often the most colorful, since they go furthest in exploring the comic and grotesque aspects of distant humanity without leaning as heavily on object lessons as would the moral philosophies of later eras.

The Blameless Ethiopians

As far back as the *Iliad* the Greeks were interested in identifying a particular race as *eschatoi andrōn*, "the furthest of men," and in Homer it is always the Ethiopians who are so designated.[9] Precisely where these Ethiopians are located is, like most questions of Homeric geography, impossible to pursue,[10] except to say that they lie far off (*tēloth'eontas*, Od. 1.22), by the streams of Ocean (*ep'Ōkeanoio rheethra, Il.* 23.205), and are split into eastern and western branches (*dichtha dedaiatai*, etc., *Od.* 1.23–24), perhaps on opposite coasts of a dimly perceived African

---

Myth of the Golden Age in the Renaissance (Oxford 1969), chaps. 1 and 2. In addition, Gilbert Highet's *The Anatomy of Satire* (Princeton 1962), esp. sections 2–4 of "The Distorting Mirror," provides many fruitful opportunities for comparison of Renaissance and Enlightenment authors with the ancient works discussed here, although its breadth is such that conclusions are sometimes limited. Some distinctions between the two eras are raised by M. I. Finley, "Utopianism Ancient and Modern," *The Critical Spirit*, ed. K. Wolff and B. Moore, Jr. (Boston 1967) 3–20.

[9] On the mythical tradition of the Ethiopians see Albin Lesky, "Aithiopika," *Hermes* 87 (1957): 27–38; Moses Hadas, "Utopian Sources in Herodotus," *CP* 30 (1935): 113–21; and Frank Snowden, *Blacks in Antiquity: Ethiopians in the Greco-Roman Experience* (London and Cambridge, Mass. 1970), esp. chaps. 3 and 6. H. Schwabl also makes some useful comments on the Homeric passages in "Das Bild der fremden Welt bei den frühen Griechen," *Grecs et Barbares* chap. 1 (Entretiens Hardt tome 8, Geneva 1961).

[10] See Ramin 73–80, who points out Ethiopians living in virtually every direction except the North; also Ballabriga 108–10, 177–92. Homer at least places them vaguely in the South, at *Od.* 4.84: "I came to the Ethiopians, the Sidonians, and the Erembi, and Libya."

continent. Their connections to the *oikoumenē* are similarly vague: On most occasions the Ethiopians seem to dwell in a never-never land accessible only to the gods, yet at one point in the *Odyssey* Menelaus mentions as an unremarkable event that he visited them on his return voyage from Troy (4.84). This curious blend of remoteness and proximity in the geography of the Ethiopians will later become an important issue for Herodotus, as we shall see shortly.

Surprisingly, Homer takes no notice of the one feature of the Ethiopians that otherwise occasioned the most surprise,[11] their dark skin (unless one considers the name *Aithiopes*—"Burnt-faces," according to its Greek etymology—to be a comment on this physiognomic feature). Instead the most prominent aspect of the race, in Homer's view, is their close alliance with the gods, who sojourn among them during "holiday leaves" from Olympus and from the world at large.[12] This closeness has been explained, for example by Frank Snowden, in terms of the Ethiopians' piety and moral virtue[13] (as suggested by their poetic epithet *amumōn* or "blameless")[14] but at the same time it partly derives from the nature of the land they inhabit, which is so prosperous as to furnish the ample sacrificial feasts which the gods relish. In fact these two explanations are in effect one and the same, since indigenous fertility and abundance, in many of the landscapes described in early Greek poetry, serve to reflect the moral virtues of the native inhabitants.[15] We

[11] E.g., to Aeschylus, fr. 389 Nauck, and to Pliny the Elder, *Hist. Nat.* 7.1.6.

[12] See J. Latacz, "Zeus's Reise zu den Äthiopen," 53–81 in *Gnomosyne: Menschliches Denken und Handeln in der frühgriechischen Literatur (Festschrift Walter Marg)*, ed. G. Kurz, D. Müller, W. Nicolai (Munich 1981), for this tradition. Didorus Siculus also discusses it at 3.2.1–4.

[13] *Blacks in Antiquity* 144–47. Snowden's analysis is partly directed at establishing a link between the Homeric Ethiopians and the historical peoples of southern Africa, but Homer's portrait is readily intelligible without such a link.

[14] Though the adjective does not always have an obvious moral force, and in fact is used of Aegisthus, a figure we can hardly see as ethically superior, at *Od.* 1.29; but see Ferguson, *Utopias* 12 and n. 20.

[15] See Lesky, "Aithiopika" and Hadas, "Utopian Sources" (above, n. 9); also A. Schulten, "Die Inseln der Seligen," *Geografische Zeitschrift* 32 (1926): 229–47; and Lovejoy and Boas chap. 1.

might compare, for example, the island of the Heroes depicted in Hesiod's *Works and Days* (170–74), which Zeus has blessed with perfect climate and boundless productivity in order to reward the semidivine beings who dwell there. The prosperity of Homer's Ethiopians, of course, unlike that of Hesiod's Heroes, cannot be said to have been "given" by the gods and does not quite so clearly represent an indwelling moral condition.[16] However, the fact remains that this prosperity forms the bond that ties Olympians and Ethiopians together, and thus the sharing of feasts by the two societies must be seen, at least in part, as a celebration of shared values.

Another interesting feature of Olympian feasting among the Ethiopians is that it removes the gods behind an opaque screen, preventing them from being seen or contacted by anyone in the world at large. At the beginning of the *Iliad*, for instance, Thetis must wait twelve days before presenting Achilles' embassy to Zeus:

> For Zeus is at Ocean among the blameless Ethiopians, gone to earth for banquets; all the gods are there with him. (1.424–25)

Nor are the gods aware, once they have entered the Ethiopian enclave, of what takes place outside it; thus at the start of the *Odyssey* Poseidon, feasting among the Ethiopians, fails to observe Odysseus getting his homeward voyage underway. The opacity of the Ethiopian retreat has traditionally been seen as a convenience of plot construction,[17] allowing Homer to take his gods "offstage" at crucial moments, but its significance surely extends beyond mere expediency. The isolation and inaccessibility of the Ethiopians' territory are part of what makes it an ideal vacation spot: Their land gives the gods a respite from tending the needs and sufferings of strife-worn humans.

The great appeal of this isolation becomes clearer in some of

[16] Aeschylus, we note, makes the link between Ethiopian bliss and divine favor somewhat stronger in his description of the "all-nourishing harbor" (fr. 192 Nauck) where Helius stops to rest his horses.

[17] For example, by W. B. Stanford, in his commentary on *Odyssey* 1. 22–23 (*The Odyssey of Homer*[2] vol. 1 [N.Y. 1959]), and by K.H.W. Völcker, as quoted by John Ferguson, *Utopias* 12.

the contrasts Homer suggests between the Ethiopian condition and that of the rest of mankind. The Ethiopians' reputation for unlimited feasting, for example, stands out sharply against the backdrop of a world where feasts are often associated with suffering and grave loss. Thus in the *Iliad* the Ethiopians are said to furnish the gods with *daita*—a word which grimly echoes the *daita* mentioned in the very fifth line of the poem (that is, provided we accept one of two variant readings of this line),[18] the carrion "banquets" furnished by the corpses of fallen heroes. Similarly in the *Odyssey*, the rich hecatombs of sheep and bulls which the Ethiopians sacrifice to Poseidon vividly underscore the pinched shortages of the human realm, where Odysseus's herds are rapidly dwindling as a result of the suitors' reckless feasts.[19] In one poem and possibly both, then, the Ethiopians' limitless abundance of food forms a marked antithesis to the suffering or privation endured in the central sphere of action.

Another, particularly striking example of this contrast occurs near the end of the *Iliad* (23.192–211), when the goddess Iris visits the West Wind to persuade him to help kindle Patroclus's pyre. Iris finds the winds at a feast, which they invite her to join; she demurs, claiming that she is on her way "back to the streams of Ocean, to the land of the Ethiopians," to partake of even more sumptuous feasting. All this recreation among the gods cannot help but put us in mind of Achilles, who just recently had refused to take any food at all so long as Patroclus's death remained unavenged. Ancient commentators, in fact, raise the issue in an even more troubling way: They understood Iris's departure "back" to the Ethiopians to mean that the gods, believing their duties in the Trojan War to be reaching an end, are here seen returning to the Ethiopian feasts they had first left

[18] The reading of this line has been contested since the time of Zenodotus, and I shall not enter into the debate over it here. Suffice it to say that modern editors are divided on the question, with Dindorf, for one, preferring *daita* (Teubner edition, Leipzig 1901).

[19] On this contrast see Vidal-Naquet, "Valeurs réligieux" (above, n. 1), and J.-P. Vernant, "Les Troupeaux du Soleil et la Table du Soleil," *REG* 85 (1972): xiv–xvii.

behind at the outset of the poem (i.e., at 1.424–25).[20] In other words, the entire involvement of the gods in the action of the *Iliad*, beginning with Thetis's embassy to Zeus and ending with the death of Hector, seems from the divine perspective to be only an interruption of an otherwise blissful Ethiopian holiday.

It should be said by way of caution, however, that these earliest contrasts between the *eschatoi andrōn* and the men of the *oikoumenē* remain implicit and veiled; Homer never brings Ethiopians into the narrative spotlight so as to offer a pointed glimpse of an alternative world, as he does with the Olympians so frequently (for instance at *Iliad* 1.570–611). Nevertheless, we are always aware of the Ethiopian retreat which lies just beyond the horizon of the poems, offering the peace and plenitude which are so sorely lacking in the world before our eyes. By glancing occasionally toward that horizon Homer seems to imitate his own Zeus, who, during a brief interlude in a pitched battle, suddenly casts his gaze far away:

> Zeus, when he had brought Hector and the Trojans near to the ships, let them remain there to endure unceasing toil and hardship, while he himself turned his shining eyes back from the battle, gazing far off to the lands of the horse-breeding Thracians, of the close-fighting Mysians, and of the noble mare-milking, milk-drinking Abii, justest of mankind. (*Il.* 13.1–6)

This interlude too, like those which take the gods to the Ethiopian land, offers a restful vision of a world defined by the contentment of its inhabitants, who in this case are portrayed as undemanding drinkers of milk rather than as sumptuous feasters.[21]

We should also be careful, moreover, not to project onto such moments of contrast too much of the satiric or ethical tendencies which later evolved out of them. For instance Homer never implies that the privation of the *oikoumenē*, as compared with the abundance of the Ethiopians, is a mark of moral in-

[20] Schol. b to *Il.* 23.296; sim. Eustathius ad loc. (1296.25).

[21] This passage has been seen as the first extant case of Greek idealization of barbarian races; see Strabo's interpretation of it, 7.3.4–9, and the discussion by Lovejoy and Boas 287–90, Bolton 71, Müller (1972) 120–21.

adequacy, or that the Ethiopians should be seen as *paradeigmata*. Rather, shortage of food, like mortality itself, is simply an unfortunate but inescapable aspect of the human condition. Homer uses the Ethiopians at most to provide an ethnologic frame that accentuates that condition, much as one might frame a painting with a contrasting color to bring out its own hues more fully.

The Ethiopians begin to take on sharper point, however, when we come to Herodotus's treatment of them, some three centuries later than the *Iliad*. In a passage of the *Histories* to which we now turn, Herodotus has not only brought the Ethiopians (or at least a branch of that race identified as Macrobian, or "Long-lived") onto the narrative stage in a way that Homer never did, but has also constructed an actual encounter between them and a people of the central *oikoumenē*, the Persians.[22] The resulting episode proves to be an exemplary case of the inverse ethnocentrism that concerns us here, juxtaposing the values of an imperfect Mediterranean society with those of divinely appointed border-dwellers.[23]

It should be observed at the outset that Herodotus employs the Persians, here and throughout the *Histories*, to represent the traditional type of ethnocentricism, which sees a central position in the world as the basis of cultural superiority:[24]

[22] I use the word "constructed" here advisedly: There is evidence that such an encounter actually took place, if we believe that an African inscription housed in Berlin (see Hennig [1936] 84–85 for a German translation) refers to this very invasion. However, we can hardly doubt that Herodotus himself is largely responsible for the elaboration of the episode, which must have reached his ears in only the sketchiest outlines (see Torgny Säve-Söderbergh, "Zu den äthiopischen Episoden bei Herodot," *Eranos* 44 [1946]: 77–80).

[23] Cited by Müller (1972) 1.126–27 as an early instance of Greek idealization of the barbarians.

[24] On Herodotus's exploration of cultural relativism see James Redfield, "Herodotus the Tourist," *CP* 80 (1985): 97–118; Rossellini and Saïd, "Usages des femmes" (above, n. 5); M. Gigante, *Nomos Basileus* (Naples 1956); J.A.S. Evans, "*Despotēs Nomos*," *Athenaeum* n.s. 43 (1965): 142–53; and Hans Erich Stier, "*Nomos Basileus*," *Philologus* 83 (1928): 225–58. Seth Benardete believes that much of the *Histories* is intended "to show the Greeks to the Greeks . . . to persuade the Greeks to look on everything as not their own" (*Herodotean Inquiries* [The Hague 1969] 14).

> They [the Persians] honor most the peoples nearest to themselves, next the people next to those, and others in proportion to their remoteness, and those dwelling furthest from themselves they hold in the least honor. (1.134)

The presumption of regarding one's own geographic position as privileged, however, represents a kind of hubris that always receives its comeuppance in Herodotus's scheme;[25] and the Persians bear out this principle every time they make war against neighboring peoples (including, principally, the Greeks).[26] In particular the wars of Cambyses in Book 3 are used to illustrate how such hubris brings disaster on itself when projected outward into the world at large.[27] It is thus peculiarly fitting that this same Cambyses, the chief representative of a worldview in which marginality translates into cultural inferiority, should be dealt his most humiliating defeat by the Macrobian Ethiopians, a people whom Herodotus explicitly locates at the borders of the earth (*es ta eschata gēs*, 3.25).[28]

The confrontation begins when Cambyses, based in occupied Egypt, decides to invade the Ethiopian land. In preparation for this he sends a delegation of intermediaries, a tribe called *Ichthyophagoi*[29] or "Fish-eaters," to present the king with four precious gifts—a dyed robe, gold jewelry, a container of myrrh, and a jar of palm-wine—ostensibly as a gesture of friendship but really as a pretext for spying on his adversaries. Cambyses also instructs these Fish-eaters, interestingly enough,

[25] See D. Lateiner, "No Laughing Matter: A Literary Tactic in Herodotus," *TAPA* 107 (1977): 173–82, and Redfield, "Herodotus the Tourist," 115. In a sense the entire *Histories* narrates the story of how the Persians get "paid back" for their self-aggrandizing arrogance, since most of their military defeats come about after they have scorned or disdained their enemy.

[26] See Susanna Stambler, "Herodotus," in *Ancient Writers*, ed. J. Luce (N.Y. 1982) 1:134.

[27] The pattern is discussed in depth by Stewart Flory in *The Archaic Smile of Herodotus* (Detroit 1987) chap. 3.

[28] For the location of their land see Ballabriga 214–15, Ramin 73–80.

[29] The Fish-eaters too were idealized in ancient ethnography, in much the same terms as the Ethiopians; see Diodorus Siculus 3.15–20, Agatharchides 49 (Lovejoy and Boas 349–50, where they are mistakenly identified as Ethiopians); Ferguson, *Utopias* (above, n. 1) 18–19.

to investigate the so-called Table of the Sun, a miraculous platform from which the Ethiopians are said to receive all manner of cooked meats. Herodotus gives no explanation for his curiosity about this wonder, but it seems to spring from a kind of jealousy: Believing his own race to be supreme on earth, Cambyses typically reacts uneasily to evidence that divine favor is in fact more in evidence elsewhere.[30]

The scene now shifts to the opposing camp where the Ethiopian king, with unexplained omniscience, sees through the sham delegation of Fish-eaters and coldly rebukes Cambyses for his treachery. He sends the spies back to Egypt bearing symbols of Ethiopian defiance, but first pauses, in a bemused frame of mind, to examine the gifts they have brought:

> Picking up the purple robe, he asked what it was and how it was made. The Fish-eaters gave him a true account of purple, and the process of dyeing, to which the king said, "These men are fakers, since the colors of their clothing are faked." Then he asked about the gold jewelry (a necklace and some bracelets). When the Fish-eaters explained the use of gold as ornament, the king laughed, and supposing them to be fetters, said, "We have stronger fetters than these among our people." Thirdly he asked about the myrrh; when they told him about its production and use in ointments, he made the same reply as he had regarding the robe. Then he came to the wine, and learned about its manufacture, while delighting in its flavor; next he asked what the king of Persia ate, and how long a Persian lived. They said that bread was the chief source of food, explaining the nature of cereal grain, and that the fullest age a man might attain was 80 years. At that the Ethiopian said he was not surprised that they lived such a short time, since they subsisted on dung; they would not live even so long, he said, if they were not sustained by that drink (indicating the wine), a product in which his own people were bested by the Persians.[31] (3. 23)

[30] Compare, for example, his resentful reaction to the Egyptians' claim of an epiphany of the god Apis, 3.29.

[31] This passage of Herodotus has been proposed as a model for an episode of More's *Utopia*, for example by Hadas, "Utopian Sources" 113–14; see pp. 152–54 of the Yale edition, *The Complete Works of St. Thomas More* vol. 4, ed.

From the detached perspective of the Ethiopians Persian ethnocentrism appears laughably presumptuous; the conquerors of the known world are here reduced to liars, cheats, fools, and eaters of dung (i.e., cereals raised from the manured earth).

Neither these gifts, nor the Ethiopian king's rebukes of them, are idly chosen; in fact what is under attack here are the most basic underpinnings of Mediterranean technology and material culture.[32] It is the artifice behind such products as dyed cloth and refined myrrh, echoing as it does the artifice of Cambyses in sending out spies, that the Ethiopian king finds so distasteful; likewise it is the use of gold for cosmetic rather than practical purposes that he sees as ridiculous. The most esteemed products of a sophisticated, manufacturing-based society suddenly lose their value when viewed through the eyes of *Naturvölker*, for whom the raw materials supplied by nature are sufficient to meet every need. Herodotus carries this contrast further in the next scene, by having the king conduct the Fish-eaters on a tour of Ethiopian life: He exhibits their food and drink (boiled meat and milk); the spring of rarefied water which gives a glossy sheen, "like that of olive oil," to those who bathe in it; the prison, where wrongdoers are bound in golden fetters; and lastly the famous meat-producing Table of the Sun. In each case the Ethiopians are seen to obtain from the environment around them the substances which the Persians can only get, ignobly, by manufacture or cultivation.

This nature-culture opposition becomes somewhat more complex in the case of the jar of palm-wine, the one token of Persian custom which wins admiration from the Ethiopian king. Herodotus here follows a long-standing tradition (dating back at least to the Cyclops episode of the *Odyssey*) according to which "primitive" peoples are unable to resist the effects of wine, that most sublime of advancements wrought by higher civilizations. Even here, however, we can see an implicit critique of Persian sophistication at work: The Ethiopian king

---

E. Surtz and J. H. Hexter (New Haven 1965), with commentary, 430–31. A different Herodotean passage (2.172) has been adduced by J. Crossett as More's source (see note of Surtz and Hexter on *matellas*, p. 429).

[32] See Flory, *Archaic Smile* (above, n. 27) 98–99.

praises wine as a salutary beverage, capable of extending the lifespan of those who drink it; whereas in fact it has the opposite effect on Cambyses, who (as we learn at 3.34) lapses into madness and violence partly as a result of his over-indulgence in wine. Alcohol can be a medicinal beverage to the Ethiopians because, in their golden-age innocence, they do not crave it immoderately; only for "advanced" races like the Persians does it pose a hazardous temptation.[33]

In matters of piety too the Ethiopians show themselves superior to their foreign invaders, in ways that are reminiscent of the Homeric tradition of Ethiopian feasting. We have already seen the importance in their realm of the Table of the Sun, a miraculous source of rich foodstuffs.[34] But Herodotus also includes another such instance of divine favor in the final scene witnessed by the Fish-eaters, that of Ethiopian coffin-making and burial rites (3.24). A local transparent stone called *huelos* is carved by the Ethiopians into chambers, and the mummified bodies of the dead are housed in them. Once inside the *huelos* a corpse is miraculously kept from decomposing, and remains visible through the glassy rock, "resembling in every way the person now dead"; the chambers are then stored upright, above ground, so that family and friends can continue to behold the deceased and offer sacrifices to them. Here the power to escape the ravages of death, which ordinarily can be conferred only by the gods (as in the case of Hector's corpse in the *Iliad*), is granted to the Ethiopians by way of the *huelos* stone, a resource which (as Herodotus specifies) is both plentiful in their region and easily obtained. Like their Homeric antecedents, then, Herodotus's Ethiopians inhabit a landscape which, with its supernatural abundance, brings them close in stature to the gods.

The impact of these disparities on the haughty Cambyses, to whom Herodotus's narrative now returns, is overwhelming.

[33] Much the same contrast emerges from Herodotus's later account of another self-destructing military leader, the Spartan king Cleomenes (6.84), who goes insane after drinking unmixed wine among the Scythians.

[34] For the connections between this table, which may in fact have been a place for the offering of sacrifices, and the Homeric tradition see Lesky, "Aithiopika" (above, n. 9) 27–29; How and Wells 261.

Having heard the taunts of the Ethiopian king from his spies, Cambyses becomes inflamed with rage and sets out at once on his planned invasion, too impatient now even to gather adequate provisions. The ill-conceived expedition becomes, in Herodotus's retelling, another study in the distance separating inner and outer worlds.[35] Although elsewhere in the *Histories* the Ethiopians had been located quite close to the borders of Egypt, so that the Fish-eaters experienced little difficulty in passing back and forth, the gulf between the two lands suddenly yawns wide when the Persian army attempts to cross it. Cambyses, who had earlier shown a fascination with the Ethiopians' meat-giving Table of the Sun, now finds his own troops running short of food before they have gone even one-fifth of the intervening distance. As he presses recklessly onward, his army regresses through successive stages of primitivism, consuming their own pack animals, then the surrounding foliage, and finally, at the last pitch of desperation, one another (3.25). At last even the distracted Cambyses gives up the invasion and returns to Egypt, the greater part of his army destroyed.

The encounter between this deranged Persian and the imperturbable Ethiopians thus ends in a pattern familiar from tragic drama, as a story of reckless daring and its disastrous consequences. But at its center lies the diatribe of the Ethiopian king, an interlude that partakes more of satire than of tragedy. We might further describe it as *ethnologic* satire, in that its point is to show the master races of the world humbled in the eyes of indifferent aliens.[36] It is because Cambyses cannot abide the implications of such satire—cannot accept any challenge to the worldview which places Persia at the all-important center of things—that the whole episode ends as a disaster for him; while on the other hand the Ethiopian king, who freely acknowledges the areas in which his culture has been bested by others (i.e., in wine-making), remains unharmed and even triumphant.

In this way Herodotus develops the contrast we saw only in

[35] The episode has been treated in some detail by J.-P. Vernant, "Les Troupeaux du Soleil" (above, n. 19).

[36] This form of humor is discussed by Riese, *Idealisierung* (above, n. 2) 14–17, and by Trüdinger 28–31.

outline in the Homeric poems into a direct and highly structured confrontation, pitting the *eschatoi andrōn*, who stand at the limit not only of geographic space but also of human perfection, against the flawed and unstable mortals of the *oikoumenē*.

The Fortunate Hyperboreans

In many ways the Hyperboreans[37] can be seen as mirror-image counterparts to the Ethiopians, inhabiting the northern edge of the world rather than the southern.[38] Thus, just as in Homer's poems the gods retire to the Ethiopians for recreation, so the Hyperboreans, according to other authors, are cherished by the gods for their moral purity and festive way of life:

> In truth, Apollo delights in their festivals most of all. . . . The Muse is never far from home among their ways, and everywhere, dances of maidens, the wail of the lyre, and the shrill ring of flutes are in the air; while they, with their hair bound in gold fillets, partake gladly of the banquets. Neither sickness, nor baneful old age, mixes with this holy tribe; far from toils and battles they dwell, avoiding the just retribution of Nemesis. (Pindar, *Pythian* 10.34–44)

Here the Hyperboreans, like the Ethiopians, are said to escape the law of Nemesis which, for ordinary species of humanity, balances pleasure with pain and satiety with want. Aeschylus exemplifies their status in the *Libation Bearers* with the phrase "hyperborean good fortune" (373): a lot which goes beyond

[37] On the Hyperboreans see Ramin 55–71; Otto Schroeder, "Hyperboreer," *Archiv für Religionswissenschaft* 8 (1905): 69–84; Grace Harriet Macurdy, "The Hyperboreans," *CR* 30 (1916): 180–83; S. Casson, "The Hyperboreans," *CR* 34 (1920): 1–3; Fred Ahl, "Amber, Avallon, and Apollo's Singing Swan," *AJP* 103 (1982): esp. 377–83; Marie Delcourt, *L'Oracle de Delphes* (Paris 1955) pt. 2, chap. 4. I have investigated Herodotus's discussion of this race in some detail in "Herodotus and Mythic Geography: The Case of the Hyperboreans," *TAPA* 119 (1989): 97–117.

[38] Ballabriga remarks, correctly, that the Ethiopians might well be considered the "Hypernotians" that Herodotus opposes to the Hyperboreans at 4.36 (215; cf. Eratosthenes fr. I B 21, Berger [1880] 76–77).

the normal human condition of good mixed with evil. It is an ideal state from which the inhabitants of the *oikoumenē* are visibly and at times even painfully excluded.

However, the mythic role of the Hyperboreans is in another sense more complex than that of their southern counterparts. Whereas the Ethiopians, as noted by their king in Herodotus's account (3.21), remain decidedly aloof from the *oikoumenē*, the Hyperboreans were thought to have traversed it in ancient times and to have left their mark on its innermost and most sanctified spaces. As a result they present a more direct and aggressive challenge to the value-systems of the central world. This is particularly true, as we shall see, in the area of religion—where the godlike Hyperboreans seem to outshine the Greeks at every turn.

It may surprise us, for instance, to discover Hyperboreans closely connected with Greece's two major sites of Apollo worship, Delphi and Delos.[39] In fact the Hyperboreans, under the leadership of a prophet named Olēn, had actually founded the Delphic oracle, according to a legend preserved by Pausanias:[40]

> Boeo, a native of the area, says in a hymn she composed for the Delphians that men who had come from the Hyperboreans, Olēn among them, had established the oracle, and that Olēn was the first to give prophecy there, and the first to chant in hexameters. Boeo's verses are as follows: "The sons of the Hyperboreans, Pagasus and godlike Aiguieus/ established upon this spot a well-remembering oracle." (10.5.9)

Boeo's strange couplet identifies the Delphic oracle as a monument, perhaps even a memorial (as suggested by the adjective *eumnēston*) of an early Hyperborean visit to the spot—as if Hyperboreans, like the gods themselves, could impart numinous power to the places which housed their relics. Delos too, like

[39] The Hyperborean role in Delphic myth has been explored by Delcourt, *L'Oracle de Delphes*, and by J. Defradas, *Les Thèmes de la propaganda delphique* (Paris 1972). For a more narrowly historical treatment see Lewis Richard Farnell, *Cults of the Greek States* vol. 4 (Oxford 1907) 100–104.

[40] Cp. Plutarch, *De Pyth. Orac.* 402d. For comment see Delcourt, *L'Oracle de Delphes* 162.

Delphi a center of Apollo's cult, claimed Hyperborean ancestry for some of its major shrines, as recounted by Herodotus (4.32–36); and here too the monuments associated with these early visitors extend the history of the shrine back to the mythic past, to a time when Hyperboreans traveled the Greek world "accompanied by the gods themselves" (4.35).[41]

The legends retailed at both Delphi and Delos, then, give the Hyperboreans a role in the worship of Apollo analogous to that of cultic heroes, mythic figures whose memorials or gravesites are thought to create a link to the divine. However, it should be noted that these Hyperborean monuments differ markedly from those of autochthonous heroes, in that they share no lineal connection with the latter-day inhabitants of the site. According to usual cultic patterns, that is, the founding hero is claimed as an ancestor by some or all of the local population; his gravesite marks the establishment of a family line in the region, often by way of a victory over the monsters or chthonic forces that originally made habitation impossible.[42] The Hyperboreans, by contrast, are not conceived of as the ancestors of any latter-day Greek peoples; their memorials do not mediate between god and man in the same way as, for example, the sites associated with Heracles' labors. We might therefore distinguish Hyperborean landmarks as the signatures of exogenous rather than indigenous heroes, recalling no familial or national triumph but only marking a spot where mysterious outsiders have come and gone.

The idea that an exogenous race thus shares in the establishment of Apollo's shrines, including Delphi itself,[43] is problem-

[41] According to the conceit, that is, that in mythic times the gods walked the earth in the company of men, whereas they have since departed to loftier retreats. In connection with the antiquarianism of the Hyperborean legends, we may note that the Delian "men and women of olden times" mentioned in the *Homeric Hymn to Apollo* (160) have been identified by some scholars as Hyperboreans; see the remarks ad loc. in the Allen and Sikes commentary (*The Homeric Hymns* [London, 1904]).

[42] The most prominent example is furnished by Apollo's defeat of the monstrous Python to establish the oracle of Delphi; see J. Fontenrose, *Python* (Berkeley 1959).

[43] The idea of Hyperborean appropriation of Delphic tradition comes out

atic in that the archaic Greeks attached great importance to the centrality of Delphi—which they saw as the "navel of the earth"—and on the special relationship to Apollo which that centrality conferred.[44] The nature of this relationship is revealed, for example, in the two parts of the *Homeric Hymn to Apollo*, both of which proudly relate how the Greeks were chosen as favored servants of Apollo and the founders of his shrines; furthermore in Herodotus, the Apollo who gives oracles at Delphi is characterized as "the god of the Greeks" by Croesus, a Persian (1.90.2). The legends in which the Hyperboreans are seen as founders of Apollo's sites, then, create a curious dissonance with these Hellenic appropriations of Delphi and of its god. Nor is Delphic mythology the only case of such dissonance: In a legend related by Pindar (*Ol.* 3), for example, the Hyperboreans are said to have bestowed upon Heracles the sacred olive spray which later became the crown of victorious Olympic athletes. Here again a sacral symbol which seems vitally Greek in spirit is found to derive from a distant race, and, what is more, a race which (as Pindar makes clear) parts with it only grudgingly.[45]

In some cases, moreover, the Greeks and Hyperboreans seem not only to divide between them the favor of the gods, and in particular that of Apollo, but actually to compete with each other for it. This competitive tendency emerges clearly, for example, in a hymn to Apollo composed by the lyric poet Alcaeus:[46]

---

even more strongly in Pausanias's follow-up to the legend recounted by Boeo, in which it is claimed that Apollo had actually sent the Hyperboreans the so-called "Winged Temple" that had been built on the site in early times (10.5.9).

[44] For the central position of Delphi see Agathemerus 1.1.2, Plutarch *De defectu orac.* 1.1 (409e), Varro *Ling. Lat.* 7.17, Strabo 9.3.6.

[45] A comparable though less clear-cut example involves the legend of Abaris, a Hyperborean wayfarer who, according to Herodotus, "travelled around the entire earth carrying an arrow, without eating anything" (4.36); later sources inform us that he was sent to dispense oracles (or perhaps medicinal cures) at the behest of Apollo, so that once again a Hyperborean was portrayed as the source of vital Greek *nomoi*. See A. Dryoff, "Abaris," *Philologus* 59 (1900): 610–14, and Bolton 157–59.

[46] Preserved by Himerius in *Orat.* 14.10; cp. Cicero, *De Nat. Deorum* 3.23.

> Oh king Apollo, son of great Zeus, whose father outfitted you at birth with a golden fillet, and a tortoise-shell lyre, and beyond these a swan-sped chariot to drive; he sent you to Delphi, and to the Castalian spring, gift of Cephissus, to proclaim a code of divine law for the Greeks. But you stepped into your vehicle and ordered the swans to fly to the Hyperboreans; and when they realized, the Delphians composed a paean and performed it to flutes and dancing, around a tripod, and urged you to come away from the Hyperboreans. But you stayed a whole year, giving laws in that country. (fr. 1.1–14)

Here Apollo's year-long dalliance in northern lands, a willful diversion from his mission to give laws to the Delphians, again makes the Hyperboreans into a people from whom essential Greek institutions must be wrested. Though it is true that Apollo finally does continue on to Delphi, and that his journey there is described in triumphant tones (in the hymn's next stanza), his return to the Greek world does not entirely resolve the tension created by the initial premise: that the Delphians are forced to wait an entire year for Apollo to leave the Hyperboreans and come their way.[47]

One factor which helps explain Apollo's reluctance to leave his northern retreat is its ideal climate: Alcaeus makes much of the fact that the god arrives at Delphi when that land is lush with summer greenery, perhaps implying that only in its best season could it lure him away from the Hyperboreans. In fact the climatic privileges attributed to the Hyperboreans,

---

The legend is discussed by K. O. Müller, *The History and Antiquities of the Dorians* (Oxford 1830) 296–97; Farnell, *Cults* (above, n. 39) 4.104.

[47] The proprietary nature of the Hyperborean friendship with Apollo is further illustrated by the story of Cleinis the Babylonian, recounted by Antoninus Liberalis from a poem by Simmias of Rhodes (fr. 2 Powell). Cleinis was a fanatical devotee of Apollo and traveled to the Hyperboreans to visit the god's temple there. He observed the sacrifice of asses which the Hyperboreans made to their patron (a detail borrowed from Pindar, *Pyth.* 10.31–36), and after returning to Babylon attempted to practice the same rite; but Apollo appeared in person and threatened him with death if he attempted it, saying "he wished only the Hyperboreans to bring him a sacrifice of asses." Later Cleinis and his sons proceed with the sacrifice anyway, and as punishment are devoured by the asses they intended to slay.

throughout their early mythology, can be seen as parallel to the superabundance of food enjoyed by the Ethiopians. The very name of this northern people, in fact, locates them *huper boreas*, "beyond the North Wind"[48]—which is to say, beyond the source of the cool, rainy weather which descends on Greece during winter months. In many accounts they are also situated beyond the legendary Rhipaean Mountains, a high northern chain which effectively seals them off from Boreas's effects. They thus inhabit a "pocket" of climatic tranquility, similar in nature to the Hesiod's Isles of the Blessed (*Works and Days* 170–74) or Homer's Olympus (*Od.* 6.43–45):

> It is not shaken by breezes nor drenched by storm, nor does the snowfall approach it; but rather, fair weather spreads cloudless upon it, and white sunlight runs up its sides.

The anomaly which allows the Hyperboreans to enjoy such perfect conditions, despite their extreme northerly locale, takes on added significance when we consider that climate, like the identification of Delphi with the "navel of the earth," allowed the early Greeks to situate themselves at the center of the globe. The Greek word for a seasonable climate, *eukrasia*, implies a moderate "blending" of southern heat and northern cold, which occurs only in the lands lying midway between these extremes; and Greece itself, in particular Ionia, was thought to occupy this median position, as illustrated by Herodotus (1.142)[49] and the author of the fifth-century treatise *Airs Waters Places* (13.15–21).[50] In fact, in a text we examined in chapter 1, Herodotus's digression on the *eschatiai* (*Histories* 3.106–

[48] Cf. Pindar *Olympian* 3.31. Modern scholars reject the etymology, preferring some derivation from *huperpherō*, "to transport," on the evidence of Herodotus's "parcel-post" story. See Daebritz, *RE s.v.* "Hyperboreer," cols. 259–61; Macurdy; "The Hyperboreans" (above, n. 37); Farnell, *Cults* 4.100–103; Bolton 195 n. 32.

[49] On this passage see Redfield, "Herodotus the Tourist" (above, n. 24) 110–11; Müller (1972) 1.126; Ballabriga 154–55. The more general question of Herodotus's notions of world climate is treated by Guy Lachenaud, "Connaissance du monde et représentations de l'espace dans Hérodote," *Hellenica* 32 (1980): 42–60.

[50] See commentary by Heidel (1937) 19–20.

16), Greece's *eukrasia* is seen as a boon given in compensation for its paucity of resources:

> The *eschatiai* of the inhabited world have been given all the finest things, whereas Greece has received by far the best mixture of seasons (*eukrasia*). (3.106)

This compensatory scheme suggests that all the regions of the earth have been allotted *some* benefit, either economic or climatic. What is remarkable is that the Hyperboreans (who go unmentioned in this passage, but are elsewhere of great concern to Herodotus) have somehow managed to obtain both at the same time.

Herodotus himself underscores the climatic privilege of the Hyperboreans in a different passage, where, as part of an ethnography of the peoples of the far Northeast, he gives the following account of southward migrations from that region (derived, as he tells us, from Aristeas's poem *Arimaspeia*):

> All the [northeastern] races, beginning from the Arimaspians—that is, with the exception of the Hyperboreans—are continually pressing upon their neighbors, so that the Issedones were pushed out of their territory by the Arimaspians, the Scythians by the Issedones, and the Cimmerians, who dwell by the southern [i.e., Black] sea, were crowded out by the Scythians and had to leave the region. (4.13)

Here Herodotus imagines a climatically structured ethnographic map, in which concentric rings of humanity press in upon one another in competition for the temperate zone at the center; but from such competition the Hyperboreans remain notably detached. For them alone any move toward the interior would entail a falling-off, a departure from limitless and pure *eukrasia*; their isolation beyond the reach of Boreas exempts them from the continuous strife and struggle that beset the rest of humanity.

In terms both of their climatic insularity and their special relationship with Apollo, then, the Hyperboreans exemplify the scheme of inverse ethnocentrism we discussed at the beginning of this chapter. Though situated at the earth's edge they manage to usurp the advantages of the center, even on occasion intruding into that center in ways that fundamentally alter its makeup. Far from being undercivilized "barbarians," they were thought to surpass the Greeks by such a vast margin as to humble all illusions of Hellenic cultural supremacy.

One final legend will serve to illustrate, by way of caricature, the inverse-ethnocentric tendency underlying much Hyperborean lore. In the fourth century B.C. the historian Theopompus invented a land called Meropis, a vast continent situated beyond the stream of Ocean; he populated it with idealized races of men, including a race of Eusebians or "Pietists" who enjoy a life much like that of the Hyperboreans. One day the inhabitants of Meropis, according to Theopompus, decided to pay a visit to the *oikoumenē*, with the following result:

> They crossed 10,000 miles of Ocean, until they reached the Hyperboreans. And, having learned that these men were the most blessed of peoples among us, they nevertheless looked with contempt on their base and wretched lot, and so disdained to go any farther. (Aelian *Varia Historia* 3.18 = fr. 75c Jacoby)

The disgruntled reaction of the Meropians to the Hyperboreans seems to have been framed as a comic extrapolation of the way the Hyperboreans, from their privileged niche at the world's edge, regard the Greeks.[51] Theopompus has wryly one-upped the archaic tradition of ethnologic satire, by moving his cultural vantage point one step further outward in space.

Arimaspians and Scythians

So much, then, for the golden-age societies at the northern and southern edges of the earth; but what of other distant-world races who inhabit harsher and less paradisical landscapes? He-

[51] See Herodotus 4.33.3–4, where the Hyperboreans are said to have stopped traveling to Delos because their messengers failed to return. Theopompus's tale of Meropis is also intimately connected with Plato's myth of Atlantis (a topic we shall come to in chapter 4), and has even been identified as a takeoff of it; see e.g., J. Bidez, *Eos ou Platon et l'Orient* (Brussels 1945) 36–40. For evidence of Theopompus's tendency to idealize the *Parōkeanitoi* or "dwellers beside Ocean" see Athenaeus *Deipn.* 526d-f (Jacoby fr. 62).

rodotus's digression on the *eschatiai*, for example—a text we examined at the end of chapter 1—entirely omits both Ethiopians and Hyperboreans, and focuses instead on such peoples as Indians, Arabians, and Arimaspians. For these races the earth does not burgeon with foodstuffs, nor do cuts of meat appear spontaneously on magic tables, but instead a bare living has to be wrested at great cost from a grudging or openly hostile environment. In other words, this less fortunate group of distant peoples can be said to embody a "hard" rather than "soft" pattern of primitive life,[52] and thus calls for a different type of discussion than the one we have followed thus far.

Hard versions of primitivism, as exemplified by that articulated in Hesiod's *Works and Days* (90–201), present an essentially ethical model of man's place in the natural world, containing an implicit object lesson. Such landscapes require man to work, or to overcome enormous hardship, in order to survive, but also hold out the promise that moral fortitude and technological advancement will emerge from his labor. Even if nature seems in the short term to throw cruel exigencies in man's path, the evolution he goes through in order to overcome them renders his suffering intelligible. In this sense the landscape of hard primitivism can be compared to the "hard road" of the archaic two-roads allegory, as found in both Hesiod's *Works and Days* (285–92) and in Prodicus's parable of the choice of Heracles (Xenophon, *Memorabilia* 2.1.21): Like Heracles primitive man stands at a crossroads, discovering that nothing of value comes easily but that hard work proves to be worth the reward.[53]

No better figure than Heracles could have been cast in this allegorical role, moreover, since many of his mythic adventures force him to fight terrible monsters for the sake of a fabulous

[52] The terms "soft" and "hard" are employed here in the senses given to them by the pioneering study of Lovejoy and Boas. While their work has no doubt overstated the "profound opposition" between these two poles, which can perhaps be seen more accurately as two sides of the same coin, the construct nevertheless remains useful.

[53] See Lovejoy and Boas 113–16.

prize.[54] Among the most prominent episodes are those which pit him against the snake of the Hesperides, guardian of the golden apples of immortality, and against the monstrous dog Orthus who tends the cattle of Geryon; but in a larger sense all his labors are part of a lifelong test of endurance leading to his divinization on Mt. Oeta. Furthermore many of Heracles' labors, especially those situated at the edges of the earth, evoke the same concerns regarding man's place in nature that give shape to the landscape of hard primitivism. His battles against the beasts, for example—dragons, boars, lions, hydras, centaurs, and monstrous dogs—all reflect, on a certain level at least, an adversarial relationship between man and the undomesticated world of nature; and his eventual divinization is in part an acknowledgment that man must summon up the noblest and most godlike elements within himself, his courage, self-possession, and intellect, in order to defeat creatures endowed with greater strength, speed, and ferocity.[55]

The Heraclean model of mankind's victory over raw nature is paralleled, albeit at a less elevated level, in much of the folkloric and ethnographic literature concerning the distant world. Depictions of the northerly, one-eyed Arimaspians, for example, show them locked in unending combat with their mortal foe the griffin, a fearsome, reptilian bird equipped with wings, talons, scales, and a powerful beak. Herodotus mentions this combat only in passing (since he refuses to believe that one-eyed men really exist, 3.115), but we know its main outlines from other sources: The griffins unearth mounds of gold in the course of digging their burrows, and this gold is stealthily pilfered by the Arimaspians, who must then escape the enraged

[54] The general outlines of the so-called quest myth are discussed by F. Vian, *Les Origines de Thèbes* (Paris 1963) 94–109, and G. S. Kirk, *Myth: Its Meaning and Function in Ancient and Other Cultures* (Berkeley 1970) 185–91; Martin P. Nilsson, "The Dragon and the Treasure," *AJP* 68 (1947): 302–9.

[55] See the discussion by Guthrie of a similar idea in Plato's *Protagoras*, *In the Beginning* 86–88. Pliny the Elder's proem to *Hist. Nat.* 7 (1.4–5) is perhaps the most memorable statement of man's defenselessness within the natural world; for others see Lovejoy and Boas chap. 13.

griffins by running for their lives.[56] The story is paradigmatic of hard-primitive lore in that it calls attention to the glittering prizes that can be won in the struggle against savage nature, as well as to the grave perils that must be faced along the way. Herodotus in fact uses the same paradigm four more times in his *eschatiai* digression, describing how the Indians battle monstrous ants, and the Arabs fight huge birds and flying serpents, in order to win the natural resources which have enabled them to thrive.[57]

Such stories of man-beast combat, it should be noted, recur countless times in countless variations throughout the long history of Greek distant-world lore, almost inevitably portraying mankind as victor in a pitched struggle with untamed nature. The Arimaspians are therefore only a single, early example of a motif which grew in popularity among the Greeks (and Romans as well) after they had themselves retreated to urban fastnesses and left such struggles behind. In fact we would do well to see this folkloric "monster-slaying" pattern as part of a general tendency, long recognized by scholars, for ancient authors to depict distant (and especially northern) barbarians as rugged ascetics as yet untouched by the vices of the *polis*.[58] The fortitude and resourcefulness which are forged in their primitive environments are precisely those which the Greeks, even as early as the archaic period, felt themselves losing; and therefore the distant races, like the "noble savage" later created by Enlightenment Europe, come to embody the virtues of a simpler, more courageous, less corrupt era of social history.

In the archaic era, however, the noble savage is in addition a comic and grotesque figure, perhaps more closely related to the

[56] The most detailed account is by Ctesias (*apud* Aelian *Nat. Anim.* 4.27). There is also a sixth-century Caeretan vase depicting a griffin chasing an Arimaspian, discussed by T.B.L. Webster in *JHS* 48 (1928): 196–205.

[57] I have analyzed these five stories at greater length in "Dragons and Gold at the Edges of the Earth: A Folktale Motif Developed by Herodotus," *Wonders and Tales* 1 (1987): 45–55.

[58] See Riese, *Idealisierung* (above, n. 2) for the early history of this *topos*; for its later development, E. Norden, *Die Germanische Urgeschichte in Tacitus Germania* (Leipzig 1920), esp. chap. 1.

medieval "wild man" than to Rousseau's Indians.[59] The Arimaspians for instance, one-eyed beings with shaggy bodies, must have figured prominently in this more carnivalesque variety of ethnographic lore. At least that is the impression conveyed by the *Arimaspeia* of Aristeas of Proconnesus, an epic dealing largely with the Arimaspians written perhaps in the sixth century B.C.[60] The poem itself has been lost, but we are fortunate enough to have Herodotus's account of its composition: Aristeas, possessed by some sort of religious ecstasy, journeyed to the land of the Issedones in the far North, precisely the point at which, according to Herodotus, the known world gives way to the unknown (4.16.1). There he halted, and during his stay learned from the Issedones about what lay beyond; on his return he recorded the whole experience in an epic devoted (as indicated by its title) to "Arimaspian matters." Whether Aristeas actually undertook such a journey is open to grave doubt,[61] but in any case the literary possibilities which were thereby created are sufficient to account for the deceit. From his vantage point among the Issedones, at the northern threshhold of the *oikoumenē*, Aristeas was able to look outward toward the hardy Arimaspians and inward toward the Greek world at the same time, a Janus-faced perspective ideally suited to the literary tradition we have dubbed ethnologic satire.

[59] The comparison between ancient "noble savages" and the Enlightenment's American Indians has been advanced by Lovejoy and Boas, 289.

[60] The date has been variously fixed. Herodotus places Aristeas about two hundred years before his own time, a date which seems impossibly early but has nevertheless been defended by Bolton chap. 1; see the reply by C. J. Herington in *Phoenix* 18 [1964]: 78–82. Suidas puts Aristeas at the beginning of the sixth century, and this has seemed a more reasonable chronology; see the discussion by Walter Burkert in a review of Bolton, *Gnomon* 35 (1963): 235–40. There is no decisive evidence within the poem to support either the earlier or the later date.

[61] Ken Dowden ("Deux notes sur les Scythes et les Arimaspes," *REG* 93 [1980]: 487–92) notes rather dryly that Aristeas couldn't have gone far in the trancelike state denoted by Herodotus's *phoibolamptos*. A later version of the Aristeas legend in Maximus of Tyre (38.3) has him flying over the lands he described, and this is thought by some to reflect the content of the original poem (see K. Meuli, "Scythica," *Hermes* 70 (1935): 154–55. On the other hand, see Bolton chap. 4 for the view that Aristeas's journey did take place.

The Issedones served as mouthpiece for this provocative cultural comparison; it was they, as we know from Herodotus's remarks, who described the griffin-Arimaspian battles, while Aristeas himself only listened to and then transcribed their stories. Thus it is interesting to note that their description of the Arimaspians, preserved in the few surviving fragments of the poem, betrays a strongly idealizing cast:

> They say there are men dwelling further up, sharing their northern borders, and that they are many, and very noble warriors, rich in horses, with many flocks of sheep, many of cattle. (fr. 4)

> Each has a single eye set in his elegant forehead; shaggy they are with hairs, the toughest of all of mankind. (fr. 5)

Here the Issedones—who are undoubtedly to be understood as the subject of *phasi*, "they say"[62]—depict their northern neighbors as a civilized people whose life, like that of any true-blooded Homeric aristocracy, is rich with the joys of horsemanship and battle. In fact, they are described as *polurrēnas poluboutas*, "owning many herds of sheep and cattle," like the wealthy Pylian lords who are tagged by Homer with the same formulaic line-ending (*Iliad* 9.154, 296). More remarkable still, the Arimaspians, despite their single eye—ordinarily a mark of grotesque ugliness—are here described as having a "handsome visage" by the Issedones. Aristeas seems to have used his alien spokesmen to elevate these far-northerly peoples, as Ephorus did his Nomads, to the status of *paradeigmata* or model human beings.

A comic inversion of this elevating movement might come, one supposes, when the Issedones turn their gaze toward the more "civilized" interior of the earth and react in horror or chagrin to what they find there. And in fact one such inversion seems to have been preserved, by purest chance, in a passage of the Arimaspeia quoted in the late-antique critical treatise *On the Sublime* (10.4):[63]

[62] The same conclusion was reached by C. M. Bowra in "A Fragment of the *Arimaspeia*," *CQ* 49 (1956): 1–10. See also the discussion by Bolton (chap. 1).

[63] Cited by the author, conventionally known as Longinus, as a failed de-

> And this too seems, to our minds, a thing of very great wonder: Men reside in water, in the sea, far from land. Pitiful fellows these are, for they endure grievous afflictions: They have their eyes on the stars, their life and soul in the sea. Indeed, one would think, they lift up their hands to the gods and utter many a prayer, while their innards are foully tossed upward. (fr. 7)

It is not entirely clear what is being described here, since the treatise's author quotes the passage out of context; modern interpretations of it have varied widely.[64] But the most defensible reading sees in this passage the attempt of a landlocked race—presumably the Issedones again—to comprehend the idea of seafaring. Having never before encountered this activity the Issedones naïvely assume that men who sail ships actually "dwell" in the water, and that the instability of such a life causes them almost constant discomfort (including sea-sickness, described here as "up-tossed innards").[65] If this reading is correct, we might further suppose that seafaring had first been described to the Issedones by Aristeas, presumably the only Hellene to visit their remote part of the world, and that therefore the grotesque image they conjure up constitutes a lampoon not just of seafaring in general but of the Greeks in particular. However this may be, the *Arimaspeia* seems in this instance to have very de-

---

scription of a seastorm, to contrast with Homer's more successful version. Longinus does not mention Aristeas by name but refers only to "the author of the *Arimaspeia*," and Bolton believes that he did not have access to the entire poem (26–27). See the discussion ad loc. by D. A. Russell, *Longinus: On the Sublime* (Oxford 1964). In any event, Longinus cannot have correctly remembered the context of the passage, since it hardly describes a storm at sea.

[64] Bethe (*RE* bd.1.2 *s.v.* "Aristeas," col. 877) believes them to be "fabulous sea-creatures," but there is no evidence elsewhere of such a legend. Karl Meuli, who discusses the passage at "Scythica" 155, suggests a race of platform dwellers, like those described in *Airs Waters Places* (15), but this interpretation leaves no good sense for *ommat'en astroisi . . . echousin*, "they keep their eyes fixed on the stars." On the other hand this line takes on a nicely pointed sense if we read it in the context of navigation.

[65] The reading was first proposed by Rhys Roberts (*Longinus: On the Sublime* [Cambridge 1899] 219) and has been supported by Bowra, "Fragment" (above, n. 62) and H. Fränkel, *Early Greek Poetry and Philosophy* (Oxford 1975) 242.

liberately turned the ethnographic tables, causing the world's central races to seem foolish while distant barbarians are raised to heroic stature.

It is significant, moreover, that seafaring serves as the pivot-point of this inversion, since it had long been associated in Greek literature with trade and commerce, social evolution, and consequent moral decline. Thus golden-age peoples are traditionally thought to be ignorant of navigation, as seen in the so-called last journey of Odysseus foretold by Teiresias in the *Odyssey* (11.121–37).[66] According to Teiresias's prophecy, Odysseus will end his life by traveling inland carrying an oar on his shoulder, until he meets a people who mistake that object for a winnowing-fan; that is, the master seaman will find a final resting place so far from the sea that the inhabitants will be innocent of even the most basic navigational tools. In other, later schemes of social evolution, it is likewise the invention of seafaring that marks the end of the golden age and the start of man's long fall from grace,[67] in the same way that the invention of money corrupts Rousseau's noble savages. Thus the Issedonean caricature of seamanship, if that is indeed what the above passage represents, would have strong ethical as well as ethnologic point: The virtuous life of primitives is here contrasted with that of the so-called advanced peoples who greedily chase profit on the seas.

If this seems an over-elaborate interpretation to construct on a few fragmentary lines of the *Arimaspeia*, we should add that a very similar lampoon of seafaring can be found in the folklore of another "hard" primitive, the Scythian sage Anacharsis. This northern barbarian was thought to have toured the Greek world as a kind of itinerant moral philosopher in the early sixth century B.C.[68] Unfortunately, the texts which relate to his visit

[66] Discussed by Jane Harrison, "Mystica Vannus Iacchi," *JHS* 24 (1904): 241–54; A. Hartmann, *Untersuchungen über die Sagen vom Tode des Odysseus* (Munich 1917), esp. 91–92, and F. Dornsieff, "Odysseus' Letzte Fahrt," *Hermes* 72 (1937): 351–55.

[67] Lucretius *DRN* 5.1004–8; Manilius Astronomicon 1.76–78; Ovid *Metamorphoses* 1.96–98; Vergil *Georgics* 3.141–42; Seneca *Medea* 301–39, 364–79. For more discussion see chap. 4, pp. 163–71, below.

[68] See R. Heinze, "Anacharsis," *Philologus* 50 (1891): 458–68; W. Schmid,

mostly derive from a later period than we are here concerned with, but the legend itself seems to date well back into archaic times, perhaps to the same era in which the *Arimaspeia* was composed.[69] Thus it is interesting to find the following barbs attributed to Anacharsis by his late antique biographer, Diogenes Laertius (1.103–4):

> After learning that a ship's thickness was only four fingers' width, he said that those who sail are only that far away from death.
>
> On being asked what kind of ship was the safest, he replied, "Those which are hauled up on shore."
>
> On being asked which were more numerous, the living or the dead, he replied, "In which group do you place those who are sailing the seas?"

In another text from the same tradition, moreover—the ninth of the *Letters of Anacharsis*[70]—the Scythian sage uses sea travel as a metaphor for greedy profiteering, describing an incident in which a band of pirates sank their own ship by taking on too much plunder; and we may further see, in the popular notion that Anacharsis had invented the ship's anchor,[71] a token of the Scythian's mistrust of seagoing vessels. In these legends, like that of the *Arimaspeia*, seafaring serves to demarcate advanced races from primitive, in a way that underscores the moral degeneracy of the former group.

The above attacks on seafaring further remind us of the anti-Persian "one-liners" Herodotus puts in the mouth of the Ethiopian king, in that in both cases a distant-world observer focuses his gaze on the most "advanced" or "sophisticated" aspects of life in the *oikoumenē*.[72] In fact in all the literature sur-

"Anacharsis," *RE* bd. 1 cols. 2017–18; and Jan Kindstrand, *Anacharsis: The Legend and the Apophthegmata* (Studia Graeca Upsaliensia 16, Uppsala 1981).

[69] As demonstrated by P. von der Mühll, "Das Alte der Anacharsislegende," *Ausgewählte Kleine Schriften* (Basel 1975) 473–81. See also Hadas, "Utopian Sources" (above, n. 9) 119–20.

[70] Edited and translated by Abraham J. Malherbe, *The Cynic Epistles: A Study Edition* (Missoula, Mont. 1977) 36–51.

[71] Diogenes Laertius 1.104, Pliny *Hist. Nat.* 7.56.209.

[72] The discussion of Scythians in this context must be qualified by their comparative proximity to the *oikoumenē*; unlike the Ethiopians and Arimaspians

rounding these *Naturvölker*, it is the pursuits that stand out as the highest achievements of Hellenic culture—seafaring, athletic contests, symposia, and the use of the marketplace as a center of trade—which come under the strongest attack.[73] Herodotus himself records an early Anacharsis story in which the satirical thrust of the Scythian's outlook is clearly revealed:

> I have also heard another story [regarding Anacharsis], told by the Peloponnesians, to the effect that Anacharsis was sent by the Scythian king to learn about Greek ways, and that on his return he reported to the man who had sent him that all the Greeks, except the Spartans, were too busy to engage in any kind of intellectual pursuits; but that the Spartans alone were capable of carrying on an intelligent dialogue. But this story is only a frivolity invented by the Greeks themselves. (4.77)

The irony behind this "ethnic joke" is easy to spot, and certainly was not lost on the Peloponnesians who (as Herodotus informs us) were its most appreciative audience. Here the Spartans, ordinarily the least inclined of any Greek citizenry toward intellectual matters, are seen by an outsider as representing the very school of Hellas; the resulting inversion suggests that all standards of human intelligence are purely subjective to begin with, and that one race's "dumb" can easily be another's "smart."

Such use of hard-primitive figures like Anacharsis as distorting mirrors, in which Greek culture and civilization gets turned upside-down, has been associated primarily with Hellenistic, and particularly Cynic, moral philosophy; but the foregoing examples show that its roots can be traced back to archaic and

---

they cannot be said to inhabit the true edges of the earth. But see François Hartog, *The Mirror of Herodotus* 12–14, for an assessment of how their extreme cultural anomalies helped situate them at the imaginary margins of humanity.

[73] Other quips attributed to this Scythian sage by Diogenes Laertius, for example, show him bemusedly wondering why Greek wrestlers insist on rubbing their skin with olive oil, since the ointment incites them to attack one another; and why Greek lawgivers punish violent attacks in the streets, yet reward the same behavior in athletic arenas. Lucian's dialogue *Anacharsis* allows the Scythian to expound on the absurdity of athletics, this time in the context of a debate with his Greek host Solon on the efficacy of the traditional Greek gymnastic education. For these themes see Kindstrand, *Anacharsis* (above, n. 68) chaps. 1.5, 2.2.

even Homeric literature. In fact, in the unique blend of fable, critical self-examination, and ironic humor that pervades such ethnologic satire can be found some of the hallmarks of the Ionian enlightenment, the great intellectual and literary movement of the late seventh and early sixth centuries B.C. The same spirit which enlivens the antiheroic poetry of Archilochus and Xenophanes, and the grotesquerie of the Homeric *Battle of the Mice and Frogs* and the Aesopic fable, can also be felt at work in much of the ethnographic literature we have herein been exploring. Animal fable in particular, a genre which in many ways typifies Ionian tastes, serves as a revealing parallel, since it uses inferior species to overturn the normal *scala naturae* in much the same way that the satiric barbarian overturns normal patterns of ethnocentrism. Thus Plutarch, for one, compares Herodotus's technique of "using Scythians, and Egyptians, and Persians as mouthpieces for his own sentiments" with that of Aesop moralizing to mankind through the personae of crows and monkeys (*De Malign.* 40, 871d).[74] Though the charge is greatly exaggerated, the comparison with Aesop reveals how different types of distance—geographic in one case, taxonomic in the other—create a similar type of satiric inversion.[75]

The *Kunokephaloi*

Below even Aesop's apes and crows on the taxonomic ladder, of course, stands the dog; and thus it was the dog, along with such unsophisticated human beings as Anacharsis, that was ultimately adopted as paradigm by the self-styled hard primitives of later antiquity, the Cynics. However the Cynics were not the

[74] An anecdote related in Athenaeus's *Deipnosophistae* (613d = Kindstrand A 11 A) has Anacharsis comparing mankind to the apes: "The ape is funny by nature; men have to work at it."

[75] The fact that the Aesopic fables were thought to have been composed by a lowly barbarian, moreover—a slave imported from Phrygia—brings them even more closely into line with the taunts of Anacharsis and his brethren. The analogy between animal fable and noble-savage literature has been suggested by a scholar who has written eloquently on both, George Boas (*The Happy Beast in French Thought of the Seventeenth Century* [N.Y. 1966] 1).

original dog-men. Long before they came on the scene the Greeks were already familiar with a race of *Hemikunes*, "Half-dogs," or *Kunokephaloi*, "Dog-heads," dwelling (in most accounts) in the remote regions of India. Let us look briefly at this curious tribe, as described by Ctesias of Cnidos in the early fourth century B.C., as a final instance of how Greek ethical models were imported at an early stage from the edges of the earth.

Here, it should be noted, we begin to turn our gaze in a new direction, toward the East—a region which shall increasingly be at issue in the chapters which follow. The archaic and early classical era with which we have thus far been concerned could not see very far into the East. Herodotus, for example, says little in the *Histories* concerning the Indians, as compared with his long accounts of the Egyptians and Scythians, inhabitants of the northern and southern climatic extremes.[76] Ctesias, however, stands on the cusp of a new era in which Greek contacts with the newly consolidated Persian empire were opening up the gateway to the Orient. In fact Ctesias himself lived at Sousa as court physician to the Persian royal family, and thus, like Aristeas among the Issedones, had privileged access to information about the distant world; and this data formed the basis of his *Indika*, a remarkable whirlwind tour of eastern lore (which we shall look at more closely in the next chapter). Unfortunately the text of this work has been lost, but a detailed summary set down by the Byzantine patriarch Photius preserves enough of its content to allow for useful discussion.

By far the most extensive of the ethnographic descriptions in the *Indika* (to judge by the space Photius's epitome allots to it) was that of the mountain-dwelling *Kunokephaloi* or Dog-heads (20, 22–23).[77] These Dog-heads, like Aristeas's Arimaspians, are fashioned after the hard-primitive ideal of moral purity and spiritual fortitude, but here the Aesopic strain of animal fable

[76] See my "Herodotus and Mythic Geography" (above, n. 37), esp. 113–17.

[77] Ctesias was not the first to describe such a race: The Hesiodic *Periodos Gēs* also glimpses *Hemikunes* or Half-dogs in the course of its aerial circuit of the earth (fr. 150 Merkelbach-West l. 8; cf. fr. 153 = Strabo 7.3.6), and Hecataeus of Miletus apparently included *Kunokephaloi* in his *Periodos* as well.

has contributed certain elements as well. As their name implies the Dog-heads represent an exotic missing link, partaking of both human and canine nature at the same time (20):

> In the mountains dwell men who have the head of a dog; they wear skins of wild beasts as clothing, and they speak no language, but bark like dogs, and in this way understand one another's speech. They have teeth bigger than a dog's, and nails like those of a dog, but larger and more rounded. . . . They understand the speech of the Indians, but cannot respond to them; instead they bark and signal with their hands and fingers, as do mutes.

Here the first feature of the *Kunokephaloi* that Ctesias chooses to focus on first is their use of speech; and since speech was often seen as a defining human attribute[78] it is significant that the Dog-heads possess it only in part, being able to understand but not replicate human language. Their mode of communication, that is, seems to be stuck midway between the human condition and the animal.[79]

This taxonomic ambiguity continues to reveal itself throughout Ctesias's description of the *Kunokephaloi*, where the Dog-heads are seen straining to achieve technological advances that are as yet beyond their capabilities. They attempt to cook their food but, lacking the means to make fires, can only broil it in the hot sun (22);[80] they have no beds but heap up litters of dried leaves to avoid sleeping on the ground (23). However in all this material Ctesias seems not to have looked down on the Dog-heads as mentally or culturally deficient creatures. In fact we note with interest in the above passage that, just after being compared to dogs, the Dog-heads are also described as "just"

[78] U. Dierauer, *Tier und Mensch im Denken der Antike* (Studien zur antiken Philosophie 6, Amsterdam 1977) 12, 33–34; H. C. Baldry, *The Unity of Mankind in Greek Thought* (Cambridge 1965) 15.

[79] In fact later writers used Ctesias' account to classify the *Kunokephaloi* both as animals and as humans. See the note ad loc. in Henry's Budé edition of Photius (vol. 1, p. 143), which contrasts Aelian's treatment (*Nat. Anim.* 4.46 = fr. 45p Jacoby) with that of Pliny (*Hist. Nat.* 7.2.23).

[80] The eating of raw food as a custom among undercivilized or bestial peoples is discussed by Vajda, "Traditionelle Konzeption" (above, n. 3) 767–69.

(*dikaioi*)—an adjective which in Greek ethnography connotes a state of supreme moral perfection.[81] Far from confirming the supremacy of man over the "sub"-human Ctesias seems instead to have used the Dog-heads to call that supremacy into question.

This questioning of the relative stature of man and beast comes through most strongly in Ctesias's final note on the Dog-heads which again juxtaposes (at least in Photius's retelling) their doggishness with their moral advancement (23):

> All of them, men and women, have a tail above their hips, like a dog's, except bigger and smoother. They have intercourse with their wives on all fours, like dogs, and consider any other form of intercourse to be shameful. They are just, and the longest-lived of any human race; for they get to be 160, sometimes 200 years of age.

To fully appreciate the irony of this passage we must bear in mind that sexual position, like speech, forms a marker by which the Greeks frequently distinguished animals from humans; thus Herodotus, for example, compares tribes which practice aberrant sexual behavior—copulating on the ground, for instance, or in public (1.203, 3.101)—to beasts. The *Kunokephaloi*, however, see things from just the opposite perspective; for them the "normal" human approach to sex becomes a badge of shame, while bestial intercourse is the only variety they deem acceptable. The subsequent observation that the Dog-heads are "just" creatures and enjoy the longest life span of all mankind completes this inversion of the *scala naturae*, undermining the validity of anthropocentrism along the same lines as the ethnocentric inversions we have looked at above.[82]

Unfortunately, the toneless and fragmentary condition of the

[81] Elsewhere too they are seen reaping the rich resources of a superabundant landscape, much like the golden-age Ethiopians and Hyperboreans: They collect huge amounts of amber and a dye-giving purple flower from the river that flows through their territory (21–22).

[82] Cp. the later texts collected by Dierauer, *Tier und Mensch* 273–84. The most famous, and most illustrative, is Plutarch's *De bruta ratione*, a dialogue in which one of Odysseus's transformed crewmen argues for remaining a pig instead of resuming life as a man.

Indika does not allow us to go further in exploring this view of Ctesias as theriophile and satirist. However, I hope to have shown at least that the Dog-heads, like other inhabitants of the world's edge, came into the *Indika* already equipped with an innate satiric potential, by virtue of their extreme cultural and taxonomic differences from inhabitants of the *oikoumenē*. If we look ahead to the "doggish" behavior of the Cynics in the Hellenistic and Imperial eras—dressing in skins, dwelling in the open or in cast-off pots, flaunting sexual mores by copulating in public—we can see the lines along which such potential could develop once it had taken root in the Hellenic imagination. It is the same sort of development that took Anacharsis, for example, from Herodotus's naïf to the curmudgeonly moralist we find in Lucian, Plutarch, and Diogenes Laertius.[83] Such distant-world figures ended up becoming *paradeigmata* in a very real sense, serving not only as vehicles for philosophic and ethical literature but as role models for daily behavior.

Looking ahead in a different direction, moreover, we can see how the grotesque and comic bestiality of the *Kunokephaloi* also followed a separate line of development: After Ctesias the word *kunokephalos* no longer stands for this half-evolved, nobly savage race of men but, more prosaically, for the baboon.[84] It is as if the human and animal components that had been so effectively fused in archaic lore later separated out, leading on the one hand to "doggish" philosophers and on the other to dog-headed apes. Yet even when seen as an animal pure and simple, the *kunokephalos* continues to fulfill some of the same satiric purposes as had its semihuman predecessor. In one of the earliest instances of the new usage (*Theaet*. 161d), for example, we find Socrates whimsically turning anthropocentrism on its ear by suggesting that the baboon, or even the pig, might more properly be considered "the measure of all things" than man.

[83] A role that continues to evolve in European literature as late as the French Revolution; see Kindstrand on "Anacharsis" Cloots, *Anacharsis* 93–95.

[84] Cf. also Aristophanes *Knights* 416, where it is not clear in which sense the word ought to be understood. For discussion see Otto Keller, *Die Antike Tierwelt* vol. 1 (repr. Hildesheim 1963) 7–9, who unfortunately fails to discuss the Ctesian use of the term.

Three

Wonders of the East

"INDIA AND AFRICA are especially noted for wonders," remarks Pliny in the seventh book of the *Natural History*, and the conjunction is a significant one. Both continents form worlds unto themselves in ancient literature, defined by the peculiar character of plant and animal life, by the bizarre behavior of springs and rivers, and by the alien races of human beings that dwell there. In fact, their similarities are such that the two continents are occasionally fused together into one,[1] despite the expanse of sea that came between them; or, in the case of the *mappa mundi* described by Herodotus in the *Histories* (4.37–42), Asia and Africa are paired as twin "down-under" landmasses which stand in opposition to northerly, and normative, Europe. As with all distant lands, that is, geographic and cartographic arrangements of these two regions depend in large part on the imaginative literature surrounding them, so that their shared mythic characteristics tend to push them together on the conceptual map of the world.[2]

Both India and Africa, moreover, unlike Europe, seemed to the Greeks to stretch out into inconceivable distance beyond the horizon, and thus, according to the scheme we examined in the first chapter, to demand some sort of artificial delimitation. The East, though, posed the problem of unboundedness even more insistently than the South. Whereas Libya was thought to have been circumnavigated by Phoenicians in early times (cf.

[1] The idea that India and Africa were joined at a point below the equator was debated as early as Polybius's time (see 3.38.1), and was later espoused by Marinus and Ptolemy (*Geography* 4.9.1, 7.3.6, 7.5.2). See Kretschmer 42–46; Berger (1898) 112–13, 130–31 (1903) 606–7, 625–26.

[2] On this tendency to make the two continents into a single place see Jean W. Sedlar, *India and the Greek World* (Totowa, N.J. 1980) 9; Albrecht Dihle, "Der Fruchtbare Osten," in *Antike und Orient* (Heidelberg 1984) 49–53 and n. 6.

Herodotus 4.44), in India no terminal (i.e., aquatic) boundary had ever been attained—even if Ocean, in this case as in others, was *assumed* to be out there somewhere.[3] As a result of this uncertainty the Greeks tended to look on their penetration of the Asiatic frontier as a daring assault on the terrors of distant space. Alexander's march to the Hyphasis, for example, becomes enshrined in Hellenistic and Imperial literature not only as a heroic military venture but as a fantastic, unrelenting quest for the eastern edge of the world, through a landscape made menacing by monsters and evil portents. Explorations of Africa, by contrast, were most often targeted at a mystery of interior rather than exterior space: the source of the Nile and the cause of its summer floodings (a topic we shall come to in the next chapter).

As a result of this distinction I have chosen to focus in what follows on India and its peculiar brand of zoological wonders, excluding African geography for the most part. But this division should not obscure the essential similarity pointed out by Pliny, that a vital interest in wonders stands behind *both* literary/scientific traditions. The wilds of Africa held animal monstrosities every bit as puzzling and freakish as those of India, as indicated by the epithet *thēriōdēs* or "beast-infested" applied to certain regions of that continent (cf. Herodotus 4.174, 181); just as the rivers of central India, in particular the Indus and Ganges, presented hydrological mysteries that were frequently compared to (and even connected with) those of the Nile.[4] Therefore in discussing the wonders of the East we shall occasionally turn our attention to the South as well, in accord with the unity of these places noted by Pliny the Elder.

Before Alexander

It is an interesting feature of the Greek experience of India that nearly all major accounts of that distant land came from agents

[3] See chap. 1, pp. 42–43, above.

[4] See Arrian, *Indika* 2.6, 6.8; Strabo 15.1.13, 16. Other sources cited by Thomson 81–82, 124, 130 and n. 2.

of the imperial rulers who invaded it. The most famous, of course, were attached to the expedition of Alexander the Great, and we shall be principally concerned with these in the second section of this chapter. But the Alexander histories were preceded by at least two other major works of Asian geography, both written by Greeks in the service of the Persian empire; and later came other, Roman accounts of military incursions into the East. In fact it can be said that the literary texts which derive from these incursions have imperial ambitions of their own, paralleling at a cognitive level the sallies of the great generals of the age. The eastern landscape presented itself to western eyes in such disorganized terms that all the resources of scientific and pseudoscientific thought—including, as we shall see, the august authority of Aristotle himself—were brought to bear in order to "conquer" its persistent strangeness.

The first Greek to visit India, according to the records of Herodotus, was Scylax of Caryanda, an Ionian sea captain pressed into service by Darius I of Persia in the early fifth century B.C.[5] Herodotus recounts that Darius, preparing to bring the western portion of India under his sway, sent out an expedition of men "whose word he could believe" to explore the Indus River and the stretch of coast between it and the Arabian penninsula. Why Darius entrusted this important task to a foreigner is unclear; Herodotus's explanation suggests that he saw the Ionians (inventors of the world map) as reliable observers and recorders of topographic data, but he must also have recognized the superiority of Greek navigational skills. Scylax acquitted himself well enough on this latter count, sailing down the Indus and westward through the Indian Ocean over the course of thirty months. However the log which came out of this voyage, to judge by the one substantial report of its contents which has survived, seems to have been less trustworthy than Darius had anticipated:

[5] *Histories* 4.44. For Scylax of Caryanda (not to be confused with the pseudonymous author of the *Periplus Maris Erythraei*) see Wilhelm Reese, *Die griechischen Nachrichten über Indien* (Leipzig 1914) 35–53; Hennig (1936) 116–20; Jacoby in *RE* bd. 7 *s.v.* "Skylax," and *Fr.Gr.H* 709; and Müller, *GGM* 1.xxxiii–li.

> The *Skiapodes* [Shadow-feet] have extremely flat feet, and at high noon they fall on the ground and stretch out their feet so as to make shade. The *Ōtoliknoi* [Winnowing-fan-ears], moreover, have huge ears, which they use like parasols to cover themselves. Scylax also writes a thousand other things, about the *Monophthalmoi* [One-eyed], the *Enōtikoitoi* [Ear-sleepers],[6] and the *Ektrapeloi* [Freaks], and a thousand other wondrous sights. (Tzetzes, *Chiliades* 7.629–36)

We can perhaps understand Scylax's log better if we see it as addressed not to the Persians, who were doubtless interested in more practical information, but to a Greek audience who delighted in marvelous tales. Archaic myth and legend had long fostered the notion that peoples of the distant world could be monstrous or deformed by comparison with those of the *oikoumenē*; we have already looked at some important examples, including the freakish races that figure prominently in Aristeas's *Arimaspeia* and the Hesiodic *Periodos Gēs*.[7] Scylax seems to have been consciously working within this tradition, gratifying his culture's expectations of the distant world as a gallery of bizarrely formed monsters and marvels.[8] In fact, later writers remark on the similarities between Scylax's log and Hesiod's fantastical poem (cf. Harpokration *s.v. hupo gēn oikountes* = F 6 Jacoby), or refer to the log's content as "songs of enchantment" more typical of poetry than prose (Philostratus *Vit. Apol.* 4.27).

Scylax was soon outdone in this type of writing by the most original and influential of the Greek Indographers, indeed the

[6] Accepting Kiessling's emendation for *Henotiktontōn*, "those who give birth once."

[7] The impulses behind such conceptions are discussed briefly by Eugene McCartney, "Modern Analogues to Ancient Tales of Monstrous Races," *CP* 36 (1941): 390–94; and by John Block Friedman, *The Monstrous Races in Medieval Art and Thought* (Cambridge, Mass. 1981) chap. 2.

[8] In fact his "log" may not have presented itself as an actual voyage account at all, at least not as a very reliable one, since no subsequent geographers make use of it; even Herodotus, who is very much at a loss for direct reports about India, seems to have left it aside. See Bunbury 1.227, 256 Note B. Jacoby (*RE* bd. 7, col. 2689) supposes that the original log was lost early on, and its information passed on in Hecataeus's *Periodos Gēs*. See also Güngerich 10.

Marco Polo of his era, Ctesias of Cnidus.[9] Ctesias, as we saw in the previous chapter, served as physician to the Persian royal family in the late fifth and early fourth centuries B.C., and so like Scylax had privileged knowledge of the East, derived in this case from reports of merchants and travelers passing through the imperial city. He compiled this material into an ethnographic and zoologic account of the Indian subcontinent called the *Indika*; the work itself is lost but its contents have been preserved in an extensive summary in Photius's *Bibliotheka* (cod. 72 45a20–50a4 = *Fr. Gr. H* F 45–52). Ctesias also wrote an important history of the Persian empire, the *Persika*, since lost, and perhaps as many as three works in the line of *periodoi* or *periēgēseis*, "journeys around" the world; very likely these latter works increased his reputation as a purveyor of marvels, since one of them seems to have contained an account of Scylax's parasol-footed men, the *Skiapodes*.[10]

Ctesias, again like Scylax, seems to have composed his *Indika* primarily to entertain rather than inform his Greek audience.[11] He claims to have gathered his information from firsthand inquiry and from reliable informants (31),[12] but this statement,

[9] On the importance of Ctesias's book in establishing many of the so-called Indian Wonders, see Jean Filliozat, "La valeur des connaissances greco-romaines sur l'Inde" (*Journal des Savants* [1981]: 97–136) 102–3, and Rudolph Wittkower, "Marvels of the East," *Journal of the Warburg and Courtauld Inst.* 5 (1942): 159–97. For more general remarks on the entire "Indian Wonders" tradition, see the recent study by Lloyd L. Gunderson of the teratological material in the Alexander Romance, *Alexander's Letter to Aristotle about India* (Meisenheim am Glan 1980), esp. chaps. 1 and 2; Albrecht Dihle, "Der fruchtbare Osten" and "The Conception of India in Hellenistic and Roman Literature," recently reprinted in *Antike und Orient* (above, n. 1) 47–61 and 89–98; and Truesdell S. Brown, "The Reliability of Megasthenes," *AJP* 76 (1955): 18–33.

[10] Cf. Suidas s.v. *Skiapodes*, Stephanus of Byzantium s.v. *kosutē*, and Pliny *Hist. Nat.* 7.2. An attempt has been made to relate these curious beings to a race of Web-feet (*steganopodes*) mentioned by Alcman (Reese 50–51). Lionel Pearson traces them back to an original Libyan home (*Early Ionian Historians* [Oxford 1939] 95–96).

[11] Reese (*Griechische Nachrichten* 77) points out that had Ctesias intended to write a truly informative or comprehensive work, he would not have omitted peoples like the Fish-eaters, Calatoi, or Shadow-feet that had been mentioned earlier in Herodotus's account of India or in other works by Ctesias himself.

[12] All chapter numbers refer to those of Müller's edition, in *Fragmenta His-*

interpreted within the terms of ancient pseudoscience, means only that he did not make things up out of whole cloth. In fact a lot of Ctesias's material seems to have been borrowed from Indian folklore and fable; some marvels, including possibly the aforementioned *Kunokephaloi*, have been traced back to legends preserved in the *Ramayana* and other Sanskrit works.[13] Whether Ctesias recognized that such stories were only fantasy and not fact is something we shall never know; but we can imagine he felt secure that his marvel-hungry audience would not ask too many questions.

Ctesias's India is a marvelous place indeed, painted in a dramatic chiaroscuro of dark and light tones. On the one hand nature seems to have shed her blessings on India more than on any other nation: There are great quantities of gold, silver, amber, and gemstones (2, 4, 12, 19); precious resources like purple dye and perfume, more exquisite here than elsewhere (21, 28); and men who live to be well over a hundred, without bodily pains or diseases (15). Moreover, the earth seems to bring forth sustenance of its own accord, as in many of the paradisic lands examined in chapter 2: fine oil can be skimmed from the surface of a certain lake, where it miraculously appears during calm weather (11); rivers flow with honey (13); sheep bear litters of four or six at a time, instead of singly (13). However there are also darker forces at work amidst this cornucopia of natural wealth. The deadly martichora, called *anthropophagon* or "Man-eater" in the Greek tongue, possesses three rows of teeth and a tail that can shoot poison darts from hundreds of feet away (7).[14] Other creatures excrete poisons so noxious that even a tiny amount, no larger than a sesame seed, can cause a

---

toricorum Graecorum, and to the translation of J. W. McCrindle, *Ancient India as Described by Ktesias the Knidian* (Calcutta 1882, repr. Patna 1987). See also the annotated edition of R. Henry, *Ctésias sur la Perse et l'Inde: Les sommaires de Photios* (Brussels 1947) and the more specialized edition in Jacoby, *Fr. Gr. H.*

[13] A detailed study of Ctesias's possible sources for the *Indika* can be found in Reese, *Griechische Nachrichten*, and in Lassen, *Indische Altertümlichkeit*[2] vol. 2 641 ff. (English translation by McCrindle, *Ancient India as Described by Ktesias* 65–91).

[14] This distressing creature is perhaps based on a distorted recollection of the Indian tiger, as first suggested by Pausanias (9.21.4).

gruesome death in which one's brain instantly dissolves and runs out through the nostrils (16).

What must have been most impressive in Ctesias's work, however—insofar as we can reconstruct it from Photius[15] and a few other sources—was the very density of its texture. In only a single book Ctesias catalogued (by a rough count) nineteen wonders associated with animals and plants; another sixteen concerning springs, rivers, and minerals; seven races of humans, and six climatic phenomena—and virtually all of these are further elaborated with a variety of properties, features, and behaviors. What emerges from a reading of the fragments of the *Indika*, then, and what surely must have emerged from the original as well, is a sense of an enormously complex landscape crowded with anomalies at every turn. This India revealed a nature which seemed to exfoliate in a limitless series of new and unexpected forms, an exuberant and creative force which defied all Greek expectations of biological normality. To quote Jean Céard's masterful study, *La Nature et les Prodiges* (14),

> Nature in India seems to play with the distinction between species. . . . Freed to exercise an irrepressible fecundity, nature amuses itself by creating new forms, by improvising on its creations; it surrenders to an alluring and terrifying anarchy.

The Greeks had a proverb to express this image of nature run riot at the edge of the earth: *Aei ti pherei Libuē kainon*, "Libya always brings forth some new thing." The saying is cited twice in the works of Aristotle, and once in more expanded form in a lost comedy by Anaxilas: "The arts, like Libya, produce some

[15] Photius's reliability as an excerpter has been attacked by Reese, who reaches the conclusion that "Just as in his excerpts from Philostratus' *Life of Apollonius*, so here Photius presents the most fabulous elements in greatest detail, and everything else only in brief" (78). More recently, however, J. M. Bigwood points out that Photius's summary of the *Indika* is more detailed than his other epitomes, and, in cases where we can check it against quotations of the original, often follows Ctesias word for word ("Ctesias' *Indika* and Photius," *Phoenix* 43 [1989]: 302–16). Photius has clearly passed over a certain amount of information about the Indians themselves in sections 5 and 6, but how much is unclear (Bigwood thinks this material may only be held off until sections 17–32; see p. 315).

new beastie (*thērion*) every year,"[16] perhaps the equivalent of our deprecatory "that's progress for you." Although the proverb in its immediate application refers to Africa and not India, we should understand *Libuē* metonymically for the southerly latitudes in general, since the saying is used by Aristotle to explain both African and Asian creatures (as we shall see in a moment). This snippet of folk wisdom nicely embodies the Greeks' bewildered response to the diversity and multiplicity they perceived in distant-world landscapes. From it we get a sense of the aetiological confusion which those landscapes inspired: For the saying seems, to judge by its use in Anaxilas's comedy, to represent a shrug of the shoulders, an acknowledgment that nature works in a certain way irrespective of human power to understand it.[17]

Nonetheless Aristotle—who never admits to being stumped in matters of aetiology, if he can help it[18]—attempts to explain the phenomenon *aei ti pherei Libuē kainon* in scientific terms, and his explanation is characteristically ingenious. It arises in a discussion of hybrid reproduction, the process by which two members of different species can interbreed to produce a third type. This process accounts for the origin of several foreign hybrids, Aristotle says, including one dubbed the "Indian dog"; and it also accounts for the dictum concerning Libya:

> The proverbial expression about Libya, that "Libya always brings forth some new thing," has been coined because of the tendency for even heterogenous creatures to interbreed there. On account of the paucity of water, different species encounter one another at the few places which possess springs, and there interbreed. (*Gen. Animal.* 746b7–13)

The same explanation, moreover, is repeated by the author of a spurious portion of the *Historia Animalium*, in discussing the

[16] *Hyakinthos Pornoboskos* fr. 27 = Athenaeus *Deipn.* 14.18.10–12.

[17] The saying later came to be particularly associated with evil schemes and contrivances; see Zenob. 2.51 and Diog. 1.68 in E. Leutsch and F. G. Schneidewin, *Paroemiographi Graeci* (Göttingen 1839).

[18] See P. Louis, "Monstres et monstruosités dans la biologie d'Aristote," in *Le Monde Grec: Hommages á Claire Préaux*, ed. J. Bingen, G. Cambier, G. Nacthergael (Brussels 1975) 277–84.

fact that "as a rule . . . in Libya all creatures are exceedingly diverse in form" (*polumorphotata*, 606b17).[19] Later, a similar notion regarding southern and eastern wildlife is adduced by Diodorus Siculus:

> [In the eastern portion of Arabia] arise goat-stags and antelopes and other types of biformed creatures, in which parts of animals which differ widely by nature are combined. . . . For it seems that the land which lies closest to the equator takes in a great deal of the sun's most generative force, and thus gives rise to species of fine beasts. It is for this reason that crocodiles and hippopotami arise in Egypt, and in the Libyan desert a huge number of elephants and variegated snakes . . . and likewise in India, elephants of exceptionally great number and bulk, as well as strength. (2.51.2–4)

Diodorus here follows the Aristotelian school in connecting the hybrid wildlife of the South with its climate,[20] though his understanding of how that climate affects reproduction follows a very different line.

Unscientific though these passages may seem from our perspective, they nevertheless offer a plausible aetiology for the biological diversity of southern lands, based on the principle that the crossbreeding of species can continually generate new animal forms.[21] What Aristotle and Diodorus have done, then, is to find a reason indigenous to the tropical Asian and African

[19] See also the explanation of the proverb *Libukon thērion* in Apostolius (10.75, Leutsch and Schneidewin 2.507).

[20] Cp. Pliny, *Hist. Nat.* 6.35.187: "There is nothing surprising in the fact that monstrous forms of animals and men arise in the extreme reaches of [Africa], because of the molding power of fiery motility in shaping their bodies and carving their forms." See Marcel Benabou, "Monstres et hybrides chez Lucrèce et Pline l'Ancien," in *Hommes et bêtes: Entretiens sur le racisme*, ed. L. Poliakov (Paris 1975) 149; Dihle, "Fruchtbare Osten" 47–49.

[21] Indeed the tendency toward hybrid morphology had long been one of the defining characteristics of the East for Greek observers. Thus Aristophanes, in the *Frogs*, associates such fantasies as "goat-stags and horse-roosters" with the figures seen on imported Persian tapestries (937–38). And the legendary Half-dogs or Dog-heads, whom we looked at briefly in the previous chapter, were variously located in either Africa or India, and in fact came to be identified by writers beginning with Plato (*Theaet.* 161c) with the baboon, an animal that dwells in both regions.

climate for this miscegenic freedom, since ordinarily (*kata phusin*, in Aristotle's terms, *Gen. Animal.* 746a29) such interspecies unions were not possible. If the wonders of the East could thus be made intelligible in scientific terms, an essential step would be taken toward normalizing and demystifying them.

The majority of ethnographic and geographic writers, however, had little interest in such scientific approaches. For them the awe which "Libyan" diversity could inspire was only dampened by aetiological or teleological explanations; the distant world assumed its most striking form when presented as an inexplicable or incomprehensible phenomenon. Hence the format in which the Indian wonders are typically recorded is that of a catalogue, a bare, reductive list which avoids all discussion of cause. Such lists present the wonders of the East as an aggregation of facts; they demand that the multiplicity of eastern nature be accepted on its own terms, in much the same way as had the expression *aei ti pherei Libuē kainon* prior to Aristotle's rationalizing explanation.[22]

Unfortunately, the works of Scylax and Ctesias have both been preserved only by later redactors, so that we cannot know for certain that they shared in this catalogic structure (although the amplitude of Photius's summary of the *Indika* strongly suggests this). However we can already perceive, as early as Herodotus, the evolution of the rhetorical pattern that would later typify Greek Indography:

> The land westward of Libya is extremely hilly, and wooded, and filled with wild beasts; in this region there are giant snakes, and bears, and vipers, and asses with horns [rhinocerus?], and dog-headed men, and headless men with eyes in their breasts (thus they are described by the Libyans), and wild men, and wild women, and other beasts in huge numbers, not at all fabulous. (*Histories* 4.191)

Herodotus's incantatory recitation of animal species grows stranger and more exotic as it lengthens, reaching a point where

[22] The following discussion of catalogic form owes much to the study by Nicholas Howe, *The Old English Catalogue Poems* (Anglistica 23, Copenhagen 1985), esp. the Introduction and chap. 1.

the author gives up all attempt at enumeration and trails off into a kind of terminal ellipse.[23] The style, moreover, is unusually clipped and breathless for Herodotus, who normally likes to examine such *thaumata* in some detail. Its effect on the reader is to create a brief, imagistic portrait of a land which does indeed produce "something new" wherever the author turns, but which cannot be scrutinized at close range (as could other places like Egypt and Scythia).

The Hellenistic genre of paradoxography or "marvel-writing," a pseudoscientific precursor of our own "believe-it-or-not" collections, is similarly constructed in great denotative lists. This genre, which emerged in the third century B.C. as a spin-off from Aristotelian biology, essentially consists of catalogues of all the most bizarre and unintelligible phenomena of nature.[24] In it item after item is ticked off with formulae like "Aristotle says . . . Theophrastus says . . . Callimachus says," or "In Cappadocia there is . . . in Boeotia there is . . . in Egypt there is . . . ." Seldom do we find any explanation of causes; indeed in some places the paradoxographers explicitly disclaim all interest in such matters (e.g., Antigonus of Carystus 60). There are strong affinities, then, between this genre and that of the *Indika*, and in fact Ctesias figures prominently in it as a source of marvelous lore.

The rhetorical strategy behind such catalogues can be ana-

[23] Remarkably, moreover, the moment at which the list becomes open-ended is accompanied by Herodotus's own finalizing *akatapseusta*, "not at all fabulous"—an assessment so surprisingly credulous that some editors (e.g., Legrand in the Budé edition) prefer emending to *katapseusta* or "entirely fabulous." A different reading is proposed by How and Wells ad. loc., who see an antithesis here between what the Libyans *claim* is true and what Herodotus himself *knows*; but the run of the sentence seems not to imply any such antithesis. I cannot explore the issue at any length here, but it seems at least possible that Herodotus meant to assert *akatapseusta* in his own voice.

[24] In fact the first example of the genre may well have been composed by the great cataloguer of the Alexandrian Library, Callimachus: His lost works include a "Collection (*Sunagōgē*) of the Wonders of the World, Arranged According to Place." On paradoxography in general see A. Giannini, "Studi sulla Paradossografia Greca," *RIL* 97 (1963): 247–66, and K. Ziegler in *RE* bd. 18.2 s.v. "Paradoxographoi" cols. 1137–66.

lyzed at a number of levels.[25] First, the matter-of-fact tone of the catalogue helps balance the exoticism of the wonders themselves: The insistence on spare linguistic structures such as the simple assertion of existence, "there is," creates a veneer of clinical, dispassionate inquiry. Furthermore, the frequent citation of sources which typifies this kind of writing also helps bolster authority—or at least relieves the author himself, and thereby his audience, of responsibility for assessing truth.[26] Beyond these strategies, however, the very density of the catalogue plays a crucial role in its effectiveness, replicating at a stylistic level the density of the Indian landscape itself. The cataloguer of wonders typically crowds his data into linguistic aggregates rather than discrete units: prolix, hyperextended sentences, or rapid-fire series of clauses. The proliferation of data dislocates its readers and overwhelms their ability to separate true from false, in effect forcing them to "swallow" whole that which would seem incredible if presented piecemeal.[27]

It was this type of dense, hypertrophic portrait of India that accompanied Alexander the Great on his march into the East, and which informed the literary works which emerged out of that expedition. In fact Alexander's march ushered in a period of intense literary activity in which Greek sojourners once

[25] In what follows I am indebted to Mary Campbell's analysis of the *Wonders of the East* tradition in medieval literature, in *The Witness and the Other World: Exotic European Travel Writing 400–1600* (Ithaca, N.Y. 1989) chap. 3. See also Ronald T. Swigger, "Fictional Encyclopedism and the Cognitive Value of Literature," *Comparative Literature Studies* 12 (1975): 354–66.

[26] Thus, page after page of paradoxographic material is cast in indirect discourse, using infinitives rather than finite verbs, to remind us throughout that nothing in it should be understood as the author's own assertion. A similar strategy is pursued by the Greek historians who assign dubious stories to an impersonal source; see H. D. Westlake, "*Legetai* in Thucydides," *Mnemosyne* 30 (1977): 345–62.

[27] As the Syrian-born satirist Lucian would later point out, tales of three-headed men begin to become credible if all the secondary details fall into line: six eyes, six ears, three foreheads, and so on (*Hermotimus* 74). In the case of the Indian wonders this principle of internal consistency applies not only to individual races and species but to the entire Oriental/African landscape, which paradoxically becomes more realistic the more it conforms to its own internal principle of *aei ti pherei Libuē kainon*.

again, following the model of Scylax and of Ctesias (who were by this time being debunked),[28] peddled oriental exotica to their countrymen back home. The influx of geographic data that the early Hellenistic period witnessed can be compared to that which followed the discovery of America—a land which, after all, was at first thought to represent only an extension of Alexander's India. What is remarkable in both cases, moreover, is the degree to which incoming reports from the edges of the earth tended to assume the forms molded for them long before.[29] Thus the imagery evoked by Scylax and Ctesias, and the expectations those authors had created of a landscape of diversity and strangeness, continued to dominate the works of post-Alexander authors like Megasthenes, Nearchus, Deimachus, and Onesicritus, as we shall see below.[30]

Marvel-Collectors and Critics

Unfortunately, most of the works of Indography from the period following Alexander's march have been lost, and their surviving fragments are scattered widely through later literature. Instead of conducting separate discussions of these fragmentary texts, therefore, I have chosen to look at the entire group through the eyes of their most famous collectors and critics,

[28] E.g., by Aristotle, *Hist. Animal.* 523a26, 606a8, and (more ambiguously) 501a25–b2. For this debunking process see my article "Belief and Other Worlds: Ktesias and the Founding of the 'Indian Wonders,'" in *Mindscapes: The Geographies of Imagined Worlds* (Southern Illinois 1988), ed. George Slusser and Eric Rabkin 122–35.

[29] See Dihle, "Der fruchtbare Osten," 59–60; Jean Filliozat, "La valeur"; and P. Pédech, "Le paysage dans les historiens d'Alexandre," *Quaderni di Storia* 3 (1977): 119–31. Pédech's study reinforces the point made by Humboldt (see Bunbury 1.574), that the reports returned from Alexander's expedition were often, paradoxically, less accurate than those which preceded them.

[30] In some cases, moreover, they survived long enough to influence Christopher Columbus and other Renaissance explorers. Columbus's reports of "dog-headed men" described by Caribbean natives, for example (entry of Nov. 26, *The Journal of Christopher Columbus*, trans. Cecil Jane [N.Y. 1989] 74), probably owe something, at least indirectly, to Ctesias.

Strabo of Amaseia and Pliny the Elder. In their assessments of the tradition Strabo calls *ta Indika*—"writings on India"—we find important analyses of how this peculiar literature functions, even if these analyses are sometimes colored by a deep-seated contempt for lying predecessors. Interestingly enough, moreover, we find that both Strabo and Pliny often indulge in the same type of tale-telling they claim to abhor in their sources, lending authority to stories of marvels even while seeming to refute them. In fact their secondhand reviews of Indographic literature often themselves adopt the form of immense catalogues, exploiting the same rhetorical mechanisms as the originals they claim to supersede.

The geographer Strabo first speaks of "the writers on India" in a discussion of the archaic poets, who, he claims, depicted such fantasies as pygmies, dog-headed men, and headless men under the pretence of not knowing any better. Strabo points out that such authors cannot be accused of true ignorance, that is, of not understanding the distinction between what is geographically real (*historia*) and what is not (*muthos*); rather they should be seen as fictionalizers, who use ignorance as a ploy in order to achieve a literary effect:

> It can be easily seen that they deliberately weave mythical material (*muthoi*) into their work, not through an ignorance of how things really stand, but through an intentional fashioning of impossible facts for the sake of startling novelty (*terateia*) and pleasure (*terpsis*). Nevertheless they feign ignorance, so that they can more credibly relate myths of this kind regarding unseen and unknown matters. Theopompus, at least, admits to this by saying that he's using myths in his histories—a better way than Herodotus, Ctesias, Hellanicus, and those who write *ta Indika*. (1.2.35)

Indography, then, like archaic poetry, is governed by a subtle strategy whereby intentional deceit (*muthos*) must be disguised as naïveté; only in this way can it properly produce *terateia*, the lurid pleasure associated with the viewing of monstrosities.[31]

[31] Strabo's implication here that early prose writers had borrowed their techniques from poetry is more fully developed at 1.2.6, where Hecataeus and Pherecydes are mentioned as transitional figures.

Unfortunately, early geographers like Herodotus and Hellanicus, and after them the writers of *ta Indika*, had tried to retain this poetic strategy long after the geographic ignorance on which it relied had been dispelled. Their technique is therefore ineffective as compared with authors like Theopompus, who openly admit their use of *muthos* rather than foisting it off as fact.

Strabo is at least able to understand the motivation of these obsolete Indographers—the desire to entertain their audience—even while condemning them for irresponsibility. However, he is at more of a loss to explain why the second generation of writers on India, those who accompanied Alexander or followed in his footsteps, also falsified *their* reports:

> All those who write about India have shown themselves liars . . . but we ought in particular to distrust Deimachus and Megasthenes. For these are the ones who tell of the Ear-sleepers and the Mouthless men and the Noseless men, and the One-eyes and the Big-legs and the Backward-fingers. Moreover they have renewed that Homeric story of the battle between the cranes and the Pygmies, a race which they claim stands only three spans high. These writers, moreover, tell of the gold-mining ants, and the wedge-headed Pans, and the snakes and cows, and the stags who drink through their horns. . . . Even though they were sent as ambassadors to Palimbothra (Megasthenes to the court of Sandracotus, Deimachus to that of his son Allitrochades), still they left behind this sort of account of their trip abroad—motivated by who knows what cause? (2.1.9 = Megasthenes fr. 27 a, Deimachus fr. 1 Jacoby)

Here Strabo's outrage over the myths in the Indographic record has increased in proportion to the degree to which these later authors ought to have known better. Megasthenes and Deimachus, after all, had actually served in the East on ambassadorial missions, yet nevertheless perpetuated reports that should have died out with Homer. Once again, moreover, Strabo contrasts these egregious liars with others less contemptible: The Macedonian admirals Onesicritus[32] and Near-

[32] On the dissemination of wonders by Onesicritus see Lionel Pearson, *The*

chus had also obtained firsthand experience of the East, but had translated that experience into reports that were at least partly accurate. For Strabo this latter group is comparable to stutterers (*parapsellizontes*), in that they try to express an intelligent meaning but garble it in the delivery.[33]

Both groups, however—deliberate falsifiers and defective reporters—look equally bad when compared with the one reliable source in whom Strabo, like his forerunner Eratosthenes,[34] puts his trust: Patrocles, a Macedonian general who served in India under Alexander's successors Antiochus and Seleucus.[35] In Patrocles' writings alone, Strabo claims, the true record of Alexander's Indian discoveries has been preserved:

> We can believe Patrocles when he says that those who followed in Alexander's train made only a cursory examination of everything, whereas Alexander himself made an accurate account, relying on the most expert observers to record the whole territory for him; and Patrocles says that this record was later handed down to him, by way of Xenocles, Alexander's treasurer. (2.1.6 = Patrocles fr. 1 Jacoby)

Thus, the evolution of *ta Indika* during the decades following Alexander appears to Strabo as a two-pronged affair: a body of outdated mythic material coexisting with a new account derived from scientific exploration. Elements like battles between cranes and the Pygmies, ants that dig up mounds of gold dust

---

Lost Histories of Alexander the Great (APA Philological Monographs 20, n.p. 1960) chap. 4 (esp. 95–105); and Paul Pédech, *Historiens compagnons d'Alexandre* (Paris 1984) 146–55. Aulus Gellius lists him among a set of worthless fabulists collected in a popular anthology of marvels (9.4.1–3; see below).

[33] Diodorus Siculus makes a similar distinction in his critique of writers on Africa, separating those who trusted in false reports from those who invented their stories with a view to entertainment (3.11).

[34] On Eratosthenes' high regard for Alexander's geographical researches see Erkinger Schwarzenberg, "The Portraiture of Alexander," in *Alexandre Le Grand: Image et Réalité* (Entretiens Hardt tome 22, Geneva 1976) 236–38.

[35] On Patrocles see Bunbury 1.568, 572–75, and Jacoby, *Fr. Gr. H* 712; for Eratosthenes' dependence on him, see Berger (1880) 94–96. In fact the data attributed to him, including a hugely misleading statement regarding the circumnavigability of eastern Asia, call his reliability into question.

in hollowing out their burrows, and giant snakes that swallow cows whole had been part of the Indographic record since the beginning, yet somehow had not been purged from that record in the wake of Alexander's conquests. At the same time, Alexander's own clinically accurate record of the East has survived in a separate line of transmission, handed down from Xenocles to Patrocles, then to Eratosthenes, and then, indirectly, to Strabo. With this account in his keeping, Strabo has the ability to expose once and for all authors like Deimachus and Megasthenes, who have—"for who knows what reason?"—kept alive the old myths.

In Book 11 Strabo again takes up the task of debunking the Indian wonders authors, this time in connection with accounts of the Caspian Sea and the Caucasus (11.5.5–6.4). Here Strabo repeats his critique of early mythographers like Ctesias and Herodotus, who had fabricated stories with an eye to pleasing their audience. The Alexander-era historians rate higher than this, but a new factor is adduced that taints them almost as much as their predecessors: Many had sought advancement by flattering Alexander or by making his exploits seem larger than life.[36] Thus, for example, they had displaced the Caucasus range into the far East, in order to allow Alexander to reach the mythical land where Prometheus had been bound to his rocky crag (11.5.5). Nor are the Alexander historians free of the original problem of Indography, a weakness for "putting one over" on the audience by exploiting areas of ignorance; for they too are said at one point to "play it fast and loose (*rhaidiourgousi*) . . . because the expedition took place at the ends (*eschatias*) of Asia, far from us; and the distant is difficult to disprove" (*to porrō duselenkton*, 11.6.4).[37]

[36] See Schwarzenberg, "Portraiture of Alexander" 244 and n. 2; and Pearson on Onesicritus (*Lost Histories* 86–88) and others (16–18, 66–67, 75–77, 150–51, 244).

[37] Strabo here echoes the critique of Homer he had earlier cited from Eratosthenes, based on the *exōkeanismos* of the *Odyssey* (1.2.19): "Distant places are better used for monstrous tales because lies are more credible there." Arrian, too, accuses certain of the Alexander historians of having deliberately made up tall tales (*Anabasis* 5.4.4).

Only in the present day, Strabo concludes, when the consolidation of the Roman and Parthian empires has laid the Orient open to view, has a truly accurate geographical account of this region become feasible (11.6.4). Thus for two reasons Strabo sees himself standing at the brink of a more enlightened epoch in Indographic writing. First, he has inherited the data gathered meticulously by Alexander the Great, and handed down by way of Patrocles; and second, he inhabits an era in which imperial ambition has opened the gates of the East even wider than under Alexander. The expansion of Western military conquest, in both cases, inexorably unveils the distant world; and since Strabo himself (as he reminds us on several occasions)[38] is the first to benefit from Rome's great leap forward, he is in a unique position to expose the fictions of the past.

Strabo's confidence in his ability to correct the Indographic record abruptly wanes, however, when, in Book 15, he actually undertakes his own survey of India. Here Strabo significantly moderates his earlier contempt for his predecessors, now urging that we read *ta Indika* with compassion (*eugnōmonōs*) since the remoteness of India has made information scarce (15.1.2). Indeed, while the geographic record has in a general way become more accurate over time—so that pre-Alexander writings can now be recognized as *tuphlotera*, "blinder," than those which came later—Strabo notes that even the observations of Roman-era merchants and sailors, who have made travel to India a routine affair, cannot always be trusted; in fact latter-day reports have sometimes corrupted older, more accurate ones (15.1.3).[39] The evolutionary scheme which Strabo elsewhere touts is here abandoned, so that the advent of the Roman Empire is no longer seen leading to the final victory of truth over fable. Instead Strabo turns back to his earlier authority Patrocles (as preserved by Eratosthenes), but even here seems unsure

[38] E.g., at 1.1.41, 1.2.1.

[39] See Bunbury 2.305–6, 309–10. Pearson (*Lost Histories* 13) observes that "it is noteworthy that the historians of Alexander made no effort to revolutionize geographical knowledge; their object, on the whole, was to make new discoveries harmonize with what was known and believed." The same point is supported by Paul Pédech in "Le paysage" (above, n. 29) 125–26.

of his principles, agreeing to accept certain stories from outside the Patroclean tradition based on what he considers "nearest to credibility" (*eggutatō pisteōs*, 15.1.10).

Strabo further compromises his standards of veracity by tempering his animus against Megasthenes and Deimachus, the lying ambassadors whom he had earlier considered the worst blights on the Indographic record. His first reference to these men in Book 15 places them, surprisingly, among "the more reasonable" (*metriasantōn mallon*, 15.1.12) of the geographers who attempted to measure the Indian subcontinent. Instead, Onesicritus (formerly one of the "stammerers" who had at least *tried* to express the truth) is here vilified as the worst liar of the Alexander group; but even the attack on Onesicritus is framed in mild, and strangely contradictory, language:

> Onesicritus might better be called the admiral of wonders rather than of Alexander; for although all those accompanying Alexander prefer the marvelous over the true, this one man exceeds all of them in his love of wonder-writing (*teratologia*). Nevertheless, he says some things that are plausible (*pithana*) and worthy of retelling, so that even a skeptic (*apistounta*) should not leave them out. (15.1.28)

Here the initial guideline of *eggutatō pisteōs*, nearness to credibility, is undercut by Strabo's own illogical tolerance of Onesicritus's lies: That which is convincing (*pithanon*) can now be written into the record even when the geographer himself, by his own admission, disbelieves it.[40] The abdication of critical responsibility which began at the outset of Book 15 has progressed even farther here, as Strabo slides from *piston* to *pithanon* in his search for a yardstick of veracity.

The final stage of this decline arrives later in Book 15, when Strabo turns his attention to the region of India beyond the Hyphasis (or Hypanis) River. This far-easterly region has a particularly significant role in *ta Indika*, since even Alexander had

[40] In fact the attack on Onesicritus's reliability is made even less forceful in that it arises in connection with a marvel Strabo believes: the tale of giant serpents dwelling in the mountains of Emodi. That is, Strabo chooses not to attack his target in one of his more vulnerable spots (such as the report of areas in India where no shadows were cast, Pliny *Hist. Nat.* 2.75.185).

not succeeded in unlocking its secrets: His restive troops had refused to cross the river, and Alexander had here turned south to begin his long trip home. We shall return to the mythology surrounding this symbolic halt further on, but for the moment let us simply note, as Strabo does, that the boundary line thus created exemplifies the rule that "the distant is difficult to disprove" (11.6.4). The fables which have been transmitted from beyond this line—principally by Megasthenes—lie outside the controls imposed by authorities like Alexander and Patrocles, and cannot be independently confirmed or refuted.[41]

Strabo begins his account of the trans-Hyphasis frontier on a skeptical note, claiming that "because of [the authors'] ignorance and [the place's] remoteness" nothing accurate had yet been set down (15.1.37). But soon he seems to become strangely captivated by his own examples of this unreliability:

> Everything about it is reported as bigger and more freakish, such as the gold-mining ants, and other beasts and men that have singular forms, or in some way have totally different qualities; like the Seres, whom they say are long-lived, prolonging their lives beyond two hundred years. They also tell of a certain aristocratic system of government, made up of 5000 counselors, each of whom furnishes an elephant for public use. And Megasthenes says the tigers among the Prasians are the largest of all . . . and that the long-tailed apes are bigger than the biggest dogs . . . and that stones are dug up which have the color of frankincense, and are sweeter in flavor than figs or honey; elsewhere there are snakes two cubits long with webbed wings, like bats, which fly by night, and let fall drops of urine (some say of sweat) which cause the skin of the unwary to rot away; and that there are winged scorpions, exceeding all others in size; and that ebony grows there; and that there are powerful dogs, which do not let go of whatever they bite until water is poured into their nostrils. (15.1.37)

Here we see Strabo moving by slow degrees from the plausible to the extraordinary, while simultaneously moving away from

[41] For the special status of the region beyond the Hyphasis, and of Megasthenes' account of it, see Arrian, *Indika* 2.9, 4.1, 6.1.

his original intention of attacking the reliability of tales from beyond the Hyphasis.[42] Like Herodotus, that is, Strabo seems to succumb to the allure of his collected wonders as his list grows longer and more exotic.[43] Were he truly concerned with the issue of credibility he need only have cited one or two exotic phenomena instead of leading us through an entire gallery of marvels.

Even when Strabo, in a later chapter, attempts to show how Megasthenes "goes overboard (*huperekpiptōn*) into the realm of the mythical," he ends up only validating those excesses in his own narration:

> He tells of the five-span and three-span men, of whom some are without nostrils, but only have two breathing holes above their mouths; and that there is a war between these three-spanners and the cranes (as Homer relates) and the partridges, which attain the size of geese; and that they seek out the eggs of these birds and crush them (since there the geese are born from eggs); and that on this account one finds no crane-eggs there, nor any young; and that frequently a crane escapes from the battles there, even after receiving a bronze dart. Similar to this are the tales of the Ear-sleepers, and the wild men, and other monstrosities. (15.1.57)

Again the momentum of the catalogue takes over as soon as Strabo begins discussing eastern fables. It is not enough to assert that the Ear-sleepers, for example, are a false invention; Strabo must also specify (later in this same passage) that they have ears that extend to the ground, and are strong enough to rip trees out of the earth and snap bowstrings. Nor is it enough

[42] Strabo "seems most attracted where he finds most to condemn," according to Truesdell S. Brown ("Reliability of Megasthenes," above, n. 9) 19. On the contradictions between Strabo's credulity and his self-avowed skepticism see Germain Aujac's introduction to the Budé edition (*Strabon* vol. 1 [Paris 1969]) xlii-xlvi.

[43] The same phenomenon has been spotted in Pliny the Elder's account of magic: "Seemingly Pliny begins within the framework of Roman hostility to the practitioners of magic; then, as he reports remedy after remedy for fear of omitting anything of value, he falls insensibly under the spell of the written word of his sources," (G. Steiner, "The Skepticism of the Elder Pliny," *CW* 48 [1955]: 142).

to provide one or two such examples, but he must also include the Swift-feet, who are faster than horses; the One-eyes, with dog's ears and shaggy skin; and the No-noses, who eat everything (even raw meat), die before they reach old age, and have an upper lip that sticks out well beyond the rest of the mouth. By the time he reaches the end of such a list he seems to have forgotten its original intent, which was not to endorse but refute the marvels it contains.

In the end, then, Strabo's attempt at revisionist Indography, with its glowing faith in the advances wrought by Alexander and Augustus, turns out to be only marginally more restrictive than the efforts of earlier writers. In fact his much-touted reliance on Patrocles may be little more than a "cover," enabling him to appear scrupulous even while indulging his obvious predilection for marvel-writers like Megasthenes and Onesicritus.[44] What is more, Strabo seems to surrender his judgement when faced with large collections of wonders and to be carried along by the catalogue, allowing its spare style and rapid momentum to carry him past all questions of credibility.

Later Greek writers continued to pass along the Indian wonders, in spite of occasional reformers like Arrian[45] who tried to stamp them out; and the Romans also cultivated the genre, thus laying the foundations of a rich literary tradition that endured through the Middle Ages and early Renaissance.[46] Because the catalogue is among the most expandable of forms, moreover, the wonder-lists continued to gather new accretions as they were transmitted. Even authors who, like Strabo, trumpeted their dislike or mistrust of Indographic writings often felt compelled to add fresh material to the heap. Aulus Gellius, for

[44] Other such strategies of deflection are discussed by Emilio Gabba in "True History and False History in Classical Antiquity," *JRS* 71 (1981): 50–62. Compare, for example, Gabba's discussion of fictional source citation among Hellenistic historiographers (54).

[45] Cf. *Anabasis* 5.4.3–5.1; discussed by Philip A. Stadter, *Arrian of Nicomedia* (Chapel Hill 1980) 119–22.

[46] For the later history of this tradition see Friedman, *The Monstrous Races* (above, n. 7); Campbell, *The Witness and the Other World* (above, n. 25) chap. 2; and Wittkower, "Marvels of the East" (above, n. 9).

example, in Book 9 of the late Roman lore collection *Attic Nights*, describes a set of Greek marvel books he had recently acquired and lists their contents for the benefit of his readers. At the end of the list he professes disgust for all such material, but does not therefore refrain from adding his own contribution:[47]

> Nevertheless it may here be permitted to set down this marvel as well, which Pliny the Elder . . . claims in the seventh book of the *Natural History* not only to have heard but to have *seen*. The words which I quote below are his own, taken from that very book. (9.4.13–14)

Gellius too, then, ends up behaving like the marvel-writers he claims to despise, cutting and pasting the wonders of the East into ever-more complete compilations.[48]

The particular book in which Gellius has here chosen to rummage, moreover—Book 7 of Pliny's *Natural History*[49]—is a wonder-catalogue conceived on a grand scale. The sweeping, synoptic opening chapters of this book list a series of monstrosities, from both human and animal realms, over half of which derive specifically from Asia and Africa (as indicated by the sentence with which this chapter began). What Pliny has here bequeathed us, then, is a rough survey of Greek Indographic writings from the fourth century onwards, thrown together in the highly reductive fashion typical of the *Natural History*. How-

[47] Cp. 10.12.1–6, where Gellius considers Pliny's marvels to be totally incredible, but insists on recording them anyway "because we ought to express our opinion about the deceitful allure of marvels of this kind."

[48] Gellius seems to want to distinguish between tales in which the teller (Pliny, in this case) has actually witnessed the wonders he describes, and those which are part of an anonymous "tradition" (cf. *traditum esse memoratumque* in 9.4.6). Such a distinction is belied by Gellius' own citation of Pliny in 9.4.7–9, however; for the material here presented as incredible is also among the phenomena Pliny claims to have witnessed himself.

[49] On Pliny's role in wonder-writing see Robert Lenoble, *Esquisse d'une histoire de l'idée de nature* (Paris 1969) chap. 4; Céard chap. 1; Marcel Benabou, "Monstres et hybrides" (above, n. 20); Olaf Gigon, "Plinius und der Zerfall der antiken Naturwissenschaft," *Arctos* n.s. 4 (1966): 23–45; and chap. 2 of L. Thorndike's *A History of Magic and Experimental Science* vol. 1 (N.Y. 1923).

ever Pliny also pauses long enough to meditate in some important ways on this welter of material; and the responses he formulates help illustrate some important new developments in the genre.

Readers of the opening of Book 7 will be struck first of all by its extraordinarily spare style: Here Pliny does not bother to subordinate, or even connect, one sentence to another, but simply tosses each new item paratactically into his grab-bag of wonders.[50] Moreover the pace of the list is frenetic, even when measured against Pliny's unceremonious prose style. The reader scarcely has time to absorb any single item before being hurried on to the next:

> There are satyrs in the easternmost mountains of India (in the region said to belong to the Catarcludi); this is a very fast-moving creature, going at times on all fours and at other times upright, in human fashion; because of their speed only the older and sick members of the tribe can be caught. Tauron says that the Choromandi tribe are forest-dwellers, have no power of speech yet shriek horribly, have shaggy bodies, grey eyes, and dog-like teeth. Eudoxus says that in southern India there are men with feet as long as a cubit, and women with feet so small that they are called Sparrowfeet. Megasthenes says that among the Nomad Indians is a tribe called the Sciritae, who have only holes instead of nostrils, like snakes; they are also club-footed. (7.2.24–25)

This mad dash through the oriental landscape continues without pause for more than seven pages of text in the Loeb edition, before Pliny finally draws breath and begins a more even-paced discussion of his next topic.

The effect created by this hypertrophy of facts and images is not only striking in itself but crucial to the larger goals of the *Natural History*, to judge by the commentary with which Pliny frames it. First, in the introduction to the catalogue, he in-

[50] Indeed, the run-on quality of this list is such that its Renaissance editors, who elsewhere divided up the *Natural History* into fairly brief chapters for reference purposes, were unable to find any convenient break and subsumed the entire list within a single, gigantic chapter.

structs the reader on how to respond to such vast assemblages of marvels:

> I don't doubt but that many people will find some of the following facts to smack of the portentous and the incredible. For who ever believed in Ethiopians before he actually saw them? Or what thing is not judged miraculous when first it comes to our attention? . . . Indeed, the power of the natural world, the majesty it expresses in all its facets, is not believable if one looks only at its particulars and does not encompass the whole with one's mind. I need hardly mention the examples of peacocks, and the spots of the tigers and panthers, and the colorings of the many species. For beyond these we note a thing which is briefly told yet immense in its implications: the great number of national languages, the number of dialects, the differences in speech so great as to make a foreigner seem scarcely human; and further the fact that though there are in our faces only ten features, or a few more, still no two of these faces in so many thousand human beings are just alike. (7.1.6–8)

The density of his text, as Pliny sees it, only reflects the condition of nature as a whole, as exemplified by the myriad variations of the leopard's spots or the features of the human face.[51] In the Indian landscape this natural diversity is seen in its most striking form, inspiring the beholder with both awe and unquestioning credulity. Pliny then returns to this idea of diversity in the catalogue's conclusion:

> In her cleverness nature has created these and other, similar things as playthings for herself, and as miracles for us. Moreover who has the power to list the individual things she creates every day, nay, almost in every hour? Let it suffice that her power is revealed by the fact that the races of men are among her marvels. (7.2.32)

Here Pliny takes a typical cataloguer's position that no explanation can be sought for the phenomena he describes, beyond the vague idea that the cosmos somehow amuses itself with "playthings" (*ludibria*).

[51] On this passage see Céard 16–17.

However lest Pliny be seen in such moments as a Roman-era Ctesias, we should note that elsewhere in the *Natural History* he looks at the Indian wonders from a more scientific, even Aristotelian, perspective. In Book 8, where Pliny turns his attention to the animal world, he seems once again to be indulging his taste for marvel-catalogues, as for example in chapters 30 and 31 where he retails many of Ctesias's Indian legends.[52] But Pliny soon transcends a simple catalogic format and introduces a discussion of cause: In describing the African lion (8.17.44) he pauses to comment on the Greek adage "Libya always produces something new," and repeats Aristotle's theory that the gatherings of species by scarce watering holes produces this differentiation.[53] Shortly thereafter Pliny cites Aristotle even more explicitly, relying on his authority to dispel a piece of popular animal lore:

> Aristotle relates a different account; and his opinion I see fit to place first, since I shall follow him in the greater part of these inquiries. When Alexander the Great became inflamed with a desire to learn the nature of the animal world, and assigned this pursuit to Aristotle, a man who excelled in every field of study, then it was ordered to the many thousands of men in the territory of all Asia and Greece to obey him: All those to whom hunting, birding, and fishing gave sustenance, and all who were in charge of pens, flocks, beehives, fishponds, and aviaries, were not to let any living thing escape his notice. And by questioning these men he laid the foundations for those nearly fifty brilliant volumes on biology. These have been summarized by me, along with some items that their author was ignorant of; I ask that my readers give them a warm reception, and, with my guidance, wander at leisure amid the universal works of nature and the central passion of the most illustrious of all rulers. (8.17.44)

[52] Examined in detail by Ermino Caprotti, "Animali Fantastici in Plinio," in *Plinio e la natura: Atti del ciclo di conferenze sugli aspetti naturalistici dell'opera Pliniana Como 1979*, ed. A. Roncoroni (Como 1982) 42–46. For Pliny's dependence on Ctesias see Céard 14.

[53] Cf. 6.35.187, Céard 16.

Thus, it is ultimately not Ctesias but a mythologized version of Aristotle, seen here as a scientific partner of Alexander the Great, whom Pliny adopts as his Indographic model.

The above account of Alexander's sponsorship of Aristotle's biology—for which, it must be said, there is not a shred of historical evidence[54]—marks an important moment in the development of the Indian wonders. As we have seen, Strabo and others had attempted to clean up the Indographic record using the new, more accurate data collected during Alexander's march. But what Strabo had tried to do by linking Alexander with Patrocles, Pliny here accomplishes even more effectively by attaching Alexander to a collaborator of unimpeachable authority: Aristotle himself. In this way he gives new substance to the vision of Alexander's conquest of the East as a scientific crusade, aimed at dispelling the cloud of fable and half-truth which had so long obscured that region. By way of this imagined partnership of omnipotent commander and omniscient philosopher, a cognitive dominion is established over the East, allowing the light of Greek rationalism to be shone under every rock and into every thicket.

This mythic partnership is only one of many attempts to accomplish in literature and legend what Alexander had failed to do in life: bring the wonders of the East under the control of western science. In the *Alexander Romance*, a text we shall examine in the next section, the greatest of explorers is again paired up with the greatest of biologists in a heroic attempt to make the distant world safe for enlightened Hellenism. But in this text, and others like it, Alexander's march across India has

[54] The issue of Aristotle's historical connection to Alexander's expedition has been debated; Werner Jaeger, for one, believes that much of the *Historia Animalium* is indeed the result of such a connection (*Aristotle*[2] trans. R. Robinson [Oxford 1948] 330). But in general there is no evidence that Aristotle obtained any data from Alexander, and plenty to suggest that he did not. See my article "Aristotle's Elephant and the Myth of Alexander's Scientific Patronage," *AJP* 110 (1990): 566–75, and P. Bolchert, "Aristoteles Erdkunde von Asien und Libyen," *Quellen und Forschungen zur alten Geschichte und Geographie* 15 (1908): 13–19. The results of Alexander's expedition had a far greater impact on Theophrastus than on Aristotle, as demonstrated by Hugo Bretzl, *Botanische Forschungen des Alexanderzuges* (Leipzig 1903).

also become something larger and more resonant: an eschatological journey which parallels the young hero's quest for immortality or divine enlightenment. In this late stratum, that is, the Indian wonders become not only a source of pseudoscientific puzzlement, but a symbolic landscape for the romance narratives which have rightly been referred to as the era's new myths.[55]

The Late Romance Tradition

Alexander's march into India had not completely fulfilled its goals, as we have seen, in that the rebellion of his troops at the Hyphasis forced the conqueror to abandon his quest for Ocean (a quest he supposedly still cherished at the time of his death).[56] But later, romanticized accounts of the expedition focused not on Alexander's retreat from the bourne of the unknown, but on his penetration into it.[57] A letter attributed to one of Alexander's cohort, already circulated as early as Strabo's day, provides some insight into how this tradition got started. According to Strabo, a letter from the Macedonian general Craterus to his

[55] E.g., by B. P. Reardon in "The Greek Novel," *Phoenix* 23 [1959]: 291–309, following Ben Edwin Perry, chap. 2 of *The Ancient Romances: A Literary-historical Account of their Origins* (Sather Classical Lectures 37, Berkeley and Los Angeles 1967).

[56] Cf. Quintus Curtius 10.1.17–18, Arrian *Indika* 1.2, Plutarch *Alexander* 68.1 The eastern coast of the Indian subcontinent seems to have been subsequently explored by one Alexandrus in the first century A.D. (see A. Dihle, "Der Seeweg nach Indien," in *Antike und Orient*, above, n. 1, 109–17), but the ancient world's knowledge of India remained frozen in essentially the state in which Alexander had left it ("The Conception of India in Hellenistic and Roman Literature," in the same volume, 89–97). Moreover, after the second century B.C. the rise of the Parthian Empire largely cut off land travel between East and West, making Alexander's feat seem all the more prodigious; see F. W. Walbank, *The Hellenistic World* (Cambridge, Mass. 1981) 67, 199.

[57] Gunderson remarks that many of the so-called Miracle-Letters in the romance tradition "tend to attribute to Alexander the achievement of those very goals that were but projected in real life" (*Alexander's Letter*, above, n. 9, p. 95). On the need to put Alexander in control of all four corners of the globe see Pearson, *Lost Histories* 13–16.

mother, Aristopatra, purported to describe an otherwise unattested leg of the eastern march:

> [The letter] says many other strange things and agrees with no one else, especially in its claim that Alexander had advanced as far as the Ganges. And Craterus himself says that he saw the river and the sea-monsters dwelling beside it. (15.1.35)

Contained in this (probably spurious) letter, then, was an account of a mythical journey Alexander had made to the Ganges, far beyond his actual turning point at the Hyphasis.[58] Behind such inventions we can sense the tendency—noted by Strabo himself at 11.5.5—for the writers on Alexander to amplify the extent of their hero's conquests to approach the dimensions of myth;[59] the region beyond the Hyphasis provided a particularly good opportunity for such amplification since it was known to be infested with terrifying freaks and prodigies.[60] In fact we can perhaps detect the Craterus's reference to "sea-monsters" on the Ganges' banks an early attempt to bring Alexander, like his mythic archetype Heracles, into confrontation with savage nature.

In later literature, moreover, we find several letters purporting to come from Alexander himself, describing similar journeys to the edge of the earth and encounters with teratological marvels along the way.[61] These missives seem to have circulated

[58] Lucan, too, assumes that Alexander had gone past the Hyphasis to the Ganges (*Bell. Civ.* 3.229–34).

[59] Exaggerations of this sort are especially prevalent in later Alexander lore (cp. Arrian, *Anabasis* 6.19.5 and *Indika* 20.2, and Quintus Curtius 9.4.18, 9.9.1), though even Alexander's contemporaries saw his journeys in mythic terms: Aeschines describes him as having gone "almost beyond the *oikoumenē*" in his northern conquests (*tēs oikoumenēs oligou dein pasēs metheistekei*, *In Ctes.* 165). See Gunderson 5–6, 84–85; R. Merkelbach, *Die Quellen des griechischen Alexanderromans*[2] (Munich 1977) 55–70.

[60] See A. Cizek, "Historical Distortions and Saga Patterns in the Pseudo-Callisthenes Romance," *Ziva Antika* 26 (1976): 363–67; idem, "Ungeheuer und magische Lebewesen in der *Epistula Alexandri*," in *Third International Beast Epic, Fable, and Fabliau Colloquium* (ed. J. Goossens and T. Sodman, Köln 1981) 78–94.

[61] The tradition is admirably summarized and catalogued by Gunderson, 32–33 and chap. 4, as a series of "miracle letters" which "report as many re-

originally in a book-length collection of letters[62] but were thereafter broken up and incorporated into various recensions of the Greek *Alexander Romance*. The longest of the epistles, and the most important for our purposes, was also published in independent form in Latin translation, probably in the second or third century A.D., though we may assume that its Greek original was considerably older than that.[63] A shorter Greek version of this letter, entitled simply *Alexander's Letter to Aristotle*, has also been included in one version of the *Alexander Romance* (ß 2.17).[64] In addition, a different Indian journey is described in both the ß recension of the Romance (2.23–31) and in two sections of the Γ recension, once in a greatly expanded version of the ß narrative (2.36–42);[65] and other jour-

---

markable experiences as possible. The setting is always in distant lands. There Alexander and his soldiers fight with monsters and undergo thrilling adventures, they see strange peoples, weird customs, and march through uninhabitable deserts" (33). Later he adds the further observation that "it is inherent in the genre to place no restrictions on the amount of confusion, distortion, and fantasy" (90). See also the useful catalogue provided by Rohde, 187 n. 1.

[62] Such is the belief of Merkelbach 56 n. 32, and Gunderson 86–88. The arguments surrounding the origin and accretion of the *Alexander Romance* as a whole are beyond the scope of this study, but it seems clear in every account of this process that the miracle letters were originally a separate element, deriving more from the stream of folktale and oral saga than from historiography. See B. Berg, "An Early Source of the *Alexander Romance*," *GRBS* 14 (1973): 382. Rohde (1914) 187 believes that the letters represent the oldest stratum of the novel.

[63] Gunderson (119) argues that the letter is in fact very nearly contemporary with Alexander himself, since the prophecies which it supplies about the fate of his sisters would only have rung true in the twenty years or so after his death. The opinion is seconded by Merkelbach (*Quellen* 60–62), who also supposes that the historical details of the prophecy would only be intelligible to an audience very close to the actual events. Neither argument seems convincing to me; see also the review of Gunderson by Cizek, *Gnomon* 54 (1982): 810. Elizabeth Haight supposes, without supplying her reasoning, that the letter to Aristotle was based on a "genuine" epistle (*More Essays on the Greek Romances* [N.Y. 1945] 4).

[64] For the relationship between the independent Latin letter and the Greek version contained in the novel, see Merkelbach 193–98 and A. Ausfeld, *Der Griechische Alexanderroman* (Leipzig 1907) 27–28.

[65] See the edition by H. Engelmann, *Der griechische Alexanderroman Rezen-*

neys to places as far afield as China and the Pillars of Heracles were narrated in other epistles.[66]

Significantly enough, the two letters of this group which are addressed to Aristotle (one of which also includes Olympias, Alexander's mother, in the address) are the two which are most concerned with animal wonders. These letters to Aristotle cast Alexander not only as a conqueror but as a champion of Hellenic science, the role which, as we saw above, was first created for him by Pliny's *Natural History*. For example, when he encounters a particularly fierce and monstrous race of semihuman creatures, Alexander's reaction is hardly that typical of a military commander: "I felt deeply disturbed at seeing such creatures; I ordered that some be taken as specimens" (Γ 2.32; cp. 2.33, 36). Indeed, empirical investigation is the activity that most characterizes the Alexander of the miracle-letter tradition: In one particularly striking episode, he descends into the depths of the sea in a primitive bathyscaph which has been fitted out with portholes to permit the collection of deep-sea specimens,[67] while in another he harnesses a team of vultures to bear him into the upper atmosphere.

The preface to the longest and most detailed of the miracle letters, titled *Alexander's Letter to Aristotle* in its Latin version, helps establish more clearly Alexander's role as Aristotle's collecting arm. This touching communiqué between master and pupil deserves quoting in full (p. 1):[68]

---

sion Γ *Buch II* (Beiträge zur klassischen Philologie 12, Meisenheim am Glan 1963).

[66] For the China journey see the Syriac version of the novel, *The History of Alexander*, ed. E. A. Wallis Budge (Cambridge 1889) 107–17; its original Greek provenance is demonstrated by John Andrew Boyle in "The *Alexander Romance* in the East and West," *Bulletin of the John Rylands Library* 60 (1977): 17–20. For the journey to the far West (among other, unidentifiable places) see rec. ß and Γ 2.27–28.

[67] Discussed by D.J.A. Ross, *Alexander and the Faithless Lady: A Submarine Adventure* (London 1967).

[68] Citations are page numbers of W. W. Boer's text (*Epistola Alexandri ad Aristotelem ad Codicum Fidem Edita* [The Hague 1953]), used here because they are conveniently keyed to Gunderson's English translation. A better text for specialists is that of M. Feldbusch, *Der Brief Alexanders an Aristoteles über*

I am always in mind of you, my dearest teacher and nearest to my heart (after my mother and sisters), even amidst the hazards of war and the many dangers that threaten us; and since I know that you are dedicated to philosophy, I decided I must write to you concerning the lands of India and the condition of the climate and the innumerable varieties of serpents, men and beasts, in order to contribute something to your research and study by way of my acquaintance with new things (*per novarum rerum cognitionem*). For although your prudence is wholly self-sufficient, and your system of thought, so fitting both for your own age and for future times, needs no support, nevertheless I thought I had better write to you about what I have seen in India . . . so that you would know of my doings (you always follow them so closely) and so that nothing here would be foreign to your experience (*ne quid inusitatum haberes*).

Here Alexander (by which name I refer to the persona of the letter) reveals the scientific basis of his project: Having uncovered a vast array of new phenomena he feels he must get them included in his master's works, although he also makes clear that his additions will supplement, not subvert, the whole system. Alexander nevertheless seems somewhat shaken by the scope of these discoveries, as indicated by his repetition of "I thought I had better write to you"—a formula that will recur several more times in the body of the letter. There is a certain urgency in his tone, a need to transmit all his findings back to "headquarters" lest this historic opportunity be lost.

Having broken the news to Aristotle that his system will need to be updated, Alexander goes on to express the overwhelming sense of wonder and confusion that the Indian environment inspires in him:

As I see it, these things are worthy of being recorded, whether singly or in great, manifold groups; for I would never have taken it from anyone else that so many wonders could exist, unless I myself had first examined them all right in front of my own eyes. It's amaz-

---

die Wunder Indiens (Beiträge zur klassischen Philologie 78, Meisenheim am Glan 1976), which is laid out so as to permit a synoptic comparison of the *Epistola* with other, related Alexander narratives.

ing how many things, both evil and good, the earth produces, that mother and common parent of beasts and fruits, of minerals and animals. If it were permitted to man to survey them all, I would think that there would hardly even be enough names for so many varieties of things. (pp. 1–2)

Here Alexander, again following a pattern we observed in Pliny, envisions the natural kingdom as an awesome totality revealing a near-infinite range of variegation. For Alexander, though, this multiplicity has become more of a problem than it had been for Pliny, in that the parameters of Aristotelian taxonomy seem now to be stretched to the breaking point. Indeed, by suggesting that man's supply of "names" (*nomina*) may not be large enough to accommodate nature's bounty, Alexander poses a rather serious challenge to Aristotle, who often refers to his own taxonomic categories as "names" (*onomata*). The Aristotelian system seems to be in danger of overload as it tries to absorb all these oriental anomalies; and Alexander, the man of action who carries that system forward into the world, fears he will be unable to hold together the rapidly diverging poles of theory and experience.

The shaky sense of control Alexander reveals in the prologue of the *Letter to Aristotle* becomes even more tenuous in the text, as he moves across the frontier encountering hostile beasts at every juncture. In the letter's first long episode (pp. 9–23), for example, Alexander, whose army has suffered from shortages of drinking water, decides to bivouac beside a stagnant pool. The error of this decision becomes apparent when swarms of scorpions arrive to drink at the pool and commence stinging the soldiers with their barbed tails (17); and no sooner have these pests been driven off than others arrive, so that the night turns into a long series of horrific incursions (pp. 18–20):

At the fifth hour of the night the trumpet signalled that those awake on watch should take their rest; but suddenly white lions, the size of bulls, arrived. . . . Also boars of immense size . . . which together with spotted lynxes, tigers, and fearsome panthers, gave us a fight worse than any previous plague. And then a huge flock of bats, similar to doves in their form, flung themselves into our mouths and

> faces, attacking the soldiers' limbs with their man-like teeth. In addition one beast of a new type appeared, larger than an elephant, and equipped with three horns on its forehead, which the Indians call a *dentityrannus*; it has a head like a horse but black in color. This beast, having drunk water, spotted us and made a charge at our camp.

This unholy *Walpurgisnacht* puts Alexander into the heart of the Indian wonders experience, surrounding him with a veritable catalogue of monstrous creatures. Indeed the setting for this night of terrors—beside a watering hole—recalls the theory put forth by both Pliny and Aristotle, that such holes formed the primary locus for the hybridization of biological forms. If the prologue of the letter portrays an Alexander struggling to hang onto his embattled Aristotelianism, then, it is not surprising to find that the narrative, shortly thereafter, thrusts him into the place where that system is most strenuously put to the test.

Following this "Night of Terrors" the *Letter to Aristotle* takes Alexander through a series of encounters with monstrous nature (far too numerous to be discussed here) and finally lands him at the endpoint of his journey, the Oracle of the Sun and Moon. Here, as in many of the miracle letters, Alexander is directed by divine voices to return to the *oikoumenē*, and at the same time receives a forecast of his own imminent death. These two messages, we note, are in fact closely related, since Alexander's trek toward the eastern edge of the world is in part a quest for divinity: As in the myths of Heracles, which Alexander's legends often reenact, the voyage beyond the *oikoumenē* comes to symbolize mankind's transcendence of the human condition.[69] Unlike Heracles, however, Alexander never quite achieves that transcendence; at the outermost limit of travel he discovers that he is not only mortal but in fact fated to die very

[69] In one episode of a different miracle letter (Pseudo-Callisthenes Γ 2.39–41), this theme is quite vividly realized as a search for the Water of Life, which imparts immortality to those who drink it or bathe in it. Alexander misses his opportunity to use the Water but his cook, whose name is given in one recension as *Andreas* or "Man," succeeds in applying it. See Gunderson 80–82.

soon. (We shall look further at the tradition of Alexander's other-worldly voyages in chapter 4.)

This revelation of mortality is in fact the primary message of *Alexander's Letter to Aristotle* and other epistles like it, and largely explains how they came to be included in the *Alexander Romance*. The novel, like the letters it contains, portrays Alexander as an Everyman dwarfed by the threatening and mysterious forces around him.[70] His journey through life parallels on a personal scale the letters' vision of his journey through India: perilous, dark, beset by portents of imminent doom. In one of the novel's many episodes of divination, for example, Alexander asks a Chaldaean sage to interpret a monstrous child that has been brought before him, whose stillborn human torso rests on legs made up of living beasts (3.29–30). The horrified Chaldaean proclaims, "O king, the human portion of this creature is you; the forms of the wild beasts are those who surround you," and predicts that, because the human half is stillborn, Alexander too is marked for an early death. In the letters from India, then, Alexander becomes precisely what this grotesque image proclaims him to be, a helpless and ultimately doomed man trapped in a world of wild animals. The landscape of the Indian wonders has become a grim allegory of the human condition, seen in its most starkly eschatological dimensions.

Nor was the author of the Alexander Romance alone in glimpsing the symbolic potential of the Indian wonders. A similar allegorizing tendency emerges in a late Greek biographical novel of a very different stamp, the *Life of Apollonius of Tyana* attributed to Flavius Philostratus.[71] In this eulogistic bi-

[70] The great popularity and wide diffusion of the *Alexander Romance* partly bears out Ben Perry's characterization of "the Hellenistic soul" in later antiquity: "Faced with the immensity of things and his own helplessness before them, the spirit of man in Hellenistic times became passive in a way that it had never been before, and he regarded himself instinctively as a plaything of Fortune" ("Literature in the Second Century," *CJ* 50 [1955]: 295–98; see also chap. 2 of *The Ancient Romances*).

[71] On this work see, most recently, Graham Anderson, *Philostratus* (Kent 1986) chaps. 11–12, and Sedlar (above, n. 1) 190–98; also Rohde (1914) 260–309; R. Reitzenstein, *Hellenistische Wundererzählungen* (Leipzig 1906) 40–53; and H. Rommel, *Die naturwissenschaftlich-paradoxographischen Exkurse bei Philostratos, Heliodoros und Achilles Tatios* (Stuttgart 1923).

ography, the last text we shall look at in this chapter, Philostratus portrays Apollonius—a mystic and philosopher roughly contemporary with Christ—as a new Alexander, making his way around the world (together with his student Damis) in search not of conquest but of sacred knowledge and wisdom. To better establish this parallel with Alexander, moreover, Philostratus begins by sending his hero into the East—so that Apollonius at first retraces the trail of the Macedonian expedition (Book 2), then plunges into the lands beyond its terminus (Book 3).[72]

No sooner has Apollonius passed this terminus, at the river Hyphasis (where a great brass column proclaims that "Alexander stopped here," 2.43), than the familiar Indian wonders begin to spring up around him.[73] In the very first chapter of Book 3, for example, Philostratus describes a wonder borrowed directly from Ctesias (*Indika* 27): a giant river-dwelling worm whose fat yields a precious incendiary oil. But lest the reader suspect that a naïve redaction of the *Indika* and similar works is in store, Philostratus quickly changes tack and brings the philosophic side of his hero into play. After introducing a second Ctesian marvel—the unicorn, with its life-sustaining horn (cf. *Indika* 25)—the author relates the following exchange between Apollonius and his follower, Damis (3.2):

> Apollonius says that he saw this creature, and admired its form; but on being asked by Damis whether he believed the story regarding the drinking-cup [carved from its horn], he said, "I will believe it, when I discover the king of these Indian tribes to be immortal; for anyone who could offer me, or whomever, a drink so health-restoring and wholesome would surely keep it for himself and drink from

[72] The historicity of this journey has been variously debated; see, for example, Jarl Charpentier, "The Indian Travels of Apollonius of Tyana," *Skrifter utgivna av. K. Humanistika Vetenskaps-Samfundet i Uppsala* 29 (1934): 6–66, and Vincent A. Smith, "The Indian Travels of Apollonius of Tyana," *Zeitschrift der Deutschen Morgenländischen Gesellschaft* 68 (1914): 329–44.

[73] Charpentier (above note) remarks on the wide gap between the relatively realistic narrative of Book 2 and the wildly fabulistic elements of Book 3 (59–66); similar comments by J. W. McCrindle, *Ancient India as Described in Classical Literature* (Westminster 1901, repr. New Delhi 1979) 195.

> this cup every day, until he became ill from the drinking. No one, I suppose, would blame him for that sort of drunkenness."

Here Apollonius, in typical fashion, plays an ironic Socrates to the admiring Damis; and like Socrates he disdains to answer his student's question directly but turns the discussion toward new and more probing concerns. Whether the unicorn's horn really does possess curative powers soon ceases to be important; the legend instead becomes distanced and objectified, serving now as vehicle for an object lesson in human mortality.[74]

Philostratus's interest in the Indian wonders as metaphors becomes even more evident in the next episode, when Apollonius joins some of the local Indians in a fabulous dragon hunt (3.8–9). This ethnographic vignette is clearly based on traditional stories of gold-guarding "ants" and griffins in the Indian hinterland, tales that were associated with both Herodotus (3.102–5) and Ctesias (*apud* Aelian *Nat. Anim.* 4.27), but Philostratus has made some important alterations in his model. First, the treasure which these dragon-hunters seek is not gold, as in earlier accounts, but a prize of loftier value: the eyes of the dragons themselves, made up of "a fiery stone which they say exerts an invincible power in many of their secret rites." In fact a particular species of dragon has eyes that are said to possess the occult powers of the ring of Gyges from Plato's *Republic*.[75] Second, the dragons of Philostratus's India are defeated not by stealth, as in the traditional tale, but by a more highly developed form of wisdom (3.9):

> On a red-dyed cloak [the Indians] weave golden letters, and place this in front of the creature's lair, after charming the letters with the power to cause sleep. By this object the eyes of the dragon—which otherwise never yield—are overcome; then they chant many bits of mystic wisdom (*aporrētou sophias*) over the beast, by which it is led to stretch its neck out of the lair and fall asleep on top of the letters.

[74] We are reminded of Plato's *Phaedrus*, in which the naïve question of whether Socrates believes the truth of a local myth is dismissed in favor of a more far-reaching type of investigation (229c–230b).

[75] Charpentier speculates that some vague recollection of an Indian legend of gem-studded cobras may lie behind the passage (60 n. 4).

The Indians fall upon him and drive their axes into him as he lays there, then cut off his head and steal the gemstones it contains.

Philostratus has here reworked a traditional gold-getting story so as to portray a battle waged by philosophers, using philosophy itself as a weapon, for the sake of a purely philosophical prize. The episode which results, we note, is perhaps closer to allegory than to ethnography;[76] at least, Philostratus seems remarkably unconcerned with demonstrating that his gem-eyed dragons really do exist.

Philostratus's most extensive exploration of the Indian wonders, however, is held off until the end of Book 3, which is also the point of Apollonius's furthest progress toward the East. Here Apollonius's interlocutor is Iarchas, the philosopher-king of a race of sages among whom he and Damis have been permitted to dwell.[77] Iarchas (like most Indian sages) possesses a superhuman wisdom, and so Apollonius's interview with him, like Alexander's visit to the Oracle of the Sun and Moon, represents the climax of a long quest for mystical knowledge. Significantly enough, Philostratus seizes this climactic moment to introduce the Indian wonders (3.45–49), and further underscores their importance with an unusual first-person aside: "Let me not leave out the discussion recorded by Damis pursuant to the fabled animals, springs, and men of India; for there would be great benefit in neither believing all things nor disbelieving."

The wonders which Philostratus chooses to discuss in this final episode do indeed seem to transcend the simple issue of belief. Merely monstrous creatures like the martichora and shadow-footed *Skiapodes* are quickly dismissed from the discussion, while sacred birds, like the griffin—here divinized as the animal which pulls the chariot of the Sun—and the phoenix, are described in greater detail.[78] By far the longest section

[76] Compare Philostratus's obviously allegorical treatment of the Lamia (4.25), a monster which uses the pleasures of the flesh to undermine a student's devotion to philosophy.

[77] On their colloquy see A. J. Festugière, "Trois rencontres entre la Grèce et l'Inde," *Revue de l'Histoire des Réligions* (1942–43) 54–57.

[78] Anderson (above, n. 71) attributes this imbalance to the fact that griffins and phoenixes "were too firmly embedded in the traditional picture of India to be dislodged," but this was even more true of the *Skiapodes* and marti-

of the interview, moreover, is given over to the *pantarbē* stone, another Ctesian wonder on which Philostratus has rung remarkable changes. Ctesias had originally described the *pantarbē* as a sophisticated "prospector's magnet": a stone which had the ability to attract gems from out of the earth (*Indika* 2). Here, some five centuries later, the *pantarbē* has entirely lost its gain-getting function and has instead become a precious symbol of divine enlightenment (3.46):

> "The largest stone is as big as the nail of this finger," [Iarchas] said, showing them his thumb. "It is conceived in a hollow space of earth, four fathoms under; yet it has about it such a great quantity of divine spirit (*pneuma*) that the earth swells a little and sometimes breaks open when the stone is conceived in it. No one can search it out, for it runs away if it is not attracted with reason (*meta logou*); but we alone, in part by rituals and in part by utterances, get for ourselves the *pantarbē*—for that is its name. In the night it shows forth daylight, just like a fire, and is red and full of rays; when seen in the day it strikes the eyes with thousands of sparkles. And the light in it is a spirit (*pneuma*) of great power, and attaches to itself everything nearby. Nay, not only nearby: You can sink as many of the stones as you like in the rivers or sea, and not even near each other but scattered every which way; and if a single stone is let down by a rope among them it collects them all by the dispersal of its spirit, and they will gather obediently into a bunch, like a swarm of bees."

Such transformations typify the way that the Indian wonders evolved as they made their way down through the ages, offering new meanings and new literary possibilities to the various eras that inherited them.[79]

---

chora. Both Anderson and Festugière (above, n. 77) mistakenly attribute Philostratus's paradoxographic excurses to a simple desire to entertain his audience; were this his main motive he would have surely supplied more examples.

[79] Later still Heliodorus, author of the Greek erotic romance *Ethiopica*, also uses the *pantarbē* in ways that suggest its mystical and religious powers: His heroine Charicleia, after praying to the gods to be delivered from an execution by fire, is rescued by her *pantarbē* ring—which in this case grants its wearer the power to withstand burning flames (8.11).

Four

Ultima Thule and Beyond

THE MACEDONIAN REBELLION at the banks of the river Hyphasis prevented Alexander from attaining the goal he cherished, the extension of his empire to the eastern edge of the world; and as a result the regions of India beyond the Hyphasis remained a source of literary exotica for centuries afterward, as we have seen in the previous chapter. In some accounts, moreover, this tendency to estrange the eastern frontier reaches a kind of hyperbolic extreme, in which the unexplored lands are seen as altogether detached from the *oikoumenē*. For example, in Quintus Curtius's *History of Alexander the Great*, a Macedonian infantryman named Coenus, who speaks on behalf of the disaffected soldiers during the Hyphasis revolt, refers to the region that lies ahead as an *alius orbis*, "another world" (9.3.8). Similarly, when Alexander later ventures far to the south and contemplates a voyage on the Indian Ocean, his restive troops complain that they are being led "beyond the stars and the sun" toward "gloom and darkness and perpetual night" (9.4.18). In such passages we see the reemergence of archaic distant-world imagery in a new and more compelling imaginative context: that of other worlds beyond the *oikoumenē*, or beyond the stream of Ocean, which now lay within reach of exploration and conquest. It is now Alexander, as a latter-day version of Heracles, who seems to have it in his power to pass beyond the boundaries of earth.

If the ends of the earth seemed to be drawing within reach in Alexander's time, moreover, the same was true to a far greater degree in the early days of the Roman Empire. The geographic keynote of the era is sounded by Ovid's grandiose claim, *Romanae spatium est urbis et orbis idem*—"The extent of

Rome's city is the same as that of the world" (*Fasti* 2.684).[1] In fact all three of the principal geographers of the early Empire—Strabo (who wrote in Greek but was nonetheless Roman in outlook), Pomponius Mela, and Pliny the Elder—seem bent on supporting this claim by showing that the *oikoumenē* (or in Roman terms the *orbis terrarum*)[2] had at last been completely circumnavigated.[3] Often they must rely on spurious or badly exaggerated legends to accomplish this feat; both Mela and Pliny, for example, cite Hanno's *Periplous* as evidence for the circumnavigation of Africa, though Hanno had in fact sailed only a short way down the coast of that continent before doubling back.[4] Such distortions attest to the enormous appeal of the "island *oikoumenē*" concept, during a time when it seemed that the earth would soon be consolidated into a single city-state.

But the Romans' vision of the *orbis* as a circumscribed *urbs* also brought with it certain problems. While on the one hand their glory was enhanced by the acquisition of an empire whose boundaries (by convention at least) embraced the entire *oikoumenē*, on the other hand this achievement imposed a spatial

[1] For other instances of the *urbs/orbis* theme, see the extensive note ad loc. in Franz Bömer's edition of the *Fasti* (*Die Fasten* vol. 1 [Heidelberg 1957]). Discussion by Philip R. Hardie, *Virgil's Aeneid: Cosmos and Imperium* (Oxford 1986) 364–66; J. Vogt, "Orbis Romanus," in *Orbis: Ausgewählte Schriften zur Geschichte des Altertums* (Freiburg, Basel, Vienna 1960) 151–71; E. Bréguet, "*Urbi et orbi*: un cliché et un thème," in *Hommages à Marcel Renard*, ed. J. Bibauw (Coll. Latomus 101, Brussels 1969) 140–52. Nicolet (33) traces the first appearance of the conceit to a passage of Nepos (*Att.* 20.5).

[2] For the equivalence of these terms see Thomson 201, Gisinger (1937) cols. 2169–70, Tandoi (1967) 49–52, and Vogt, "Orbis Romanus," 153–54 and n. 8. Vogt also outlines several other senses of the term.

[3] Actually Strabo (1.1.8) admits that the southernmost and northernmost tips of the *oikoumenē* have yet to be sailed around, but deduces logically that they too must be bounded by sea.

[4] Pliny *Hist. Nat.* 2.67.168, Mela *De Situ Orbis* 3.90–91. On the Plinian passage see Bunbury 2.382–84; Robert Lenoble, *Esquisse d'une histoire de l'idée de nature* (Paris 1969) 149–52; K. G. Sallmann, *Die Geographie des älteren Plinius in ihrem Verhältnis zu Varro* (Untersuchungen zur antiken Literatur und Geschichte 11, Berlin and N.Y. 1971) 144 n. 57. For Mela see the notes ad loc. in the edition by P. Parroni, *De Chorographia Libri Tres* (Storia è Letteratura 160, Rome 1984) 434–35.

limitation which their expansionist spirit could not easily accept. If the world were truly to become an enormous walled city, where then could Roman legions find new lands to conquer? It was in response to this perceived limitation that Roman writers of the late Republic and early Empire began to look longingly at the few frontiers still remaining to them: the northern coast of Germany, the upper reaches of the Nile, and the mysterious island of Thule located vaguely in the North Atlantic. Beyond these, moreover, they imagined other lands, as yet unnamed and undiscovered, which seemed to beckon Rome with the promise of unceasing geographic expansion.

Of course, the fact that the Romans conceived of a manifest destiny drawing them on to distant parts of the globe will hardly seem a novel idea to readers of Latin literature; it has been investigated in numerous scholarly works including, most recently, Claude Nicolet's *Space, Geography and Politics in the Early Roman Empire.*[5] What we shall focus on here, rather, is how Hellenistic lore surrounding "other worlds" and Alexander's supposed plans to conquer them set the pattern for later myths of lands beyond the Roman frontier. Germany and the upper Nile, for instance, though known to be quite securely attached to the *oikoumenē*, seem to become *alii orbes* in much the same way as had Alexander's India, as if to provide a new and more compelling challenge to the outward movement of Greco-Roman culture. A similar *plus ultra* impulse, moreover, made Thule, an otherwise obscure island glimpsed in the seas beyond Britain, into a powerful symbol of Rome's renewal and future greatness. At the same time, however, the idea of Roman conquest beyond Ocean had its darker side, especially to those who saw Alexander's exploits as a paradigm of reckless greed: Thus the philosopher Seneca and others see Rome's maritime expansion as the final stage in a long slide toward reckless ambition, amorality, and self-annihilation.

[5] Originally published in French under the title *L'Inventaire du monde: Géographie et politique aux origines de l'empire Romain* (Paris 1988). I am grateful to Ellen Bauer of the University of Michigan Press for making a preliminary copy of the English-language version available to me.

Antipodal Ambitions

Plato was the first writer whom we know to have thought seriously about worlds beyond the *oikoumenē*, though there is evidence that here, as elsewhere, he owes much to the Pythagoreans.[6] In the *Timaeus* and *Critias* Plato describes the enormous island of Atlantis, formerly located in Ocean outside the Pillars of Heracles, and claims that the subsidence of that island has left the seas there shallow and unnavigable. The *Timaeus* portion of the myth also goes further and imagines a chain of islands stretching away to the west of Atlantis, leading by stages to an enormous mainland forming the opposite bank of Ocean (24e–25a); this region is not named but is described as the "true sea, and the land enclosing it, that which one might in complete truthfulness call a continent" (25a3–5). It is this trans-Oceanic element of the Atlantis myth that has especially interested students of ancient geography, since it seems wholly superfluous within its context: The farther continent is (as far as we know) uninhabited and plays no part in the central story of the war between Atlantis and Athens.[7] Why then did Plato bother to include his famous[8] sentence describing these far-western lands? Are we here entitled to speak, as has Paul Friedländer,[9] of "Plato as geographer," a man interested in putting

[6] Cf. Alexander Polyhistor *apud* Diogenes Laertius 8.26 (= Pythagoras fr. B1a Diels-Kranz), who credits the "Pythagorean Memoirs" with the doctrine of an earth "inhabited all around."

[7] In fact, Plato omits it entirely in his "reprise" description of Atlantis in the *Critias* (108e), though he does later recall the existence of the other mid-Ocean islands (114c). See Paul Friedländer, *Plato: An Introduction*[2] (Princeton 1969) 274.

[8] We cannot begin here to deal with the long and vigorous afterlife this sentence has enjoyed, especially in the era following the discovery of the New World; but see José Imbelloni, "Las 'Profecias de America' y el Ingreso de Atlantida en le Americanista," *Boletin de la Academia Nacional de la Historia de Buenos Aires* 12 (1939): 115–48, and (with A. Vivante) *Le Livre des Atlantides*, tr. F. Gidon (Paris 1942); Ida Rodriguez Prampolini, *La Atlantida de Platon en los Cronistas del Siglo XVI* (Mexico 1947). Briefer comment is provided by Thomson (90–93).

[9] *Plato: An Introduction* chap. 15; discussion of *Timaeus* 273–77. See also

across earnest (if highly speculative) theories about the structure of the globe?

Before attempting to answer these questions let us look briefly at another "geographic" myth in the *Phaedo*, to which that of the *Timaeus* and *Critias* has often been compared. Here Plato, using Socrates as mouthpiece, envisions an earth so vast that it makes the *oikoumenē* and all its inhabitants seem only "ants or frogs dwelling around a pond" (109b). The simile is intentionally pejorative, for Plato's point is that we who live in the *oikoumenē* are lowly creatures compared with other inhabitants of the globe; while we reside in a huge crater, our atmosphere clogged up by the silt and mud that has collected there, they dwell on mountaintops, breathe pure ether, and commune with the gods themselves. This scheme has much in common with the legends of Hyperboreans and Ethiopians we examined in chapter 2, but assumes an even greater discontinuity between the *oikoumenē* and its surrounding spaces: Our sky is so occluded by the impurity of the air that we have no perception at all of the world above it, any more than a fish can perceive the terrestrial realm from below the surface of the sea. In this way we are cut off from what Plato again describes as the "true" regions of the earth (109e7–110a1).

It is this discontinuity, I would argue, which forms the most significant link between the *Phaedo*'s geography and that of the *Timaeus* and *Critias*; for in both our passageway to the other world is blocked by "impassable mud" (*aporos pēlos*, *Crit.* 108e8, cf. *Tim.* 25d5; *pēlos amēchanos*, *Phaed.* 110a6). We can scarcely ignore the metaphysical implications of this "mud," a substance which is associated elsewhere in Plato with base materialism and inability to perceive a higher reality.[10] Therefore,

---

F. Gisinger, "Zur geographischen Grundlage von Platons Atlantis," *Klio* 26 (1932): 32–38, where Friedländer's approach is cited approvingly.

[10] The word *pēlos* occurs in the *Theaetetus* among a list of things so lowly and ignoble that they are assumed not to have correlates in the world of forms (130c7). See also *Republic* 533c, where the eye of the soul is said to be mired in "barbaric mud" (*borborōi barbarikōi*) when it fails to glimpse true reality (connected by Adams with the Orphic conception of human ordure as a form of

the fact that Plato, in both his geographic schemes, imagines an *oikoumenē* cut off from "true" places by a curtain of mud has a clear application within the realm of epistemology: An understanding of the "true" earth cannot proceed from the data gathered by the senses, any more than astronomers (as Plato suggests in the *Republic*, 528a-531a) can come to know the heavens merely by watching the sky. To live in the *oikoumenē*, then, is equivalent to living in the darkness of the famous Cave—indeed the parallels between the Cave allegory of the *Republic* and the mythic geography of the *Phaedo* have already been well established.[11]

The Atlantis myth of the *Timaeus* and *Critias* should therefore be seen not as a philosopher's experiment in geography, as Friedländer suggests, but as pseudogeography in the service of philosophy. The Greek tradition of fabulous islands beyond the Pillars was indeed well suited to this sort of epistemological development, since as we have seen such places were typically thought to be fenced off by impenetrable barriers. In fact one tale prominent within this tradition seems to have circulated during Plato's day—it is recorded in a wonder-book usually dated to the fourth century, *On Marvelous Reports*—and has therefore been tentatively identified as one of Plato's sources for the Atlantis myth:

> They say that in the sea outside the Pillars of Heracles an uninhabited island was discovered by the Carthaginians, many days' sail from shore, which has all kinds of trees, and navigable rivers, and a marvelous variety of other resources. When the Carthaginians began going there often on account of its fruitfulness, and some even emigrated there, the Carthaginian leaders decreed that they would put to death anyone who planned to sail there, and got rid of all those who were living there, lest they spread the word and a crowd

---

punishment in Hades; see notes to 363d, 533d in *The Republic of Plato*² [Cambridge 1969]).

[11] Frutiger (*Les Mythes de Platon* [Paris 1930] 61–66) and Schuhl (*La Fabulation platonicienne* [Paris 1947] 50–51) concur in comparing the *Phaedo*'s geography with the allegory of the Cave in the *Republic*. See also Bluck's note in *Plato's Phaedo* (London 1955) 200–201.

> gather around them on the island which might gain power and take away the prosperity of the Carthaginians. (84, 836b30–37a7)

In this story, as in the myth of Atlantis, the pathway connecting one world to another has been forever sealed shut, though this time by political rather than perceptual boundaries.[12] Moreover, in both cases the world which has been lost is described as paradisical or divinely blessed, as if to equate the geographic limits imposed by the Mediterranean with mankind's exclusion from the world of the golden age.[13]

Plato does, however, furnish an example of what it would be like to escape these limits and recover our lost connection to "true" geography. In the *Phaedo* myth discussed above he has Socrates imagine that a crater-dweller could sprout wings and fly above the atmosphere, and from that vantage point behold the cosmos in its actual splendor (109e). No sooner has this case been put, moreover, than Socrates himself becomes that winged being, describing a remarkable vision of the earth "as one would see it from above" (110b): a brightly colored spherical[14] object adorned with gold, silver, and jewels. In this

[12] The story is repeated in much greater detail by Diodorus (5.19–20), who adds a second motive for the quarantine: The Carthaginians wished the island to remain unknown (to all but themselves) so that, if threatened by enemies, they could escape there and not be pursued. Diodorus may well have invented this second explanation, since, as noted by Oldfather in the Loeb edition (vol. 5 [Cambridge 1939] 150 n. 2), it does not square with the rest of the narrative. We might contrast the "closed-door" policy of Carthage here with a different chapter of *On Marvelous Reports* (136), where the Phoenicians are reported still to be sailing to unknown islands four days west of the Pillars in order to catch the huge tunas that congregate there.

[13] Cf. Diodorus Siculus 4.18.4, where the Pillars of Heracles are seen as a memorial of the ancient closing of the straits (in this case, to prevent "sea-monsters" from entering the Mediterranean).

[14] I do not intend to enter into the debate over the shape of the earth in the *Phaedo*, except to say that I am persuaded by Calder's point ("The Spherical Earth in Plato's *Phaedo*," *Phronesis* 3 [1958]: 123) that Plato would never have used the analogy of a ball here if he did not intend us to imagine a spherical planet. For the other side of the debate see T. G. Rosenmeyer, "*Phaedo* 111c4 ff.," *CQ* n.s. 6 (1956): 193–97, and "The Shape of the Earth in the *Phaedo*: A Rejoinder," *Phronesis* 4 (1959): 71–72; also J. S. Morrison, "The Shape of the Earth in Plato's *Phaedo*," *Phronesis* 4 (1959): 101–19.

transcendent description Plato follows a tradition we have looked at above in connection with the Hesiodic *Periodos Gēs*, and which would go on to become hugely popular in the period with which we are now concerned. Only by flight—whether the actual, airborne journey of the Boreades or the mental and imaginative ascent of the dying Socrates—could one break through the barriers of perception and attain a glimpse of worlds beyond the *oikoumenē*. And the panorama thereby achieved was often strikingly beautiful and mysterious, a visible revelation of ultimate truth.

Eratosthenes, for example, employs the same technique in his poem *Hermes*,[15] a work strongly influenced by Plato which would in turn inspire a long passage of Vergil's *Georgics* (1.231–56).[16] In this poem Eratosthenes uses Hermes—another being endowed with wings—to attain a vision of the whole earth, which he sees divided by climate into horizontal zones:

> Five encircling zones were girt around it: two of them darker than greyish-blue enamel, another one sandy and red, as if from fire. . . . Two others there were, standing opposite one another, between the heat and the showers of ice; both were temperate regions, growing with grain, the fruit of Eleusinian Demeter; in them dwelt men antipodal to each other. (fr. 16 ll. 3–5, 16–19)

With this snippet of verse we begin to turn our attention to a new tradition, which located the other world not in the West—as had been true in Greek myth and literature up to Plato's time—but in the South. It was in this direction, below the equator, that Hellenistic and Roman writers looked when seeking an alternate continent, and when pondering the alien race

[15] Fragments in J. Powell, *Collectanea Alexandrina* (Oxford 1925) 58–63. For commentary see Berger (1903) 398–99.

[16] For the Platonic influence see Friedrich Solmsen, "Eratosthenes as Platonist and Poet," *TAPA* 73 (1972): 192–213, esp. 206–10; for Vergil's use of the poem see Richard Thomas, "Virgil's *Georgics* and the Art of Reference," *HSCP* 90 (1986): 195–98, and the same author's notes to the passage in question in his commentary on *Georgics* 1 and 2 (Cambridge 1988).

who are very nearly christened in the final line above: the Antipodes.[17]

Beginning with Aristotle, Greek geographers speculated about a second habitable world in the southern hemisphere matching the *oikoumenē* in the North.[18] The supposition that such a world existed was based, as indicated by Eratosthenes' poetic version above, on the then-emerging picture of a large and spherical earth divided into climatic zones. It had long been theorized that the *oikoumenē*, stretching roughly from the arctic circle to the Tropic of Cancer, constituted a single habitable zone bordered by two uninhabitable ones;[19] more recently the new science of earth measurement had demonstrated that this entire landmass took up only a small portion, certainly less than half, of the global surface. The conjunction of these two hypotheses then gave rise to a third, that is, that a congruent *oikoumenē*, stretching from the Tropic of Capricorn to the antarctic, formed the mirror image across the equator of the one formed by Asia, Africa, and Europe.[20] Whether the two habitable worlds were separated by sea (as supposed by Crates and other Stoics, who thought that Ocean occupied the entire

[17] The use of the adjective *antipodes* here seems to antedate its first use as a proper noun (see below). Diogenes Laertius attributes the invention of the word to Plato (3.24), but he is probably thinking of a passage in the *Timaeus* (63a) which designates a geographic position rather than a people.

[18] Aristotle, *Meteor.* 2.5.11, 16; see Bunbury 1.397, Thomson 90, Berger (1903) 301–2. The history of ancient theories of the Antipodes is surveyed by Armand Rainaud in *Le Continent austral: Hypothèses et découvertes* (Paris 1893; repr. Amsterdam 1965) chap. 1; see also Kretschmer 53–59, Wright 17–19 and 156–61, and G. Boffito, "La leggende degli Antipodi," in *Miscellanea di studi critici ed. in onore di Arturo Graf* (Bergamo 1903) 583–601.

[19] The theory of zones has been tentatively assigned to Parmenides and the Eleatics, but its origins are obscure and several philosophic schools probably shared in its development. See Kretschmer 49–53; Berger (1903) 197–218, (1898) 94–97, and "Die Zonenlehre des Parmenides," *Berichte über die Verhandlungen der königlich-sächsischen Gesellschaft der Wissenschaft zu Leipzig* (Philol.-Hist. Classe) 47 (1895): 57–108.

[20] It is the same sort of symmetrical thinking, we note, which had led Herodotus to suppose that the Hyperboreans in the North must be balanced by Hypernotians in the South (4.36), and that the Nile must run parallel to the Danube (2.29), now projected onto the newly expanded scale of global geography.

breadth of the equatorial zone),[21] or by an intolerably hot stretch of desert, was open to debate (cf. Strabo 2.5.3); but in either case the two worlds were cut off from each other with equal finality (more on this point below).

In the century following Aristotle's, moreover, the two-world scheme was taken a step further by Crates of Mallos, who imagined not only paired *oikoumenai* in the North and South but a second pair in the western hemisphere. Two branches of Ocean were imagined to run between these four worlds, creating perpendicular "rings" of water at both the equator and the meridians.[22] Strangely enough, Crates, as we shall see in more detail in the next chapter, supported this four-world scheme with citations from Homer: Thus, the famous "double-dwelling Ethiopians" of the *Odyssey* could be explained as living on the coasts of both northern and southern continents, separated by Ocean, and the homeward voyage of Menelaus could be plotted on a course that took him from one world to the other (Strabo 1.2.24 = Crates fr. 34c Mette). It is Crates' four-world scheme that was canonized for later antiquity and the Middle Ages by Cicero's Dream of Scipio, a text we shall come to shortly, and by the commentary added to it by Macrobius in the fifth century A.D.

Opinions differed widely in antiquity as to whether these other worlds were inhabited, and if so, by what type of people. Aristotle says only that the southern continent *could* support

[21] See Geminus 16.21–22 (= Crates fr. 34a Mette), Macrobius *Commentum in Somn. Scip.* 2.9.1 (= Crates frs. 35–36); Diels, *Doxographi Graeci* 467.5. The problems of reconciling such a theory with reports of Africa's transequatorial extension were obviously great, and some scholars, like Rainaud (*Le Continent austral* 33–34 and n. 5) wrongly suppose that all geographers before Marinus and Ptolemy simply ignored that extension; but cf. Thomson 70–71, Berger (1898) 120–21. The vagueness of ancient geographers regarding the southern extension of Africa is indeed a troublesome issue, and deserves a longer discussion than I can give it here; it probably results in part from the ambiguities inherent in the term *oikoumenē*, which could be used to refer both to the habitable *portion* of the landmass defined by Europe, Asia, and Africa, or to the landmass as a whole.

[22] Thomson 202–3, Berger (1903) 215–18, Mette (1936), and Nicolet 63.

life, not that it actually did so.[23] But Cleomedes, summarizing Crates' scheme of a four-part earth in late Hellenistic times, claims that "Nature is life-loving, and reason requires that she has filled all the world, wherever possible, with creatures both possessing intellect and not" (*De Motu Circ. Corp.* 1.2). If these continents *were* inhabited, then a second question arose as to whether the beings that dwelt there looked like ordinary humans—as implied by Eratosthenes' above use of the adjective *antipodes* for both northern and southern races, implying a strict symmetry across the equatorial plane[24]—or entirely dissimilar, as assumed by Strabo (2.5.13) and the Stoics generally.[25] As the latter theory gained currency the word Antipodes evolved from an adjective into a proper noun, denoting either the inhabitants of the "down-under" continent, in the two-world scheme, or of the landmass transverse to the *oikoumenē* (modern-day South America) in Crates' quadrate division.

The southerly continent could also be referred to as Antichthon or "Counterworld"[26] and its supposed inhabitants as Antichthones—a term which attests to their remoteness, since it derives from the Pythagorean term for an alien *planet* located behind the "dark side" of the earth.[27] The Antipodes or An-

[23] By contrast the author of the pseudo-Aristotelian *Problems* assumes quite off-handedly that the southern continent is indeed populated (26.21, 942b9–13). An interesting passage of Pliny's *Natural History* (2.65.161) refers to a debate on this point between scholars and the unlettered masses, the crux of which was whether "down-under" peoples would fall off the bottom of the world.

[24] Lucian's Demonax entertains a similar notion when making fun of a scientist who believes in the Antipodes, proposing that the true Antipodes are our own reflections at the bottoms of wells (*Demonax* 22).

[25] Cf. Cicero, *Academica* 2.39; Lucretius, *DRN* 1.1052–67; and Plutarch, *De Facie* 924a (with further citations in the note ad loc. in Cherniss' Loeb edition, *Moralia* vol. 12 [Cambridge, Mass. 1957] 63).

[26] Cf. Achilles Tatius, *Isagōgē ad Arat.* 30, Cicero *Tusc. Disp.* 1.28.69, Mela 1.4. The schemes by which the alternate continents were named became highly confused, since most of the names involved, like *Antichthones*, *Antipodes*, *Antoikoi*, were functionally interchangeable; cp. Geminus 13, Cleomedes 1.2.

[27] Cf. Aristotle *Metaphysics* 1.5 (986a8–13), *De Caelo* 2.13 (293a18–b8); both passages in Kirk and Raven, frs. 328–29, 331. See the discussion by D. R. Dicks, *Early Greek Astronomy to Aristotle* (Ithaca, N.Y. 1970) 65–68, who

tichthones might indeed have dwelt as far away as another planet, for all that ancient geographers ever hoped to contact them. To the south, the burning heat of the torrid zone was assumed to render travel past the equator impossible;[28] while the intervening expanse of Ocean to the west was (as always) too wide or too dangerous to cross.[29] As a result these worlds had to remain entirely in the realm of hypothesis, and it became fashionable for empirically minded writers to refuse to discuss them. Strabo, for instance, reminds us on several occasions that "geographers have no business pondering what lies beyond our *oikoumenē*" (2.5.34; cf. 2.5.8, 13). Pliny, for his part, concludes his aforementioned discussion of the "island earth" with this remarkable meditation:

> Thus the seas poured everywhere around us, by dividing the globe, have robbed us of a portion of the world; there is no region that permits passage from here to there or from there to here. Indeed this thought, so well suited to dispelling the vanity of mortal existence, seems to demand that I now reveal the whole of *this* world, whatever it is, and display its length and breadth to your eyes. (2.67.170)

Yet in spite of this empiricist view that worlds which could not be approached should not be discussed, the Antipodes always bulked large in the popular imagination of both Greeks

notes that the moon was similarly referred to as *antichthōn* by the Pythagoreans (according to Simplicius).

[28] Mela 1.4, Manilius 1.377–78, Hyginus *Astronomica* 1.8.3; see Rainaud 50–53, Wright 158. The implications of this idea for reports of the circumnavigation of Africa, as noted by Thomson (262), seem never to have been clearly thought out. An amusing passage in the *De Natura Novi Orbis* of José de Acosta (1580) records the author's amazement when, during a passage across the equator on his first voyage to America, he found the weather so cold that he had to put on extra layers of clothing (see Acosta 2.9 in *Historia Natural y Moral de las Indias*, repr. Valencia, Spain, 1977; and Barbara Beddall's introductory article, "Father José de Acosta and the Place of his *Historia Natural y Moral de las Indias* in the History of Science," 12–98).

[29] Aristotle *Meteor.* 2.5.13, Strabo 1.4.6, Cleomedes 1.2; see Kretschmer 58–59, 71–73. Crates managed to combine the perils of heat and navigation in his scheme, by assuming that the entire torrid zone at the equator was occupied by Ocean.

and Romans. We are surprised to discover a note in Pliny, for example, indicating that Taprobane (modern-day Sri Lanka) was mistaken, prior to the coming of Alexander, for the land of the Antichthones; that is, since its insularity had not yet been proved, geographers assumed that it represented the northernmost tip of that southern continent (*Natural History* 6.24.81).[30] Pliny's younger contemporary, Pomponius Mela, moreover, feels inclined to agree that Taprobane represents "the closest part of another world" (*De Situ Orbis* 3.70), attributing this theory to one of two alternatives proposed by Hipparchus.[31] Other curious notions concerning these other worlds indicate that they were felt to be closer than the geographers claimed; for example, Herodorus of Heracleia maintained that vultures, rather than being hatched from eggs like other birds, instead fly into our world from "another world invisible to us" (Aristotle, *Historia Animalium* 563a5 = Herodorus fr. 22a Jacoby).[32] A late antique poet named Tiberianus capitalized on such notions, publishing what he claimed was a letter from the Antipodes which had wafted across Ocean on the breeze.[33]

The Antipodes exerted their most prominent allure, however, in the context of Roman military expansion, especially during the period from the first century B.C. to the first century A.D. In this era a series of texts, which we shall now briefly

[30] The attractiveness of this idea becomes apparent a few paragraphs later, where Pliny himself refers to Taprobane as a land "banished by nature outside the world" and hence free of the vices that plague other countries.

[31] The name of Mela's source is unfortunately misspelled in the text as "Ipparchius," and the reconstruction to Hipparchus is rejected by some (see the note to Parroni's edition, 420–21), but accepted by D. R. Dicks in *The Geographical Fragments of Hipparchus* (London 1960) 58 and 115–16; cf. Thomson 208 and n. 2, Berger (1903) 462 and n. 2, Tandoi (1967) 57.

[32] Cf. Plutarch *Romulus* 9 (= Herodorus fr. 22b), Pliny *Hist. Nat.* 10.7.19. Marcel Détienne believes that the "other world" referred to by Herodorus is actually the moon (*Les Jardins d'Adonis* [Paris 1972] 48–49).

[33] Quoted by Servius on *Aeneid* 4.532; see J. W. Duff, *Minor Latin Poets* vol. 2 (Cambridge, Mass. 1982) 566–67, Boffito 587 n. 1. A new edition of Tiberianus by Silvia Mattiacci, as yet unavailable to me, undoubtedly deals with the fragment at greater length (*I carmi e i frammenti di Tiberiano*, Florence 1990).

survey, depict archetypal conquerors—Scipio Africanus, Messalla Corvinus, and, as always, Alexander—contemplating whether the southern *oikoumenē* could be bridged to the northern as part of a globe-spanning extension of empire. The positions they adopt on this question vary widely, and indeed much can be learned from these variations concerning the expansion of the Roman world picture during this period. For example, the contrast between the first two texts we shall examine, the Republican-era Dream of Scipio and an Augustan ode to Messalla, attests to the sudden growth of Rome's antipodal ambitions that accompanied the emergence of the principate.

In the so-called Dream of Scipio, the mythic finale to the dialogue *De Republica*, Cicero sends Scipio Aemilianus into the sky by way of a dream vision; his goal, following the model Plato had established with the Myth of Er in the *Republic*, is to teach the future statesman the ethical lessons he will need to govern well. From his perch in the skies Scipio is allowed to look down on the earth he inhabits, while the shade of his grandfather, Scipio Africanus, explains its true nature:

> You see that the earth is girt and surrounded by certain zones, of which the two that are most widely separated . . . are rigid with ice, while the one in the center, the largest, is scorched by the heat of the sun. There are two that are habitable,[34] and of these the southern zone, in which the inhabitants press their footprints opposite to yours, has no contact with your race; as for the other, northern zone, which you inhabit, look what a small part of it touches you. Indeed the entire stretch of land that you cultivate . . . is but a small island, surrounded by that sea you on earth call the Atlantic, or the Great, or Ocean; yet look how small it is in spite of its great names! (*Republic* 6.20)

[34] Africanus had earlier (chap. 19) described a four-part world, similar to that of Crates, but here shifts to a two-part model; perhaps he is focusing his grandson's attention on the one hemisphere visible to him, leaving the "dark side" out of account. For other explanations of the discrepancy see Karl Büchner, *Somnium Scipionis* (Hermes suppl. 36, Wiesbaden 1976) 38–39 and n. 31, 50–51 and n. 52; R. Harder, *Über Ciceros Somnium Scipionis* (Halle 1929). In other works Cicero prefers to think in terms of a two-part world (see *Tusc. Disp.* 1.28.69, *Acad.* 2.39.123).

The lesson which the great Africanus—who was himself reputed to have conquered much of the territory he here reveals[35]—derives from this vision is that earthly fame cannot travel far, and that the young Scipio should therefore pursue wisdom rather than glory in his statecraft.

The five-banded earth Cicero here envisions obviously owes much to Eratosthenes' *Hermes*,[36] but the fact that geographic revelation is now placed in the mouth of a world-bestriding general rather than a god gives it new political significance. The Antipodes have for Cicero become an exemplary case of lands that can never be conquered, a visible symbol of the limits to Roman expansion. That those limits are exhibited before the young Scipio, moreover, reflects the fact that, at the time of the *De Republica*'s composition, two other military leaders were emerging as the inevitable inheritors of the Roman state. Though it would be parochial to suggest that the Dream of Scipio is addressed specifically to Pompey and Julius Caesar, nonetheless the lesson of the Antipodes could have no better application than to their careers, which (as Cicero claims elsewhere) had already brought Roman arms to the very bourne of Ocean.[37] Where geographic reach has become a measure of political power, Cicero's focus on the lands that must remain out of reach translates into a warning that the limits of power must not be transcended.

[35] See the fragments of Ennius describing the extent of Scipio's conquests, discussed by F. W. Walbank in "The Scipionic Legend" (*PCPS* n.s. 13 [1967] 57–58).

[36] For the sources of the *Somnium* see Büchner, *Somnium Scipionis* 47–59; Pierre Boyancé, *Études sur le Songe de Scipion* (Bibliothèque des Universités du Midi 20, Bordeaux and Paris 1936). On the tradition of astral ascents in ancient literature and Cicero's use of it, see A. J. Festugière, "Les thèmes du Songe du Scipion," *Eranos* (1946) 370–88; R. Lamacchia, "Ciceros *Somnium Scipionis* und das sechste Buch der *Aeneis*," *Rh. Mus.* 107 (1964): 261–79; R. M. Jones, "Posidonius and Cicero's *Tusculan Disputations* 1.17–81," *CP* 18 (1923): 202–28.

[37] *Prov. cons.* 29, 31, 34; *Marcell.* 28. See R. Frénaux, "Géographie Cicéronienne: La notion d'*Oceanus* dans les *Discours*," in *Littérature Gréco-romaine et géographie historique: Mélanges offerts à Roger Dion* (Caesarodonum 9 *bis*, Paris 1974) 131–41.

However, if the Scipios, and by extension Caesar and Pompey as well, are here seen as inexorably circumscribed by Ocean, the same was no longer true of one of their successors in world conquest, Messalla Corvinus. At least that is the impression conveyed by a eulogy of Messalla ([Tibullus] 3.7), composed by an unknown author shortly after 31 B.C.[38] This eulogy forecasts that Messalla, after surpassing Odysseus in the scope of his far-flung conquests (49–81), will cap his career by conquering the Antipodes:

> Wherever Ocean rings the world with seas
> no land will bring against you hostile arms.
> The Briton, as yet unbeaten by Rome's wars, awaits you,
> and the other part of the world, beyond the sun's path. . . .
> So, when your deeds have at last gained glorious triumphs,
> you alone shall be equally called great in either world. (148–50, 175–76)

The Antipodes have here been moved very much within the ambit of Roman conquest, posing a challenge only slightly greater than the as-yet unconquered British Isles; even the scorching heat of the equator (blithely glossed over with the phrase *interiecto sole*) seems not to present any difficulty for Messalla.

Naturally we must chalk much of this up to hyperbole, but nevertheless the opposition this poem creates when paired with the Dream of Scipio, a text which preceded it by only a few decades, is remarkable. What had intervened was the Battle of Actium and the forging of a new imperial program which promoted the goal of global, even extra-global, expansion as the natural concomitant of autocratic rule. It was not long after this that Vergil, in a passage of the *Aeneid* that we shall look at below, envisioned Augustus extending Roman power "beyond the stars, beyond the course of the sun" (6.785–88; cp. 8.226–27). Limitless, ever-expanding empire was the prize which the

[38] The date is established by lines 121–34, where the author refers to Messalla's installation as consul in 31 B.C. as a recent event.

new regime offered its citizens, as both a recompense for and a distraction from the loss of republican government.[39]

Underlying this Augustan program for world-spanning empire, of course, lay the Hellenistic mythology surrounding Alexander the Great; and so it is not surprising to find Alexander too, in legends that became increasingly prominent during the late Republic and early principate, preparing to extend his conquests beyond the seas. In a rhetorical textbook dated to about thirty years before Cicero's *De Republica* (and in fact falsely attributed to Cicero for some time), we find the first extant traces of this myth: "If Alexander had lived longer, he would have brought the Macedonian armies across Ocean" (*Rhetorica ad Herrenium* 4.31).[40] The legend was probably elaborated out of Alexander's actual exploration of "Ocean" at the mouth of the river Hyphasis, with an additional glance at his supposed plan to circumnavigate the southern half of the *oikoumenē*.[41] Indeed most of the lore concerning Alexander's so-called last plans depicts the conqueror extending his rule to the edges of the earth,[42] but this new and perhaps specifically Roman contri-

[39] Another early Imperial poet, Manilius, takes a very different approach, glorying in the fact that his own hemisphere lies under Augustus's rule while the Antipodes are deprived of it (*Astronomicon* 1.384–86). On the whole topic see chap. 2 of Nicolet. Also, the contrast between the expansionist and restrictive impulses in Roman treatments of the Antipodes has been dealt with by Gabriella Moretti in a forthcoming article, "The Other World and the Antipodes: The Myth of Unknown Countries Between Antiquity and the Renaissance," pt. 4 (*The Classical Tradition in the Americas*, vol. 1, Boston [1992]).

[40] Text is that of Marx's Teubner edition (*Ad C. Herennium Libri IV* [Leipzig 1894] 322), which supplies the word "armies" (*acies*); the manuscripts give a variety of unintelligible readings which have Alexander crossing a "Macedonian ocean."

[41] Cf. Diodorus Siculus 18.4.2–5, Quintus Curtius 10.1.16–18, Arrian *Anabasis* 4.7.5, 5.26.2.

[42] See the discussion by Tarn in Appendix 24 of *Alexander the Great* vol. 2 (Cambridge 1948) 378–98; idem, "Alexander the Great and the Unity of Mankind," *Proc. British Acad.* 19 (1933): 123–66; F. Hampl, "Alexanders des Grossen *Hypomnemata* und letzte Pläne," *Studies Presented to D.M. Robinson* vol. 2 (St. Louis 1953) 816–29; and Fritz Schachermeyr, "Die letzten Pläne Alexanders des Grossen," *Jahreshefte des österreichischen archaeologischen Inst.* 41 (1954): 118–40. The latter three of these articles have also been reprinted in

bution takes the tradition a quantum leap further. It portrays Alexander as a hero capable of crossing Ocean, a feat which only Heracles—another hero who served as a prominent archetype for Augustus—had achieved before him.

The idea of Alexander's plans for an expedition beyond Ocean grew in importance at Rome as the Roman Empire grew. In the late first century A.D., for instance, Quintilian lists as a typical example of a conjectural issue the question "whether Alexander is going to find lands beyond Ocean" (*Inst. Orat.* 3.8.16); the context here and in related passages (7.2.5, 7.4.2) suggests that this was a stock theme for rhetoricians of the time. In fact, a rhetorical exercise dealing with just this theme is among the *Suasoriae* collected by Seneca the Elder; and a reference to the same theme in another of Seneca's rhetorical works (*Controversia* 7.7.19) demonstrates, again, its topicality in Rome of the first century A.D. Lucan, in Book 10 of his epic poem *Bellum Civile*, claims that Alexander at the time of his death

> was preparing to bring his fleet into Ocean,
> there by the outer sea; neither fiery heat nor sea-swell
> nor desert Libya, nor Ammon with its Syrtes, could stop him.
> He would have gone into the West, following earth's declination,
> rounded the poles, and drunk from the Nile at its source,
> but his dying day prevented it. (10.36–41)

—though it is not clear whether this alludes to crossing Ocean or simply coasting the southern portion of the *oikoumenē*,[43] while Lucan's contemporary, the younger Seneca, speaks of Al-

---

Alexander the Great: The Main Problems, ed. G. T. Griffith (Cambridge and N.Y. 1966).

[43] The former view is adopted by Bourgery and Ponchont in the Budé edition (Paris 1929), where the phrase "following earth's declination (*mundi devexa secutus*)" is interpreted to mean "en passant par les antipodes et en faisant le tour de la terre d'orient en occident." Much depends on how we take the phrase *mundi devexa*; it may only refer to a voyage southward, just as Vergil describes the earth's surface as *devexus in Austros* (*Georgics* 1.241). See Rainaud, *Continent austral* 47–50 for the idea of the North as higher in elevation than the South (strangely enough, though, Tiberianus's letter from the Antipodes began with the heading: "Those above greet those below").

exander "exploring unknown seas, sending new fleets onto Ocean, and breaking through, as it were, the very bounds of the world" (*Ep*. 119.7).

That the theme of Alexander's designs on the Antipodes became popular during the Roman Empire's greatest period of expansion can hardly be coincidence. The juncture reached by Alexander as he stood at the shore of a subjugated world was, in effect, the same one that his Roman successors could see looming ahead of them; it is their concerns that we hear in the words of Alexander reported in the elder Seneca's first *Suasoria* (3): "Whatever has reached its peak has no room left for increase." In fact, the relevance of this theme to the contemporary geopolitical situation is brought home by Seneca's discussion of this particular *Suasoria*, in which a poem describing Germanicus's expedition into the North Sea is quoted as a follow-up to Alexander's crisis at Ocean (15). We shall look at this poem in more detail below, but for now let us simply note the message behind its inclusion here: that imperial Rome was carrying forward the goals left unfulfilled by the dying Alexander.

One final text, a Greek work in this case, will serve to complete the foregoing series, though it derives more from the tradition of mental and conceptual "voyages" to the other world than from that of military conquest. It is difficult to date the pseudo-Aristotelian treatise *On the Cosmos* with any precision, but scholarly consensus places it in the period of the late Roman Republic or early Empire.[44] It takes the form of a letter from Aristotle to Alexander (the converse, in other words, of the *Letter of Alexander to Aristotle* we looked at in the previous chapter). In this epistle "Aristotle" invites his one-time pupil to join him in a mental survey of the universe, leaving the earth behind so as to observe it from the heavens "with the divine eye of the soul" (391a15). He then points out the features of the earth as seen from above, as had Scipio Africanus for his grand-

[44] A survey of opinions on the question is provided by David Furley in the introduction to his Loeb edition, *Aristotle: On Sophistical Refutations*, etc. (Cambridge, Mass. 1955) 337–41. Furley gives 50 B.C. and A.D. 140 as the probable *termini* within which the date must be fixed.

son Aemilianus; but the configuration of the planet is very different in this case than it had been in Cicero's *De Republica*:

> The *oikoumenē* is really all one island, encircled by the sea called Atlantic, despite the ignorance of public opinion which divides it into islands and continents. And it's likely that there are other such islands lying far off, on the opposite side of the straits (*antiporthmous*); some are bigger than it, and some smaller, though all but this one are invisible to us. For just as our *oikoumenē* is situated in the Atlantic in the same way as islands are in our seas, so are the other *oikoumenai* within the entire ocean; for they too are great islands, washed all around by great seas. (392b24–30)

It is not clear where the author of *On the Cosmos* got this picture of multiple inhabited worlds of varying sizes, so markedly different from the symmetrical two-world and four-world constructs of Hellenistic geography;[45] nor is it clear whether, by describing these worlds as *antiporthmoi*, literally "at the other end of a ferry voyage," he means to suggest that they were near enough to the *oikoumenē* to be accessible by ship. But it is certainly significant, within the context we have been looking at thus far, that Alexander is designated as the recipient of this privileged knowledge. The man who, after the conquest of India, was said to have wept for lack of new worlds to conquer, is once again asked to cast his gaze beyond the *oikoumenē*, and to consider that there are after all many further frontiers.

The North Sea Coast

If Alexander's greatest challenge had been met on Indian shores, however, that of the Romans of the early Empire lay in the opposite corner of the world. Here too was found an enormous island, Britain, which like Taprobane was at first identified as another world, that is, not an island at all but the tip of

[45] Berger suggests a connection with Poseidonius, (1898) 101–2.

a giant continent.[46] This similarity suggests that "other worlds" tend to crop up in places where the limits of conquest most need to be breached; as one Roman elegist says in regard to Claudius's conquest of Britain, "Ocean, the bounds of the world, is no longer bounds to our empire" (*qui finis mundo est, non erat imperio, Anthol. Lat.* 419.4). In fact, Julius Caesar's invasion of Britain is quite clearly framed by Florus, a second-century epitomizer of Roman history, as an Alexander-style search for new worlds to conquer: "Having traversed all lands and seas Caesar faced Ocean and, as if the Roman world were no longer enough, contemplated another" (*Epitome* 1.45.16).

That Britain should be portrayed as an antipodean world is scarcely surprising, since this island was genuinely separated from the *oikoumenē* by a swath of Ocean; Vergil amplifies only slightly when he speaks of "Britons, wholly cut off from the entire world" (*Eclogue* 1.66).[47] However, the English channel was crossed at a fairly early stage in Rome's growth, and thereafter its waters never again presented much of an impediment. Therefore, Roman authors looked instead to the North Sea for a true horizon of conquest; Tacitus, for example, opens his *Germania* by portraying these waters as a completely alien realm:

> I believe the German race is indigenous and very little adulterated by the influx and commerce of other races; for migrant peoples used to travel by ships instead of overland, whereas the immense Ocean on Germany's further side, which one might call antipodal (*utque sic*

[46] Dio Cassius 39.50.3, Velleius Paterculus 2.46.1; discussed by Gisinger (1937) 2138–39, Vogt, "Orbis" (above, n. 1) 153 and n. 6. According to Pliny the Elder the "island" of Scandinavia—for so he regarded this enormous penninsula—was likewise considered "another world" by its own inhabitants (*Hist. Nat.* 4.13.96). On the whole topic of Roman *alii orbes* see pt. 7 of Tandoi (1967) 46–64.

[47] Cf. Catullus's references to *ultima Britannia*, 11.12, 39.4; Horace, *Odes* 1.35.29–30, 4.14.48–49, etc. The location of Britain "beyond Ocean" was played upon in efforts to enlarge the stature of those who conquered or surveyed it, especially Claudius, for example, in the play *Octavia* (26–30, 38–44) and in the elegies of the *Anthologia Latina* (419–26). Livy carries this conceit to an absurd extreme, at one point describing Mago's flight to Gades, an island only a few miles off the coast of Spain, as a journey *extra orbem terrarum in circumfusam Oceano insulam* (28.32.8).

dixerim adversus), is entered only rarely by ships from our world (*ab orbe nostro*). (2.1)

By combining in this sentence the use of *adversus*, a term normally applied to antipodal worlds,[48] and the phrase *ab orbe nostro*—which can be taken to mean simply "from our region"[49] but which also carries overtones of the more sweeping *orbis terrarum*—Tacitus stresses the idea that the North Sea is entirely separate from the *oikoumenē*.[50] That idea is further strengthened when Tacitus goes on to report that Odysseus, of all people, had sailed German waters "during that long and fabulous wandering" (3.3)—evoking the surreal seascapes of the Phaeacian tales in connection with his chosen topic.[51]

Like Odysseus, moreover, the latter-day navigators who entered the North Sea were elevated by Roman writers to the stature of epic heroes. We have already alluded to one of the earliest texts in this mythicizing tradition, the poem of Pedo

[48] Cp. Cicero, *De Rep.* 6.20, Pliny *Hist. Nat.* 10.7.19.

[49] The passage usually adduced by commentators for comparison is *Agricola* 12.3, but since *noster orbis* is there used in contrast with Britain—an island which, as noted above, really does stand outside the *oikoumenē*—the parallel serves only to underscore the degree to which Tacitus is here distancing the Germans. The unknown author of the pseudo-Ovidian *Consolatio ad Liviam*, for example, refers to this region as a *Germanus orbis* (391) and an *orbis novus* (313); cited by E. Norden, *Die Germanische Urgeschichte in Tacitus Germania*[2] (Leipzig 1922) 96 n. 2. The fact that the Germans were partly separated from Roman lands by the Danube, a river which Seneca, for one, associates with Ocean as one of earth's primordial waters (*NQ* 3.22), may have contributed to this conception. But Ovid also speaks of a *Scythicus orbis* (*Tristia* 3.12.51) while Lucan creates *orbes* in Libya, Iberia, and Thessaly (*Bell. Civ.* 7.223, 9.547, 5.343, 7.6). See Vogt, "Orbis Romanus" (above, n. 1) 165 and n. 57.

[50] See notes ad loc. by D.R. Stuart (*Tacitus: The Germania* [N.Y. 1916] 27), J.G.C. Anderson (*De Origine et Situ Germanorum* [Oxford 1938] 38) and H. Furneaux (*Cornelii Taciti de Germania* [Oxford 1894] 39–40).

[51] Cp. Juvenal's 15th satire, where the same sort of juxtaposition is used in order to render the Egyptians a strange and alien race. The adjective used by Tacitus here, *fabulosus*, recurs in the last sentence of the *Germania*, in another context reminiscent of the *Odyssey*: "[Beyond this region] everything else is *fabulosa*: The Hellusii and Oxiones have human faces and visages, but the bodies and limbs of beasts; but since this has not been proven I leave it an open question."

Albinovanus[52] depicting the wreck of Germanicus's fleet in the North Sea (A.D. 16). Here Pedo, who had served under Germanicus[53] and was probably an eyewitness to this maritime disaster, cloaks the episode in imagery borrowed from the *Odyssey* and from archaic Greek and Punic *periploi*:

> Now they see daylight and sunshine abandoned behind them
> so quickly; while they, exiled from the world's known bounds,
> dare to pass through the shadows whose realm is denied them
> toward the end-points of things, the final shores of the world.
> Now that body which holds, beneath its slow waves, huge monsters—
> Ocean—which holds savage sea-beasts in every direction
> and sea-dogs, begins to rise up, the ships going with it,
> which noise redoubles their fears; the ships, they believe, are now sinking
> in mud, and the fleet deprived of its swift-blowing breezes,
> themselves by the chances of drift to be left to the sea-beasts
> to be torn in pieces forthwith, a grim kind of death. (15)

Pedo's poem continues with a speech by a tormented crewman who demands to know why the Romans are thus risking their lives, and whether they are seeking "a race dwelling beneath another pole, another world untouched by [freemen?]."[54] The language of this unknown sailor closely resembles that which

[52] A friend of Ovid's (*Ex Ponto* 4.10) and an epic poet (Quintilian *Inst. Orat.* 10.1.90) who was admired by Seneca as a brilliant raconteur (*Ep.* 122.15).

[53] Tacitus, *Annals* 1.60. There is needless dispute as to whether the elder or younger Germanicus is referred to in the poem (both made voyages in the North Sea): Vincenzo Bongi ("Nuovi esegesi del frgm. di Albinovano Pedone," *Istituto Lombardo Rendiconti* 3.13 [1949] 29) and Winterbottom, editor of the Loeb edition, believe, correctly, that the latter individual is meant; William Edward opts for Drusus Germanicus (*The Suasoriae of Seneca the Elder* [Cambridge 1928] 96), but on the basis of a curious notion that "there is no evidence here" of the disasters which befell the younger Germanicus's fleet. Furneaux in fact quotes Pedo's poem as a "contemporary account" of exactly this event (*The Annals of Tacitus*,[2] vol. 1 [Oxford 1896] 386).

[54] The text here is corrupt, and the best available reading (though still inadequate) is *liberis*, following the note by Bongi (38). See discussion by Tandoi (1964) 143–44, 147–51, and sources cited in n. 2 p. 147.

Quintus Curtius puts in the mouth of Coenus, the rebellious Macedonian soldier,[55] and indeed the two rhetorical situations are remarkably alike: Not since Alexander's halt at the Hyphasis had any army known so little about what lay ahead of them.

Beyond its obvious parallels with archaic *periploi* and Hellenistic Alexander legends, however, Pedo's poem is also noteworthy for the way it animates Ocean as an enemy attacking the Roman fleet. For example in line 7 the sea's waters are said to *consurgere* ("rise up"), a verb that strongly suggests the onslaught of a hostile army.[56] In this personification too, we note, Pedo may have been following Greek precedent. Strabo, writing at about the same time as Pedo, records a legend that the Cimbri tribe, dwelling on the shore of the North Sea, actually took up arms against the flood tides that inundated their homes, and that a cavalry force that was sent against these tides was very nearly drowned by a sudden inrush of water (7.2.1). A similar though less vivid legend, attributed by Strabo to Ephorus, relates that the Celts, another coastal tribe whose land was subject to Ocean floods, "suffer more destruction from water than from war" (ibid.). Such images of Ocean as a military foe offered Pedo a superb means of glorifying his senior officer Germanicus: Like Achilles battling the river Scamander the Roman general is here pitted against the most implacable of enemies, so that his subsequent loss of the fleet becomes a tragic rather than merely embarrassing event.

A different account of Germanicus's shipwreck recorded by Tacitus, moreover, goes even farther than Pedo's in casting Ocean as the cosmic nemesis responsible for the disaster.[57] In fact the passage of the *Annals* where this wreck is described (2.23–24) seems to be part of the larger scheme we have al-

[55] Tandoi (1964) 143–45.

[56] See Edward's note ad loc., with a reference to Johannes Schultingh's commentary in the 1672 Amsterdam edition; Tandoi (1964) 134–38.

[57] It is common to see Pedo cited as one of Tacitus's sources for this episode; but since both authors rely on a fairly broad literary tradition we need not assume any direct link between them. The relationship between the two authors is explored at length by Tandoi (1967) 7–14.

ready seen in the *Germania* and which in fact underlies all of Tacitus's writings: The Romans, though victorious across the rest of the globe, are continually denied access to the waters of the North Sea and the North Atlantic. Significantly enough, Tacitus never uses the name "Ocean" except when referring to these waters,[58] as if reserving the mythic aura of that name for the region that most merited it. Like Pedo, moreover, Tacitus sees this region as the seat of a divinely centered, retributive scheme of justice, where the *Romanitas* that had forged a world-spanning Empire is destined at last to receive its comeuppance.[59]

In Tacitus's account Germanicus's fleet is lost when the ships, beset by a violent storm but still holding their own, are suddenly overwhelmed by an influx of tide (*Annals* 2.23). As in the legends recounted by Strabo, that is, the very impetus of Ocean's waters is portrayed as its greatest weapon of destruction. Nor does Tacitus allow the circumstance to pass unnoticed: In a grandiloquent sentence (the text and meaning of which have been matters of dispute) he moves from this particular instance of Ocean's power to the more general hydrologic principle:

> To the same degree that Ocean is more turbulent than the rest of the sea and that Germany exceeds other places in the harshness of its climate, to that degree did this disaster exceed all others in novelty and severity; enemy shores all around or else a sea so wide and

[58] The one apparent exception is at *Annals* 15.37, where a bizarre flotilla assembled by Nero is accompanied by animals imported *abusque Oceano*—presumably from Ocean in general rather than the North Sea in particular. However, this usage too can be seen as a deliberate tactic of estrangement, making Nero seem connected to remote and alien waters (as demonstrated by A. J. Woodman in a recent, as yet unpublished, paper, "Tacitus as Paradoxographer").

[59] Cf. the remarks of Anderson on *Germania* 2.1, concerning "Tacitus' bold personification of Ocean as an enemy which resists the investigation of men and over whom victories are won" (*De Origine* 38). The idea has not, to my knowledge, been developed by subsequent writers on Tacitus.

> deep that it is thought to be the final one, unbounded by land. (2.24.1)

Here Ocean—by which name Tacitus again means "the North Sea," as is clear from the contrast with *cetero mari*—is explicitly marked as the agent of Germanicus's disaster, and at the same time is given the terrifying attributes of the archaic Greek *apeirona ponton* or "boundless sea." In fact Tacitus's reversion to a mythic view of Ocean, stressing its finality and limitlessness, has seemed unacceptable to some scholars, who argue for changes in the Latin text or for an interpretation which would have Tacitus looking askance at the view he here expresses.[60] Nevertheless, the above version (that supported by Furneaux) hardly seems anomalous when compared with Tacitus's mythicizing portrait of the North Sea elsewhere, for instance in the opening of the *Germania* quoted above.

In fact the remaining portion of this very episode attests to Tacitus's deliberate use of archaism in describing the North Sea's power. Following the above sentence Tacitus goes on to describe the fate of Germanicus's men: Some were drowned, he reports, but most were washed up onto desert islands where they either starved to death or survived by consuming the bodies of their horses (2.24.2). After the few survivors were later recovered by Germanicus, Tacitus continues,

> all who returned from far away told tales of wonders (*miracula*), such as powerful whirlwinds, unheard-of birds, sea-monsters, and ambiguous creatures partway between human and animal; they either saw such things or believed them in their terror. (2.24.6)

Again Tacitus deftly evokes archaic distant-world imagery to lend color and mystery to his narrative. In this case the vaguery of the phrase *ex longinquo*, "from far away," serves to make these North Sea islands seem immeasurably remote;[61] and the

[60] The fomer approach is that of F.R.D. Goodyear, *The Annals of Tacitus*, vol. 2 (Cambridge Classical Texts and Commentaries 23, Cambridge 1981) 250–52; the latter, of Erich Koestermann, *Cornelius Tacitus Annalen*, bd. 1 (Heidelberg 1965) 293.

[61] Cf. Ulpian, *Digest* 2.13.6.9: . . . *in longinquo habere, veluti trans mare*.

reference to man-beast hybrids, clearly recalling the Ctesian tradition of Indian-wonders monstrosities, serves to further distance and alienate the entire episode. The last sentence of the passage thus carries through the program begun in the first, the conversion of the northern Ocean into a strange and forbidding mythic landscape.

The same program, moreover, can be observed in Tacitus's discussion in the *Germania* of the North Sea explorations of Germanicus's father, Drusus. Drusus had apparently become the first Roman to sail these northern waters during his command of the German frontier in 12–9 B.C.,[62] although detailed information regarding the voyage is lacking. Tacitus alludes to it briefly and mysteriously in a digression from his ethnographic survey of Germany, when he comes to the region where the Rhine empties into Ocean:

> But to be sure, in this region we have made attempts on Ocean itself; and beyond our reach are rumored to lie the Pillars of Hercules, whether it is the case that Hercules journeyed there or that we have agreed to attach every sort of marvel, in whatever region, to his fame. Nor did Drusus Germanicus lack daring, but Ocean blocked him from investigating either Hercules or itself. Soon thereafter we stopped trying, and it was deemed more reverent and more pious to believe in the works of the gods than to know about them. (34)

This passage too has given commentators some trouble: It is surprising for one thing that Tacitus places the Pillars near the mouth of the Rhine rather than at Gibraltar, and for another that he claims Drusus's expedition as the final Roman trial of the North Sea, ignoring the above-mentioned operations of Germanicus (as well as others conducted by Tiberius in A.D. 5). Once again, however, we can ascribe these distortions to Tacitus's deliberate mythopoiesis. Clearly he means to personify Ocean in this passage as a stubborn and imperturbable foe, for

[62] See Suetonius, *Claudius* 1, and Dio Cassius 54.32–55.1. Discussion by Hennig (1936) 264–65.

example by making it the object of the verb *temptavit*[63] and the subject of *obstitit*; and this characterization takes on greater force if he imagines the Romans having been forever repelled from its bounds after their first, fruitless approach. The odd reference to northerly "Pillars of Hercules" can likewise be explained, in accordance with Tacitus's own observation about the god's prominence in marvelous tales, as part of an attempt to surround this frontier with the mystique of archaic *periploi*.

To this pair of defeated North Sea voyagers, Germanicus and Drusus, Tacitus also adds a third, his own father-in-law, Agricola. Though Agricola's fleet had succeeded in circumnavigating Britain (c. A.D. 80) and in conquering the islands off its northwest coast, Tacitus nevertheless manages to focus attention on the one place it could not reach, the island of Thule:

> Even Thule was seen in the distance, but their orders bade them go only so far; and besides winter was coming on. But they did report that the sea was sluggish and hard to row against, and was barely stirred even by the winds. I believe this is because lands and mountains, which are the cause and origin of storms, are sparser, and the deep mass of unbroken sea is more slowly moved. (10)

Once again it is the very waters of Ocean that stand as an impenetrable bar to Roman exploration, forming a torpid mass that cannot be rowed or sailed across.[64] Here Tacitus has borrowed a page from Himilco as well as from Pytheas of Massilia, who, as we saw in chapter 1, described a similarly impassable sludge in the waters around Thule.

Such glances into the murky distance show Tacitus romanticizing and distancing the Northwest frontier, much as the historians of Alexander had done with the Southeast. But in drawing this parallel I do not mean to imply that Tacitus saw this region as a frontier to be conquered, or wished to foster a *plus ultra* spirit among his Roman readers. Indeed, although his

[63] See Tandoi (1967) 9 and n. 3. Tacitus's phrasing here recalls Seneca's grandiose description of Alexander at *NQ* 6.23.3: [*Oceanum*] *ipsum temptavit novis classibus*.

[64] Cp. *Germania* 45, where the Baltic Sea is similarly described as *pigrum ac prope inmotum*.

views on foreign policy are markedly pro-expansionist elsewhere,[65] the passages discussed above show the opposite inclination: Tacitus seems to believe that this one region of the world, where Rome faced a boundary imposed by nature rather than by barbarian armies, must remain forever closed, and that divine anger would destroy any further expeditions sent out to explore it. In fact, by supplying a religious motive for the Roman retreat from the North Sea, in the *Germania* passage quoted above, Tacitus echoes the pious injunctions of Pindar against voyaging beyond the Pillars (see chap. 1, pp. 17–18). He also reveals a fundamental connection with his near-contemporaries Seneca and Pliny the Elder, whose views we shall come to at the end of this chapter.

The Headwaters of the Nile

Like Germany the river Nile would seem to be too much a part of the *oikoumenē* to qualify as an *alius orbis* or "other world"; yet here too the Hellenistic and Roman geographic imagination situated one of its most remote and alien frontiers. Since archaic times Greek thinkers had tried to plot the upper course of the Nile and to explain its anomalous yearly floods; their efforts had generated a wide array of hypotheses, all of which, according to later writers who compiled them into great lists, ultimately fell short of the truth.[66] The problem of the Nile thus took on the stature of a mythic riddle—Diodorus Siculus, for example, remarks on the appropriateness of the river's Egyptian name, "Water from Darkness" (1.37.9)—and mythic solutions

[65] Cf. Furneaux in vol. 1 of *The Annals of Tacitus*,[2] vol. 1 (Oxford 1896) 138–39: "His disdain is natural for the old 'narrow limits of empire' . . . and for the prince who 'cared not to extend the frontier.' " Both Furneaux and others remark on Tacitus's contempt for Augustus's dying injunction against expanding the limits of empire, which Tacitus says was delivered "either out of fear or jealousy" (*Annals* 1.11; cf. Cassius Dio 56.33.5).

[66] See Diodorus Siculus 1.37–41, Seneca *NQ* 4a, Aëtius 4.1.1–8, Aelius Aristides *Orat.* 48 Dindorf. Discussed by H. Diels, *Doxographi Graeci*[4] (Berlin 1965) 226–29, and Brigitte Postl, *Die Bedeutung des Nils in der römischen Literatur* (Dissertationen der Universität Wien 40, Vienna 1970) 74–84.

were called in to solve it, including one which traced the Nile's peculiar behavior to its origin in the Antichthones.

This curious notion was apparently based on a theory put forth by Eudoxus of Cnidus in the fourth century B.C.,[67] and attributed by him (probably in an attempt to mystify) to a sect of Egyptian holy men.[68] Eudoxus reasoned that since the Nile rose in summer and fell in winter, the opposite of the pattern followed by other rivers, its waters must originate in the southern hemisphere where summer and winter were reversed. It was only a short step from this theory to an assumption that the Nile's source lay in an antipodal continent, separated from the *oikoumenē* not only by the equator but by Ocean as well.[69] The problem of how the river could then reach the *oikoumenē* was solved by means of an underground channel passing beneath Ocean, the same sort of conduit that was thought to connect the spring Arethusa in Sicily with its source in mainland Greece. Bizarre though this explanation may seem it was preferred[70] in the first century A.D. by Mela, the same geographer who also (as we saw above) felt inclined to credit Hipparchus's other-world view of Taprobane:

[67] Aëtius 4.1.7; cf. Schol. Hom. *Od.* 477, Diodorus Siculus 1.40.1 (frs. 287–89 in François Lasserre, *Die Fragmente von Eudoxos von Knidos* [Texte und Kommentare 4, Berlin 1966]).

[68] On the fictionality of this attribution see Heidel (1937) 101 n. 220. The conceit whereby Plato's Solon received the myth of Atlantis from Egyptian priests may rightfully be compared.

[69] Geminus 16.26, *Doxographi Graeci* 386. For the connection between this theory (sometimes attributed, though probably falsely, to Nicagoras) and that of Eudoxus see Thomson 117–18 and Lasserre 246–48. Eudoxus's version seems to have assumed that Africa extended below the line of the equator.

[70] Since Mela clearly does believe in the Antichthones, as he indicates right at the outset of his work (1.4), it follows from the conditional quoted here that he also believes the Nile originates among them. Later Mela adds a different theory he also considers *credibile*, tracing the Nile to an obscure West African fountain named Nuchul (3.95–96); but this account too has the effect of removing the river's source to a remote never-never land, since its waters are said to pass beneath the sands of a vast desert before arriving in their known location. Cp. Pliny, *Hist. Nat.* 5.10.52; Hennig (1936) 100–106.

> But if there is another world, and there are Antichthones opposite us across the equator, then even this would not be far removed from the truth: that the river rises in their land, whence it penetrates under the seas by way of a hidden channel, then emerges again in our land; and that because of this it swells in midsummer, when it is winter in the land of its origin. (1.54)

This link between the Nile and the Antichthones, moreover, is only one of a set of theories which traced that river to a mystical and unseen source; others derived it from aquifers under the earth, or from a freshwater stretch of Ocean reported to lie off the southern coast of Africa.[71] Even the sober-minded Ptolemy, who came closest to the truth by tracing the Nile to melting snows atop an African mountain range, imparted his own touch of mystification: he records the name of that unseen range as "Mountains of the Moon."[72] In any case what is of concern to us here is that the Nile, like the North Sea coast, presented the Romans with the challenge of a seemingly unattainable goal, the kind of place that was most vividly imagined as an alien or even antipodean world. Hence it too served, in a number of early imperial texts, as the object of imaginative expeditions of conquest seeking to extend Roman power beyond the edges of the earth.

As before the pattern for these imagined projections of imperial power can be found in the Hellenistic lore surrounding Alexander the Great, since by Roman times Alexander's brief sojourn in Egypt (333–31 B.C.) had been made the occasion for various researches into the mysteries of the Nile. Legend held that Alexander had sent Callisthenes, the nephew of Aris-

[71] The theories of Oenopides of Chios and Euthymenes, respectively. For a survey of these and other relevant theories see Postl, *Die Bedeutung des Nils* 11–36; more briefly in Rainaud, *Continent austral* 46–48.

[72] *Geog.* 4.8.3; see Bunbury 2.617–18, who supposes this to be Ptolemy's translation of some native African name, and Thomson 277 and n. 2. The name was exploited by Heliodorus in the *Ethiopica* for its obvious romantic appeal; it was still current in the nineteenth century, when British explorers traced the White Nile to the lake system of the Mitumba Mountains in present-day Uganda.

totle, to explore the upper Nile, or that Aristotle himself had directed Alexander to investigate this region on his behalf.[73] The orator Maximus of Tyre suggests that Alexander had used his famous interview with the oracle of Zeus at Ammon to inquire into this age-old riddle (41.1). A variety of sources report that Alexander, having come to the banks of the Indus River, claimed to have found the origin of the Nile there; after all the Indus too swelled in the summer, and was seen to contain the crocodiles traditionally associated with Egypt.[74]

These legends concerning Alexander's Nile explorations become particularly prominent in the tenth book of Lucan's epic poem *Bellum Civile*. In one passage we have looked at already, for example, Lucan claims that Alexander "would have drunk from the Nile at its source" had he lived long enough to complete his designs; shortly after this he relates that Alexander had sent a band of men into southern Ethiopia to uncover the well-springs of the Nile, but that the blazing heat of the torrid zone had blocked their progress (10.272–75). Such myths concern Lucan in Book 10 because they provide a parallel to the career of his own epic conqueror, Julius Caesar, who has also at this point made Egypt the seat of a campaign for global hegemony.[75] The parallels between the careers of the two figures are in fact highlighted when Caesar, newly arrived in Egypt, visits the grave of Alexander (an episode we shall return to below), and shortly thereafter undertakes his own inquiry into the sources of the Nile.

The scenario of the latter episode is as follows: Caesar, while

[73] According to a "Life of Pythagoras" epitomized by Photius (cod. 249 = Aristotle fr. 246 in V. Rose, *Aristotelis qui ferebantur librorum fragmenta* [Leipzig 1886]).

[74] Strabo 15.1.25 (= Nearchus fr. F 20 Jacoby); Arrian *Indika* 6.1.2–3, 5–8. See Lionel Pearson's discussion in *The Lost Histories of Alexander the Great* (APA Philological Monographs 20, n.p. 1960): 121–23, and, for the widespread impact of this conception, J. André, "Virgile et les Indiens," *REL* 27 (1949): 160–62.

[75] That global mastery is the prize that the civil wars are being fought over is clear from 1.290–91, 2.583–84, 3.295–96. On Lucan's use of Alexander as a parallel for Caesar see chap. 2 of M.P.O. Morford's *The Poet Lucan: Studies in Rhetorical Epic* (Oxford 1967).

enjoying himself at a banquet thrown by Cleopatra, enters into a conversation with an Egyptian priest named Acoreus. Casting himself as a latter-day Plato in search of mystical wisdom, Caesar begs Acoreus to reveal to him the secrets of the Nile: "Give me hope of seeing the Nilotic springs, and I shall abandon this civil war" (10.191–92). The priest, to our great surprise, replies in ponderous tones that he will do exactly that:

> It is lawful for me to disclose, O Caesar, the secrets of our great parents,
> things that before this age were unknown to the uninitiate.
> Let others believe it pious to keep silence on such great wonders;
> I, for my part, believe that the gods take pleasure in this:
> that their works be made open to all, their holy laws known to the people. (10.194–98)

There follows a long (125-line) excursus in which Acoreus reveals all that he knows about the Nile, while Caesar and the rest of the dinner guests, and presumably Lucan's audience as well, attend in astonished silence.

The explanation contained in this excursus is trotted out in three segments, each one preceded by fanfares extolling the occult nature of the revelations they contain. In the first section (199–218) Acoreus discusses the astral and planetary influences on the Nile, and compares the moon's role in the river's risings to its influence over Ocean tides.[76] The second (219–67) refutes a set of ancient theories concerning the Nile's floods and, again, compares that river to Ocean—in this case because both go back to the beginning of time.[77] Following this Acoreus introduces a digression on the reckless kings who have sought the Nile's secrets before Caesar, a list which includes not only Alexander but Sesostris and the madman Cambyses (268–85). Finally in the third segment Acoreus reveals the greatest

[76] For discussion of this highly confused passage, see the "Astronomical Appendix" to A. E. Housman's edition of the poem, *Marci Annaei Lucani Belli Civilis Libri Decem* (Oxford 1926) 334–37.

[77] A doctrine that Lucan may have picked up from his uncle Seneca; see *NQ* 3.22.1. Postl sees much of the Nile excursus in the *Bellum Civile* as borrowed from Seneca, as does Housman ("Astronomical Appendix" 335).

mystery of all, the location of the river's headwaters (298–302):

> You [Nile] are permitted to rise at the summer solstice,
> to swell in a foreign land's winter, and import your own snow-
> storms;
> you alone are allowed to wander through both hemispheres.
> In *that* one your sources are sought, in *this* one the goal of your
> waters.

In the end Acoreus's much-heralded "secret" amounts to little more than a rehash of the Eudoxan theory, but with high rhetorical color added (including a stunning description of the great river snaking its way through equatorial deserts) to lend mystique to its otherwise predictable contents.

Unfortunately nothing more comes of this episode, perhaps as a result of Lucan's failure to complete Book 10; we never hear Caesar's response to Acoreus's revelation or learn what, if anything, he intends to do with his new knowledge. However, if we are to avoid seeing the Nile *logos* simply as a "purple patch" sewn onto the poem we must bring it into the larger context of Caesar's similarities to Alexander the Great, which as mentioned above emerge as a principal theme of the tenth book of the *Bellum Civile*. Caesar's visit to Alexander's grave at the beginning of the book, for example, occasions a long diatribe from Lucan against globe-spanning imperial ambition (10.20–52)—a topic which touches Caesar as nearly as Alexander.[78] Are we meant, then, to see the Nile excursus which follows as an instance of that ambition, a case of reaching out (if only in cognitive terms) for regions that ought not be approached? Or is it rather the sort of effort in which ambition might work toward the good, as suggested by Caesar's pledge to Acoreus that he would renounce further wars if he could learn the secrets of the Nile?

In attempting to answer these questions we should take note of another passage which mentions the Nile in a very different context: In the proem to the *Bellum Civile* Lucan ruefully lists

[78] See the analysis by Morford in *The Poet Lucan* (above, n. 75) 17–19.

"the race (if any there be) which knows the birthplace of the Nile" (1.20) as one of the regions which Rome could by now have conquered, had her energies not been squandered on the civil wars. Even while endorsing such ambitions, however, Lucan inveighs against the self-aggrandizing figures who had caused those wars, thus seeming at the same time to condemn and to ennoble the spirit of empire-building. The same paradox recurs in the scene of Caesar's visit to Alexander's grave in Book 10, where Lucan, in the midst of his polemic against Alexander's ambition, suddenly expresses regret that Alexander had bettered the Romans in subduing the East. In both passages, there seems to be a distinction at work between good and bad forms of expansion, the former undertaken for the benefit of an entire society, the latter arising out of the self-serving impulses of an Alexander or a Caesar. Because the source of the Nile has always been the objective of megalomaniacs, Lucan implies, it has remained unattainable for the more unified Rome governed by the current emperor, Nero.[79]

Perhaps, too, Lucan wished to draw an implicit contrast with the Nile expedition recently sent out by Nero, which may in fact have done more to bring the river's sources to light than had Alexander or Julius Caesar. Indeed Lucan's uncle, Seneca, pointed to this expedition in his *Natural Questions* as one of the most glorious achievements of Nero's reign:

> You must know that, among the various theories regarding the summer flooding of the Nile, there is this one: The river bursts forth from the ground, and swells not because of waters that fall from above but those that issue from the earth's interior. Indeed I myself have heard the story of two centurions sent by Nero—who is especially devoted to truth, as he is to the other virtues—to investigate the source of the Nile: They had gone a long way, and, having been furnished with provision by the king of Ethiopia and commended to the neighboring kings, they penetrated to the outermost regions. They said, "We came to some vast marshes, of which the natives did

[79] Morford rightly compares a passage of Livy (9.17–19) where the one-man leadership of the Macedonian army is contrasted with Rome's decentralized structure.

> not know the egress, nor could anyone hope to know it; the water was so clogged with plants and could not be struggled through either by foot or by ship, since the muddy and overgrown swamp does not support ships except perhaps small ones, big enough for one man. There," they said, "we saw two rocks, from which the massive flow of the river cascaded." (6.8.3–4)

If this report can be trusted, Nero's emissaries reached a point about 9 degrees north of the equator, where the marshes they described were rediscovered by an Egyptian expedition in 1839.[80] Aside from its historical interest, however, Seneca's account is noteworthy in that it too, like Lucan's *Bellum Civile*, portrays Nero as the right type of explorer-ruler, in contrast to Alexander (who is vilified at *NQ* 5.18.10). Seneca insists that Nero had dispatched his explorers out of intellectual curiosity, a motive which, in the scheme of the *Natural Questions* (cf. 7.30.3–32.4), ranks at the very top of the scale of human virtues; at the same time he makes no mention of what Pliny the Elder reports as the military objectives of the mission.[81] The reasons for this careful retouching of geographic history will become clearer in the next section, where we shall look more closely at Seneca's attitudes toward exploration and the growth of empire.

The Atlantic Horizon

In all the ways discussed above, then, Roman writers of the first century of empire gave mythic dimensions to the frontiers that surrounded their world. Let us turn, in this final section, to the one frontier which had dwelt in the province of myth since long before the advent of Rome: the western Atlantic. We have already looked at Plato's myth of Atlantis and the various older legends this myth relies on, including the Isles of the Blessed,

[80] Casson 126. See also Bunbury 2.347–48 and n. 4.

[81] According to Pliny (*Hist. Nat.* 6.35.181) the centurions in question had been sent out to reconnoiter for an invasion of Ethiopia. Pliny's version is deemed more credible than Seneca's by Hennig (1936) 308–9.

the Fortunate Isles, and the alleged Carthaginian discovery of an unnamed land outside the Pillars of Heracles. In Roman literature all of these westerly islands, like other idylls of Greek myth, were subsumed into the scheme of territorial expansion which dominated the worldview of the age; and in addition a new objective, Thule, was added to their number, reportedly located at a six days' sail from the west coast of Britain.[82] Such islands, moreover, were typically imagined not just as other worlds but as *new* worlds; their pure vistas had remained unsullied by commerce with the *oikoumenē* and (in some cases) unspoiled by human habitation.[83] Thus they seemed to offer Rome the possibility of social and cultural renewal, of escape from the decline of Mediterranean civilization, or even—in the extreme view of the philosopher Seneca—of the final, apocalyptic metamorphosis of the human race.

The island of Thule has already been mentioned above in a different context, in our discussion of Tacitus: Agricola had glimpsed Thule during the course of his circumnavigation of Britain, but had deemed it unreachable on account of Ocean's viscosity. This is indeed a characteristic image of Thule, since from its first appearance in geographic writings, about 300 B.C., the island presents itself as a place which can be perceived but not approached. Even its discoverer, Pytheas of Massilia, seems only to have heard about its existence from the natives

[82] I shall not pursue here the question of Thule's identity, but favor the view of Bunbury (1.594 n.4) that such an identification is impossible given our body of evidence. Attempts have nevertheless been made; the favored candidates are Iceland, the Shetland Islands, and the coast of Norway. Discussion by Carpenter 173–80, Hennig (1936) 129–34, Cary and Warmington 51–52, and recently C.F.C. Hawkes, *Pytheas: Europe and Greek Explorers* (J. L. Myres Lectures 8, Oxford 1975). The Middle Ages, beginning with Dicuil in A.D 825, usually used the name Thule to refer to Iceland (see Wright 75).

[83] Pliny the Elder records Juba's account of the Fortunate Islands (*Hist. Nat.* 6.37.203–5), which showed them to be deserted, though the traces of buildings on some indicated a previous inhabitation. Plutarch's description of the "Atlantic Islands" to which Sertorius tried to flee (*Sertorius* 8.2–3) leaves the question of their inhabitation ambiguous. The island discovered by the Carthaginians is described as uninhabited by pseudo-Aristotle (*On Marvelous Reports* 136), but Diodorus gives it an indigenous population (5.19). Other relevant texts collected by Lovejoy and Boas 290–303.

he encountered in his North Atlantic voyage;[84] like Agricola he found the seas in its vicinity too thick and sluggish to be navigated (Strabo 2.4.1; see chap. 1, pp. 22–23, above). Beyond Thule, moreover, lay a region which Pytheas's informants called the Frozen Sea[85]—a name which again suggests the impossibility of crossing northwestern waters.

After Pytheas no Greek or Roman explorer learned anything more about Thule, so that later writers sometimes felt unsure as to whether it even existed (See Strabo 2.1.13, 2.1.17, 2.5.8; chap. 5, pp. 197–98, below). And since it had never been visited, no one knew whether it was, or could be, inhabited. Surrounded by these uncertainties, Thule soon took on symbolic rather than geographic resonance, as attested by the epithet attached to it by Vergil and Seneca, *ultima* or "furthest."[86] By a kind of metonymy this one island came to represent all the most distant regions to which exploration and conquest could aspire. Furthermore, its far-westerly location held a strong historical significance for the Romans, a people who portrayed their own arrival on the stage of history as a migration from a collapsing East to an unspoiled Italian "Hesperia."

It is these connotations, at any rate, that lie behind Vergil's use of the phrase *ultima Thule* in the proem to the *Georgics* (almost certainly its first occurrence). Here, in an elaborate hymn to Augustus as savior of Rome, Vergil imagines the young ruler becoming a god after his death, and wonders whether he will choose earth, sea, or sky as his domain; that is,

> whether you will look after cities, O Caesar,
> opt for the care of the lands, and the great world receive you
> as powerful giver of nurture to crops and to seasons,

[84] Strabo 2.4.1 (fr. 7a in H. J. Mette, *Pytheas von Massilia* [Berlin 1952]); see Carpenter 173. Cleomedes, by contrast, reports that Pytheas had "been there" (*en hēi gegonenai*, fr. 14), but this is only a vague assertion, as noted by Bunbury (1.594 n. 3).

[85] Fr. 6a = Strabo 1.4.2; cf. Pliny *Hist. Nat.* 4.16.104.

[86] Carpenter (173) calls this phrase "a synonym for 'world's end.' " Juvenal refers to Thule at *Satires* 15.112 as the most remote outpost to which Greco-Roman culture might reach, jokingly suggesting that even this distant island may soon import a teacher of rhetoric.

your head bound with myrtle, the plant of your clan's mother,
Venus;
or whether you come as a god of the wide sea, and sailors pay
reverence
to your divine presence alone, farthest Thule obey you,
and Tethys bequeath all her waters to you, as her daughter's new
bridegroom. (1.25–31)

Thule is here seen not as a nation but as an embodiment of the Ocean in which it lies; like Ocean, the greatest tribute such a wild and remote place can offer is to "obey" (*serviat*) its master. But this obedience will be won not primarily by force of arms, as Vergil makes clear in the next line, but by the more gentle and restorative yoking of the marriage bond.[87] Looking ahead to the *Aeneid*, we are tempted to see *ultima Thule* in the same light as the Hesperia promised to the fleeing Trojans: For in that later poem Aeneas, like Augustus here, would win a pure western land for his people by marrying into its dynastic line.

Indeed the parallels between the *Georgics* proem and the new-world themes of the *Aeneid* help explain why Vergil here chooses to foreground Thule, an otherwise obscure island with no prior literary tradition behind it. The realm promised to Augustus in this proem is a cultural blank slate, in contrast to the many old-world ethnographic vistas described elsewhere in the *Georgics*;[88] it seems to stand outside the cyclical patterns of

[87] In fact, by juxtaposing the distinctively feminine phrase *ultima Thule* with the idea that Augustus will soon become son-in-law to Tethys, the sea-goddess traditionally associated with the far West, Vergil may intend us to perceive Thule, if only subliminally, as Augustus's new bride. For the historical evidence surrounding Augustus's Atlantic ambitions see Józef Wolski, "Auguste, l'Océan et l'impérialisme romain," *Ktema* 8 (1983): 261–68.

[88] For example, a long excursus of *Georgics* 2 shows "the world subdued by distant husbandmen" (114–35), including in its scope most of the traditional landscapes cherished by Greek ethnographers (Arabia, Ethiopia, India, and the like); and similarly a description of Libya and Scythia in Book 3 (339–83) draws on standard *topoi* of mankind's subjugation of the elements. For a more detailed analysis of these traditional elements see R. Martin, "Virgile et la Scythie (*Géorgiques* 3.349–83)," *REL* 44 (1966): 286–304, and chap. 2 of Richard Thomas's *Lands and Peoples in Roman Poetry: The Ethnographic Tradition* (Cambridge Philological Society suppl. 7, Cambridge 1982), esp. 51–52.

progress and decline that are everywhere in evidence in the body of the poem. That Vergil was deeply concerned about the inescapability of such patterns is clear from his fourth *Eclogue*, where he predicts that a new golden age will be disrupted by the arrival of a new *Argo* and a new Achilles; the same concerns emerge too from a reading of the *Aeneid*, where Aeneas's marriage to the princess of Latium is described as a new rape of Helen leading to a new Trojan War. The Thule of the *Georgics* proem can be better understood when viewed against the background of such concerns: Only in a place outside the *oikoumenē* and therefore outside the cycles of history could Augustan society make a true new beginning, without fear of repeating the errors of the past.

The *Aeneid*, too, holds out to Augustan society the promise of an as-yet untainted western home, in this case in a world so new that it lacks even a name. The place is described by the shade of Anchises at the climax of his Book 6 speech predicting the future course of Roman conquest:

> [Augustus] will carry imperial rule past the Indians,
> past the Garamantians—there lies a land outside the heavens,
> outside the pathways of day and of sun, where Atlas, sky-bearer,
> turns on his shoulder the wheel inlaid with bright stars. (794–97)

The visionary quality of this passage has rendered its meaning obscure, and we get no clear sense of where the land it describes is to be found; "beyond Indians and Garamantians" points vaguely to the East or Southeast,[89] whereas "outside the heavens" (*sidera*, probably = "constellations," i.e., the zodiacal belt), "outside the paths of sun and day" have been interpreted since Servius and Donatus to mean "below the Tropics."[90] Fi-

[89] Vergil's vagueness as to where the Indians were located, and his tendency to associate them with Africa, are discussed by André in "Virgile et les Indiens" (above, n. 74).

[90] See Donatus, *Interpretationes Vergilianae*, vol. 1 (ed. H. Georgius, Leipzig 1905) 609. Quintus Curtius similarly refers to Alexander's planned journey beyond the Hyphasis as taking him *extra sidera et solem* (9.4.18). Lucan places Ethiopia so far south that only the hoof of Taurus extends above it (*Bell. Civ.* 3.253–55), but he probably imagined the zodiac to lie no further south than the Tropic of Cancer, an error in which Vergil may here concur (see the "As-

nally, the reference to "sky-bearing Atlas" seems to indicate the far West,[91] making for a total of three out of a possible four cardinal directions within as many lines of verse. It seems likely that Vergil means to signify "beyond the known world" in general terms rather than in one particular direction,[92] but the Atlas line gives a decided tilt toward the West: A passage of Book 4 where the same line recurs (480–86) situates Atlas near both the setting sun and the Hesperides.[93]

In both the *Georgics* and the *Aeneid*, then, Vergil expresses the idea that Augustus's destiny will carry his rule beyond the western Ocean, a final extrapolation of the movement that had first brought the Trojans to Rome; and he holds out the hope that this westward expansion will also usher in a new order of things. This powerful vision, we note, was to have an impact far beyond what Vergil himself could foresee. Some fifteen hundred years later an emperor who styled himself after Augustus, Charles V of Spain, would send out fleets to the New World using *tibi serviat Ultima Thule* ("Let farthest Thule obey

---

tronomical Appendix" to A. E. Housman's edition of Lucan [above, n. 71] 327–29).

[91] Cf. the passages collected by Ramin, 27–39. A. E. Housman, on the other hand, claims that Vergil has here moved Atlas to the south, and compares a passage of Statius's *Silvae* (4.3.153–57; see "The *Silvae* of Statius," *CR* 20 [1906]: 44–45, and "Astronomical Appendix" [above, n. 71] 328–29); but the juxtaposition of *Nili caput* and *nives Atlantis* by Statius does not seem to imply a collocation of the two places. Austin notes that *Atlas* refers here to the giant, not the mountain, but both entities were primarily associated with the far West.

[92] See Philip Hardie, *Vergil's Aeneid: Cosmos and Imperium* (Oxford 1986) 195, and R. G. Austin, *Publii Vergilii Maronis Liber Sextus* (Oxford 1977) 244–45. For a different view, E. Norden, "Ein Panegyricus auf Augustus in Vergils *Aeneis*," *Rh. Mus.* 54 (1899): 466–82. Both Austin and Norden note the influence of Alexander legends on this passage.

[93] In imitation of Hesiod, *Theogony* 518. That this earlier *Aeneid* passage, which describes the land from which Dido plans to obtain a narcotic potion, also speaks of "the furthest spot in Ethiopia" (481) has been the source of some confusion; but the Ethiopians were so vaguely located in antiquity that they could be situated almost anywhere, including the far West (see notes ad loc. by A. S. Pease, *Publii Vergilii Maronis Aeneidos Liber Quartus* [Cambridge 1935] 391; and by Austin on 6.797). Norden ("Ein Panegyricus," 470) notes that a passage of Lucan's *Bellum Civile* describes Ethiopia as lying almost entirely outside the zodiacal belt (3.253–5).

you") as one of his rallying cries.[94] And the *Aeneid* lines concerning a "land beyond the stars," identified in the early sixteenth century as a reference to the Americas, would be seized upon by the monarchs of Renaissance Europe as a justification for their own programs of transatlantic conquest.[95] We shall look in more detail at such transformations in the epilogue that follows this study.

If Vergil saw the western horizon as promising the renewal and restoration of Roman society, however, others saw the same horizon in more pessimistic terms, as offering the possibility of a final and irrevocable flight from Rome. This escapist vision is developed most fully in Horace's sixteenth *Epode*,[96] a poem written shortly before the *Georgics*, when Rome was still embroiled in some of the worst fighting of its civil war. In this poem a nameless speaker, whom we might think of as Horace's mask, addresses his fellow citizens in the fervent tones of a forensic orator,[97] bemoaning the ruin wrought by decades of bloody conflict. Finally he proposes his solution to the present crisis:

[94] See Robert Rawlston Cawley, *Unpathed Waters: Studies in the Influence of the Voyagers on Elizabethan Literature* (N.Y. 1967) 67–74. Charles's more famous motto, the *Plus Ultra* inscribed on his coat of arms, also takes Augustan imperial propaganda as its model (see Earl Rosenthal, "*Plus ultra, non plus ultra* and the Columnar Device of Emperor Charles V," *Journal of the Warburg and Courtauld Institutes* 34 [1971]: 204–8).

[95] First correlated with the Americas by Glareanus in *De Geographia* (Venice 1527) chap. 11; seen as an imperative for Spanish conquest by Erasmus Schmid, "Oratio de America," appended to *Pindarou Periodos* (Amsterdam 1616) 259–60. See section 2 of my "New World and *novos orbes*: Seneca in the Renaissance Debate over Ancient Knowledge of the Americas," forthcoming in vol. 1 of *The Classical Tradition in the Americas* (due 1992).

[96] On this poem see Eduard Fraenkel, *Horace* (Oxford 1957) 42–55; also Kurt Witte, "Horazen's sechzehnte Epode und Vergils Bucolica," *Philologische Wochenschrift* 41 (1921): 1095–1103. The escapist theme of the poem has often been correlated with a historical incident recorded in Plutarch's *Sertorius* (8–9), probably borrowed from a lost work of Sallust: The aging Sertorius, deeply embroiled in the Social Wars of the early first century and weighed down by strife, contemplates a voyage to the idyllic "Atlantic Islands" described to him by Iberian merchants.

[97] For the assembly setting see Fraenkel 43–46.

Encircling Ocean awaits us; let us fly to the fields,
the blessed, fortunate fields, and the fertile islands. (41–42)

In the next twenty or so lines the speaker paints a dreamlike picture of the life that can be had in this new world: As in all golden-age landscapes the weather will be perfect, food will be plentiful even without cultivation, and the animals will be at peace with one another and with man. Horace urges his fellow Romans, or at least their "better part" (16), to flee to this western[98] utopia, and to swear never to return until the Apennine Mountains fall into the sea and timid deer mate with fierce tigers.

Horace's view of the West is not only darkened by the finality of this drastic solution, moreover, but also tinged with bitterness as a result of the inaccessibility of the proffered goal.[99] Throughout the rapturous description of the new world to come we remain aware of the distance that lies between it and present-day Rome, so that by the end of the poem Horace's speaker begins to sound more like a deranged millenarian than a visionary leader. The gap between ideal solutions and real limitations becomes particularly obtrusive in a passage where the speaker describes the isolation of his island paradise:

No bark raced here impelled by *Argo*'s oars,
nor did the tainted Colchian woman land here;
Phoenicians turned not their sails in this direction
nor did Ulysses' crewmen, full of labors. (57–60)

The idea that no one, not even the most far-traveled sailors of myth and fable, has yet visited these islands raises the implicit question of how everyday Romans are to get there; but the speaker remains notably silent on this question, and in that si-

[98] Though he does not give a name or a locale to these utopian islands, his description of them overlaps so closely with Greek accounts of the Fortunate Isles that it is impossible not to identify the two. (Both Fraenkel and Lovejoy and Boas [293] take *divites insulas* as a proper noun, but the sense of the passage does not seem to call for any specific toponym.)

[99] See Fraenkel 46–47 on "the complete unreality of the poet's proposal." My own reading differs from Fraenkel's in that it does not attribute this proposal to Horace himself, but to a character created by him.

lence lies a very grim assessment of Rome's actual prospects for redemption.

More troubling still is the possibility raised in the above lines that any crossing to the other world would corrupt the very purity it seeks to attain: The pointed reference to the *Argo* and to the *impudica Colchis* who accompanied it imparts to the whole project of discovery a moral taint which is fundamentally out of harmony with its utopian goals. The contradiction, in fact, is one which closely concerned poets and moral philosophers in the first century of the Roman principate. On the one hand it was only by means of oceanic voyages that the new worlds of the West could be reached, if they could be reached at all; but on the other hand such voyaging was seen as a violation of the natural order which had separated the regions of the globe with seas.[100] Indeed Horace himself gives voice to this latter, moralistic view of navigation in another poem, *Odes* 1.3 (21–26): "For no purpose did a wise god divide the lands with estranging Ocean, if our impious ships nevertheless race across waters that should be left untouched; recklessly braving all, the human race rushes through forbidden sin." Later, Pliny the Elder expands on the theme in a famous meditation on the flax plant, source of the linens from which sails are made:

> Our life is reckless and filled with sin, in that something can be grown to catch the winds and buffets, and that it is not enough to be carried by the waves alone . . . and finally that out of so small a seed something should be born that can carry the whole world back and forth. (*Hist. Nat.* 19.1.5)

Both authors use the word *audax*, "daring" with an additional connotation of "impious," to condemn man for crossing seas that were meant to remain uncrossable.[101] By contrast, how-

[100] On this contradiction see F. Desbordes, *Argonautica: Trois études sur l'imitation dans la littérature antique* (Brussels 1979) 77–78.

[101] For other relevant passages and brief discussion see Lovejoy and Boas 37–38, 146–51, 225–28, 370–71; Tandoi (1964) 153–56. The specifically Roman provenance of the theme is demonstrated by G. G. Biondi, "Il Mito Argonautico nella *Medea*: Lo Stile 'Filosofico' del Drammatico Seneca," *Dioniso* 52 (1981): 421–26.

ever, the early imperial poet Manilius was capable of portraying exploration in far more positive terms, seeing man's progress in shipbuilding as a victory over the "stubborn sea" which had "stolen away new worlds" from his inquiring mind (*Astronomicon* 1.76; cp. 1.87–88).[102]

No author concerns himself more closely with this ambivalence than the philosopher Seneca (the last writer we shall examine in this chapter). Like Horace and Pliny, Seneca in the tragedy *Medea* condemns the first navigator as an *audax*, a word he renders even more pejorative by the addition of the modifier *nimium*: "*Too* daring was he who first broke through/the perilous seas with so fragile a ship" (*Medea* 301–2).[103] In other writings though, principally in Book 5 of the *Natural Questions*, he concurs with Manilius in seeing the positive and progressive aspects of overseas navigation. In both cases Seneca's approach to the topic is the most far-reaching, and in the former case also the most negative, of any of the authors we have examined thus far.

Let us look first at the *Natural Questions*, where Seneca, like Pliny, conducts a meditation on seafaring as a digression from natural science—in this case in connection with a lengthy discussion of winds (Book 5). After considering the climatological ways in which the winds benefit mankind (dispelling heat, bringing rain to nourish crops, etc.), Seneca turns to look at their more harmful consequences:

> What of the fact that the winds have allowed all peoples to traffic with one another and has mixed races from disparate locales? A great kindness on nature's part, if the madness of the human race did not turn it toward self-destruction. As it is, though, one could say of the winds what people said of Julius Caesar, according to Livy: It's not certain which way the republic would be better off, if Caesar had been born or not. (5.18.4)

[102] The Manilian passage has been specifically contrasted with Horace's ode by Loretta Moscadi, "A Proposito di Manilio 1.96–104 e Orazio, *Carm.* 1.3.37–40," *Atene e Roma* 25 (1980): 163–66.

[103] The recollection of Horace's *audax* in *Odes* 1.3 is remarked by C.D.N. Costa in his note to this passage, *Seneca: Medea* (Oxford 1973) 99.

Seneca goes on to resolve this ambivalence by asserting that humanity would indeed be better off without the winds, since they are so often used for the wrong purposes; and the most prominent example of such misuse lies in the idea we have been concerned with throughout this chapter, the extension of imperial power beyond the sea:

> Providence, and that god who orders the cosmos, in giving the winds the power to move the atmosphere and in pouring them out in every corner (lest anything stagnate and become rank), did not intend this: That we should fill ships with armed legions and send them to conquer a portion of the deep, or that we should seek enemies upon the sea or beyond it. (5.18.5)

Seneca then cites Alexander the Great (along with Xerxes and Crassus) as an example of such reckless ambition, adducing the scenario his father had depicted in the first *Suasoria* in a new and more damning context: "Alexander will fly beyond Bactria and India, will seek what is beyond the great sea, and will think it unworthy that there is something he cannot pass beyond" (*esse aliquid ultimum sibi*, 5.18.10).

Having thus resolved his initial question—it would in fact be better for humankind if the winds did not blow (5.18.11)—Seneca turns to examine a new aspect of the problem, one which is in effect the converse of the Alexander scenario. Not only do the Romans show impious daring by attacking lands beyond the seas, they must also live in fear that some transoceanic power will one day attack *them*:

> No land is so far distant that it cannot send out some evil of its own contriving. How can I know whether even now some chief of a great nation in some hidden place (*in abdito*), his courage swollen by the complicity of fortune, ceases to restrain his armies within their borders or makes ready his fleets in quest of parts unknown? How can I know whether this or that wind brings war down upon me? The greatest contribution to human peace would be for the seas to be closed off. (5.18.12)

Here Seneca, with remarkable catholicity, imagines that even at the height of her power Rome is subject to the same invasions from abroad that she has thus far inflicted on others. Moreover, his abrupt shift in emphasis in the final line of this passage, from man's misuse of the winds to the crossing of the seas, reveals that his major concern throughout is with expeditions across Ocean. The "hidden" region beyond the Atlantic, seen by other authors as the locus of Rome's greatest promise, is here depicted in ominous tones as her gravest threat.[104]

Surprisingly enough, though, Seneca concludes this discussion by returning to the beneficial aspects of the winds, claiming now that god had created them not only for climatic reasons but also

> so that we might come to know regions beyond our own; for man would have been an unschooled animal without wide experience of things if he were confined within the limit of his native soil. He gave us winds so that the benefits of each region might be shared in common, not for the transport of legions and cavalry or the ferrying over of weapons of human destruction. (5.18.14)

The sudden introduction of this new theme, man's need for maritime exploration as a spur to intellectual progress, reveals just how complex the issue of distant seafaring has become for Seneca. Though sea voyages in one sense represent a step away from the purity of the golden age, they also represent a step forward in human evolution;[105] the sundering of earth's lands by water can be seen both as a natural bar to man's development and as a challenge he must learn to overcome. In this latter view, as we have already noted, Seneca was preceded by the *Astronomicon* of the poet Manilius.

The problematic nature of transoceanic travel adduced in the

[104] This passage too took on new meaning in the Renaissance, when Lipsius, for one, mused that the Indians of South America had seen its meaning demonstrated all too clearly. See his *Physiologiae Stoicorum libri tres* (Antwerp 1604) pt. 2, chap. 19, pp. 122–26.

[105] The same paradox is evident in Pliny the Elder, who complains of "the seas that rob us of half the world" (2.67.170) even while condemning the technology that would eventually repair that loss. On Seneca's glorification of technological progress see the finale of the *Natural Questions* and F. Morgante, "Il progresso umano in Lucrezio e Seneca," *Rivista di Cultura Classica e Medievale* 16 (1974): 3–40.

Natural Questions also becomes a central theme of Seneca's tragedies, following the pattern of overlap between the two bodies of work explored most recently by Giuseppe Biondi and Thomas Rosenmeyer.[106] I have here elected to focus on the one play in which it stands out most clearly, the *Medea*, but we should not therefore lose sight of the fact that Ocean and the lands beyond it loom large in many Senecan dramas. It is to such lands, for example, that Hippolytus (*Phaed.* 929–37), Oedipus (*Oed.* 1016–18), and Hercules (*Herc. Oet.* 742–44) are imagined to flee in order to escape the horror of their crimes; and it is to Ocean itself that various other heroes turn in order to cleanse themselves of sin (*Herc. Fur.* 1321–25), or from which they invoke their punishments (*Phaed.* 1159–63, 1204–6). In such passages Seneca can be said to combine the redemptive view of Ocean we have seen in Vergil with the retributive scheme advanced by Tacitus: Ocean does indeed bring renewal but only by way of a harsh purgation, a remorseless swallowing up of moral pollution. It cleanses in the same fashion as the fiery conflagrations of Stoic cosmology, that is by returning the world to ancient chaos in order to start anew.

The *Medea*, in particular, exemplifies this use of Ocean as a cosmic nemesis toward which moral evil inexorably tends. To some extent this scheme was inherent in the outlines of the myth: The fact that Medea had been brought into the Greek world by way of the first overseas voyage naturally lent itself to moralizing treatments, as we have already seen in Horace's 16th *Epode*. But Seneca foregrounds the navigational theme of the Medea story to a greater degree than any previous writer, certainly more so than Euripides had done in his version of *Medea*.[107] In the second and third of the play's choral odes (301–

[106] Biondi, "Il mito argonautico," above, n. 101, and *Il nefas argonautico: Mythos e logos nella Medea di Seneca* (Edizioni e Saggi Universitari di Filologia Classica 33, Bologna 1984); Rosenmeyer, *Senecan Drama and Stoic Cosmology* (Berkeley, Los Angeles, London 1989).

[107] Biondi ("Il mito argonautico") 422–26. The author (425) rightly raises doubts as to whether any ethical critique of seafaring lies behind the famous opening of Euripides' *Medea*, in which the Nurse laments the building of the *Argo* in preparation for Jason's voyage.

79, 579–669) Seneca casts his mind back from the scene of action to the original voyage of the *Argo*, and in particular to the *audacia* shown by the ship's navigator, Tiphys, in undertaking it:

> Too bold was he who first broke through
> the perilous seas with so frail a ship,
> who saw his own lands vanish behind him
> as he trusted his life to the uncertain breezes. (301–4)

> Whoever it was who on that bold ship
> put hands to the famous oars, stripped Mt. Pelion
> of the thick tree-shade of her sacred groves . . .
> he paid for defiling the laws of the sea
> with an ignoble death. (607–9, 614–15)

These two odes have been examined in detail by Biondi and we need not repeat his analysis here, but we should note that Seneca, by thus foregrounding Tiphys's role in the Medea story, frames the action of the play as an expiation of the *Argo*'s original sin—a working out of the moral scheme expressed in Book 5 of the *Natural Questions*. In the third choral ode, for example, he introduces a previously unattested aspect of the *Argo* legend, the idea that Tiphys (as well as other Argonauts) had died at sea in atonement for insolent daring. The suffering which now awaits Jason is seen as a further stage of this retributive process; in fact Medea is virtually made to personify Ocean's vengeance when she is described as "a force more evil than the sea, a prize worthy of the first ship" (362–63), or when she compares her own destructive power to Scylla, Charybdis, and other navigational perils (407–14).

What, then, does this retributive scheme imply for imperial Rome, which by the first century A.D. had sailed into seas more distant than those crossed by Tiphys and Jason? Seneca turns to address this question at the end of *Medea*'s second choral ode. In an unusual break from dramatic convention, he suddenly has his Corinthian chorus speak in terms that apply to his own place and time:[108]

[108] See notes ad loc. of Costa and Biondi (*Il nefas argonautico*), which cor-

Now has the sea grown tame, and it suffers
every restriction; no famous *Argo*
(built by Minerva's hand, shipping the oarage
of princes) is needed to sail it;
every small skiff roams at will on the deep.
All boundaries have shifted, and cities have set
their walls in a new land; the all-travelled world
lets nothing remain in its previous station;
The Indian drinks from Araxes' cold waters,
The Persians drink from the Elbe and Rhine. (364–72)

Here the increase in travel and exploration under the Romans is described as a perversion of world geography, confusing the order of nature and interchanging peoples on opposite sides of the globe. And what is worse, the trend is increasing rather than diminishing, leading humanity toward a further and more terrible voyage of discovery:

An age shall come, in later years,
when Ocean shall loose creation's bonds,
when the great planet shall stand revealed
and Tethys shall disclose new worlds,
nor shall Thule be last (*ultima*) among lands. (376–80)

In language that conflates nautical exploration with the Stoic vision of the cyclic destruction of the cosmos,[109] Seneca here depicts the crossing of Ocean as a final, cataclysmic step in human moral decline.

What is most remarkable about this famous passage, how-

---

rectly observe that not many years have elapsed since the return of the *Argo* and the time of the play; it would be absurd to suppose that navigation had become so widespread in so little time.

109 See Biondi ("Il mito argonautico") 428–30. At the end of Book 3 of the *Natural Questions* (30.1–8) Seneca describes this final cataclysm as an inundation of the seas, using imagery strongly reminiscent of the above passage; cp. in particular *cum . . . ex hac idonea diligentia remiserit mundus* (*NQ* 3.30.5) with *laxet Oceanus vincula rerum*. The Stoic "binding" metaphor for the cohesion of the universe has been explored by M. Lapidge in "A Stoic Metaphor in Late Latin Poetry: The Binding of the Cosmos" (*Latomus* 39 [1980]: 817–37); see esp. the passage of Avitus describing the Biblical flood in terms strongly reminiscent of Seneca.

ever, is that Seneca chooses to include the Vergilian phrase *ultima Thule* in its final line, allowing us to measure the true depth of his brooding pessimism. Aware that he is confronting one of the most cherished ideals of the Augustan age, the dream of an empire reaching "beyond the stars," he partly imitates the language of that dream[110]—so that an incautious reader might suppose that he too, like Vergil, is celebrating its imminent fulfillment. But his technique is actually closer to that of Horace in the 16th *Epode*: He surrounds this shining vision with a black background, thereby transforming it into a moment of dissolution and despair. In this case the larger themes of the *Medea*, with their harsh lesson in the moral degeneracy of navigational daring, form the dark field against which these lines must be placed. Rome's voyages into the West, like Jason's into the East, will undo the order that holds the world together; the passing of Thule will indeed usher in a new age for humankind, but one which will return us to the ancient chaos of the *apeiron* rather than to the golden age of Vergil's *Georgics* and *Aeneid*.

[110] The Vergilian echo behind the phrase *ultima Thule* is further supported by Seneca's 1.375, *venient annis saecula seris*, with its clear evocation of *Aeneid* 1.283 (*veniet lustris labentibus aetas*), part of Jupiter's grand prophecy of a coming *imperium sine fine*. See pt. 4.2 and n. 33 of Moretti, "Other World and Antipodes" (above, n. 39).

Five

Geography and Fiction

In the opening chapter of this study we looked at the earliest extant Greek inquiry into the nature of Ocean, that conducted by Herodotus in Books 2 and 4 of the *Histories*. We saw that Ocean exemplified for Herodotus the question of how the earth's boundaries were to be determined, mythologically or empirically; and in subsequent chapters we have seen how this question was advanced and elaborated by the writers who followed Herodotus, in regard not only to Ocean but to other distant-world legends as well. However, we have yet to explore in full the theoretical and critical implications of such discussions, the topic to which we turn in this final chapter. Debunking a myth necessarily involves debunking the author who records it, after all; and thus it may be said that Herodotus and his successors, in questioning the existence of entities like Ocean, formulate an approach not only to geography but to a kind of imaginative literature we might loosely call fiction.

Herodotus himself seems aware of some of the theoretical issues involved in his Ocean critique. In his first attack on the myth, directed against an unnamed author (perhaps Hecataeus)[1] who has connected Ocean with the mysterious flooding of the Nile, Herodotus complains that such theories take refuge in the remoteness of distant space and hence "do not admit refutation"[2] (*ouk echei elenchon*, 2.23). That is to say they must be approached by way of arguments from plausibility and internal coherence, for example by an examination of the idea of Ocean's circularity, rather than by the sounder route of empir-

[1] See Lionel Pearson, *Early Ionian Historians* (Oxford 1939) 87; Alan B. Lloyd, *Herodotus Book 2* (Etudes preliminaires aux réligions orientales dans l'empire romain, vol. 43, Leiden 1976) ad loc.

[2] The meaning of *elenchos* here is correctly explained by G.E.R. Lloyd in *Magic, Reason and Experience* (Cambridge 1979) 253 and n. 118.

ical evidence. This "credibility shield" provided by distant space becomes even more of a concern in cases where no arguments from plausibility exist; in his inquiry into the Hyperboreans, for example, Herodotus seems completely at a loss for reasons either to believe or disbelieve the traditional stories, and settles for repeating them without taking any position at all.[3] At such moments Herodotus relies on the storyteller's prerogative of "saying what is said" (*legein ta legomena*, 7.152.2; cf. 2.123.1) without necessarily affirming it—the same strategy, it should be noted, with which Aristotle urges writers of fiction[4] to countenance their inventions (*Poetics* 25.12–13).

The idea that distant space could become a "cover" for fictional narratives again becomes an issue in Strabo's analysis of the Indian wonders, as we have seen in chapter 3. Indeed the principle Strabo expresses in connection with tales of India, *to porrō duselenkton* ("the distant is difficult to disprove," 11.6.4), is remarkably similar to Herodotus's protest of *ouk echei elenchon* in his critique of Ocean. And much the same principle is articulated by Eratosthenes in a debate over the Phaeacian tales of Homer's *Odyssey* (a text that will be at issue in much of the chapter which follows). Homer had removed the wanderings of Odysseus into Ocean, Eratosthenes claims, because that region of the earth was *eukatapseuston*,[5] literally "easy to lie about" (fr. I A 14 = Strabo 1.2.19). Here, we note, the inaccessibility of distant space is seen from the poet's rather than the critic's viewpoint and is therefore regarded in a positive light, as an artistic resource rather than an investigative obstacle.[6]

[3] The passage is discussed in greater detail in my "Herodotus and Mythic Geography: The Case of the Hyperboreans," *TAPA* 119 (1989): 97–117.

[4] That the terms *poiēsis* and *poiētēs* in the *Poetics* refer primarily to the category of literature we call "fiction," rather than to "poetry" as it is usually translated, has been asserted by L. J. Potts (*Aristotle on the Art of Fiction*, Cambridge 1968).

[5] The word seems to have been original to Eratosthenes, but may have been inspired by Herodotus's curious use of *akatapseusta*, "not at all fictional," at *Histories* 4.191.

[6] See the epilogue below for the ways in which Renaissance theorists, notably Tasso and Lopez Pinciano, echoed this critical stance.

The critical methodology evident in all these passages, based on the sorting out of geographic fact from fictional invention, may seem pedestrian enough to modern readers, who are accustomed to subtler explorations of literary meaning than a simple true/false distinction. Yet we must not lose sight of the fact that the boundary between *historia* and *muthos* (or *historia* and *fabula* to the Romans) was an issue of prime importance in ancient, and later in Renaissance, literary criticism.[7] Since self-acknowledged fictions like the modern novel as yet had no place in the literary taxonomy, invented tales had to be cloaked in various historical guises in order to win acceptance, and their degree of success was largely dependent on how well they maintained these impostures. The importance of this credibility ethic to readers of ancient fiction has been demonstrated by a number of recent studies[8] and I do not intend to discuss it at any length here, beyond briefly setting the stage for the discussion which follows. For I hope to show that the literature of geography and exploration, as attested by Herodotus, Strabo, and Eratosthenes above, provided a means of circumventing this ethic, and thereby opened a path for the most radical experiments in prose fiction ever attempted by ancient writers.

Nor should we look upon the process of sifting truths from fictions as an unsophisticated or antiquarian approach to narrative, since the same process continues in our own century in

[7] These terms, plus a third intermediate rubric (*plasma* or *argumentum*) were brought over into literary criticism from rhetorical theory, where they served to classify legal arguments according to truth content. See Cicero *De Inventione* 1.27, *Rhetorica ad Herrenium* 1.12–13, Schol. ad Dionysius Thrax 449.10, Sextus Empiricus *Adversus Grammaticos* 263–64. Discussion by K. Barwick, "Die Gliederung der Narratio in der Rhetorischen Theorie," *Hermes* 63 (1928): 261–87. For earlier examples of the truth-fiction issue in Greek literature see Wolfgang Rösler, "Die Entdeckung der Fiktionalität in der Antike," *Poetica* 12 (1980): 283–319, and Chester G. Starr, "Ideas of Truth in Early Greece," *Parola del Passato* 23 (1968): 348–59.

[8] Most notably Jack Winkler's *Auctor et Actor: A Narratological Reading of Apuleius' The Golden Ass* (Berkeley and Los Angeles 1985), esp. pt. 1 (though the concerns of this book also go far beyond the simple *historia-muthos* dichotomy I have outlined here). See also A. W. Gomme, *The Greek Attitude to Poetry and History* (Berkeley and Los Angeles 1954) and other sources cited below.

contexts very much like those we are concerned with here. Thus, contemporary readers have tried to extract an accurate record of early navigations from the Phaeacian tales of the *Odyssey*, closely paralleling the efforts of Stoic Homerists of the Hellenistic era; for instance, Tim Severin in *The Ulysses Voyage: Sea Search for the Odyssey* (London 1987) claims to have completely retraced the route of Odysseus using a reconstructed bronze-age ship.[9] At the same time, moreover, modern scholars have called into question the veracity of some seemingly reliable accounts of discovery, such as Robert Peary's record of his journey to the North Pole.[10] The reversibility of this critical process, which can recategorize invented travels as real or real accounts as inventions,[11] invites us to consider more closely the literary status of the explorer text and its relationship to other, more overtly fictional narratives. Indeed the groundwork for such an investigation has already been laid by Erwin Rohde, who in the landmark book *Der griechische Roman und seine Vorlaüfer* treated the travelogue as a principal antecedent of the ancient novel.[12]

[9] The most famous of these attempts to reconstruct Odysseus's route, on paper if not on the high seas, are those of the French scholar Victor Bérard, in *Les Phéniciens et L'Odyssée* (2 vols., Paris 1902–3) and *Les Navigations D'Ulysse* (3 vols., Paris 1927–29).

[10] See Wally Herbert, "Did Peary Reach the Pole?" in *National Geographic* 174.3 (Sept. 1988): 387–413, though the issue in this case is more one of accuracy than veracity—Herbert only questions whether Peary in fact reached the true Pole, rather than whether he ever made a journey across the Arctic ice cap. Perhaps a more telling, though less well known, example of a disputed travelogue would be the journals of the sixteenth-century Portugese adventurer Fernão Mendes Pinto: The introduction to a recently published translation (*The Travels of Mendes Pinto*, trans. Rebecca D. Katz, Chicago 1989) leaves completely open the question of whether many of Pinto's travels ever took place.

[11] Carpenter (183) remarks on this reversal in connection with Pytheas of Massilia, and compares the way in which Marco Polo's travel narrative, though currently accepted as true, was derided as "a thousand lies" by contemporary readers. J. H. Parry in *The Age of Reconnaissance* (N.Y. 1964, 23–24) points to a further irony in the case of Polo—that even while "Il Milione" was being laughed to scorn, the utterly mendacious *Travels* of Sir John Mandeville were given complete credence.

[12] See also Percy Adams's two studies of the relationship between travel nar-

Ocean and Poetry

When Herodotus claims that "some poet or other" invented the name Ocean and inserted it into his poetry, his critical task is complete; he does not bother to ask *why* this entity was invented or what it is doing in so much early Greek literature. We can, however, glean some of his thoughts on these questions from the language in which he frames his refutation of the myth. At one point he attacks the theory connecting Nile and Ocean as "more wrongheaded . . . but also more wondrous (*thaumasiōterē*) to relate" than other explanations of the river's flooding. The antithetical contrast of the two terms seems to imply a causal explanation, that is, "This theory got started because it inspires wonder, not because it's true." Despite its geographical vagueness, that is, Homer's Ocean constitutes a *thauma* of the first order, the same kind of grand and absorbing spectacle that Herodotus himself often takes evident delight in. (In fact we may further speculate that Herodotus's animus against the Ocean myth derives in part from his frustration at not being able to tap its thaumastic potential. One can only imagine, based on his extensive treatment of the Nile in Book 2, what Herodotus might have done in a *logos* based on a river encircling the entire earth.)

Herodotus's *thauma*-based understanding of Ocean's role in early poetry, however, was not enough to satisfy later literary critics. For them Homer's Ocean became not just a marvel but a hermeneutic mystery, and moreover a key to larger mysteries of the Homeric corpus and of archaic poetry as a whole. In particular, the two lines of the *Iliad* where Ocean is described as "origin of the gods" and "begetter of all things" (14.201, 246) provoked a long debate among readers of Homer, and led to some of the earliest attempts at an allegorical reading of his

ratives and early English fiction, *Travelers and Travel Liars* (Berkeley 1962) and *Travel Literature and the Evolution of the Novel* (Lexington, Ky., and London 1973); and for France two books by Geoffroy Atkinson, *The Extraordinary Voyage in French Literature Before 1700* (N.Y. 1920), and *Les relations des voyages du XVII siècle et l'évolution des idées* (Paris 1924).

text. These lines (which we looked at in chapter 1 as evidence for a cosmogonic conception of Ocean) are also sometimes conjoined with a similar, and perhaps derivative, passage from the Orphic hymn to Ocean (84), of uncertain date but earlier than the fourth century B.C.:[13]

> Ocean I call upon, father unperishing, always existing, origin of immortals and mortals, who sends his waves round about the farthest circle of earth.

As mentioned earlier in chapter 1, Plato is perhaps the first writer to look at these passages from a critical perspective, and his analysis prefigures that of many later readers.[14] He wrestles with the *Iliad* lines twice in the *Theaetetus* (152d7–e7, 180c8–d3), and once again in the *Cratylus*, this time in conjunction with the Orphic hymn (402b1–c3). On each occasion he has Socrates find in these passages a veiled description of the Heraclitean "flux" governing the cosmos. Nor does he treat this as a subjective or arbitrary interpretation, but one based on the explicit intentions of the early poets:

> Have we not heard something else regarding this question [of a universal flux] from the ancients, who baffled the masses by way of their poetry: that Ocean and Tethys, both flowing streams which do not stand still, are the source of all other things? (*Theaet.* 180c8–d3)

Here Plato suggests that the "ancients" (*hoi archaioi*) had deliberately hidden allegorical meanings in entities like Ocean by a kind of encryption, as if to keep their truths out of reach of the

[13] The *terminus ad quem* is established by Plato's citation in the *Cratylus* (see below).

[14] Cf. Vergil's phrase for Ocean in the *Georgics* (4.382), *pater rerum*. An array of late Greek commentaries and handbooks, including Stobaeus's *Eclogues* (1.10.26) and the pseudo-Plutarchan *Life of Homer* (93), adopt the same reading as an article of scientific dogma. Diels (*Doxographi Graeci* 91–94) derives both passages, as well as a similar citation in Sextus Empiricus (*Adv. math.* 10.313–18), from a lost intermediary source, Heracleon. A different reading of the same passage, hearkening back to Plato's comparison with Heraclitus, refers to Ocean as "the source of all the gods, which is to say, the elements" (cf. Schol. ad. Dionys. Perieg. l. 1, Müller *GGM* 2.428).

unlettered public; he goes on to contrast this with the technique of modern-day teachers (like Socrates) who express their meanings openly, "so that even the cobblers may hear." It is not clear whether Plato himself took such a view seriously (it sounds like the same sort of labored hermeneutics he allows Socrates to scoff at elsewhere, e.g., *Phaedrus* 229c–230a),[15] but the frequency with which it recurs and the degree of its elaboration indicate that some of his contemporaries probably did so.

Aristotle, although skeptical of Plato's Heraclitean reading of Homer's Ocean,[16] proposes an allegorizing interpretation of his own, grounded this time not in cosmology but in meteorology. In his *Meteorologica* he introduces Ocean as a figure for the circulation of water vapor in the earth's atmosphere:

> We should think of [the hydrologic cycle] as a river, running in a circle high and low, composed of air and water together: When the sun is near, a river of vapor runs upward, and when it sets a river of water runs down. And this cycle keeps going continually in the same order. Thus, if the men of old were speaking in riddles (*ēinittonto*) when they mentioned Ocean, then perhaps they referred to this river which flows in a circle around the earth. (347a2–7)

This solution may strike us as contrived, perhaps even more contrived than Plato's; what is interesting, however, is that Aristotle here agrees with Plato in supposing that early poets deliberately "wrote in riddles,"[17] and in seeing Ocean as a prime example of such encryption. As to the question of what purpose this riddling style would have served, however, beyond

[15] See M. L. West, *The Orphic Poems* (Oxford 1983) 118 for the view that Plato was not proposing this as a serious interpretation. Also Robert Lamberton in *Homer the Theologian: Neoplatonist Allegorical Reading and the Growth of the Epic Tradition* (Berkeley 1986) 252, assumes in connection with the *Theaetetus* passages that "Socrates is parodying Theaetetus' teachers."

[16] He refers to it obliquely in the *Metaphysics* (983b27), though here Thales rather than Heraclitus supplies the cosmological correlate.

[17] Strabo, we note, uses a compound of the same verb *ainittomai* in describing the vagueries of Homeric geography (1.1.3), as well as the verb *allēgoreō* (1.2.7).

providing colorful metaphors for later cosmologists, Aristotle gives no clues.

In these and other[18] cosmologically grounded readings of Ocean we can see the rudiments of what would later become a full-scale allegorical system, transforming the *Iliad* and the *Odyssey* into poems of natural science. The landscapes and even characters and plots of these poems were eventually construed as references to the terrestrial globe and the movements of airs, waters, and heavenly bodies, thanks to the principle that archaic literature hid its meanings in code. At the culmination of this system's evolution stands the magnificent *Homeric Allegories* attributed to Heraclitus, to be dated perhaps to the first century A.D.,[19] but its principal exponents were Stoic critics of the third and second centuries B.C.: Zeno, Cleanthes, Chrysippus, and others (whose writings are now mostly lost). These critics were driven by the principles of their school to put all great art and literature on a utilitarian footing; only if the *Iliad* and *Odyssey* were found to contain "lessons," useful or enlightening information couched amid their poetry, could they be deemed acceptable from an ethical standpoint.[20] Herodotus's initial critique suggesting that poets had merely "invented" the name Ocean, that is, had to be invalidated at all costs; to accuse Homer of indulging in useless *thaumata* was to attack the very foundation of his artistic stature.

A good example of the ingenuity—some might say perversity—of these Stoic readings of Ocean is provided by Crates of Mallos, a highly eccentric geographer-critic of the third century

[18] Ocean as metaphor for the terrestrial horizon: Schol. Anonym. 3 on Aratus *Phaen.* 26 (E. Maass, *Commentariorum in Aratum Reliquiae* [Berlin 1898] 343); Strabo 1.1.6; Schol. Venetus on *Il.* 5.6 (also Eustathius 514.32). For discussion see Buffière, *Les Mythes d'Homère* 216–17, Berger (1904) 1–2, Gisinger (1929) cols. 2311–12.

[19] See the introduction to the Budé edition by F. Buffière, *Heraclite: Allégories d'Homère* (Paris 1962), esp. xx-xxxix.

[20] On the importance of utility in Stoic aesthetics see Phillip DeLacy, "Stoic Views of Poetry," *AJP* 69 (1948): 241–71; for Strabo in particular, see W. Aly, "Aut prodesse aut delectare volunt poetae," in *Strabo von Amaseia*, vol. 4 (Bonn 1957) 376–84, and G. Aujac in the introduction to the Budé Strabo, vol. 1, xxv-vi.

B.C. Crates often used Homeric poetry to support the Stoic geographic theories he favored, for example the scheme of a four-part earth separated by two rings of Ocean (see chap. 4, pp. 131–33, above). When Homer did not bear out Crates' point clearly enough, moreover, he was fully prepared to emend the text of the poems to make them correlate more clearly. One such emendation concerned the very *Iliad* passage we are here examining; according to Plutarch[21] Crates added an otherwise unattested line to this passage, so that it read:

> Ocean, who was framed the begetter of all things,
> [both men and gods, spreads over the greatest part of the earth.]

Since Crates' geography (derived in this case from Cleanthes and Zeno) called for a very wide Ocean, filling the entire region between the tropics, it seems likely that he supported (or created) this extra line so as to make Homer a firmer advocate of his beliefs.[22]

This and other pseudoscientific interpretations would seem to leave little room for attempts, like that of Herodotus, to treat Ocean as a purely aesthetic or imaginative literary property. Yet if we move forward in time to the first and second centuries A.D., we find several instances of a curious literary conceit which partly recapitulates the Herodotean view: Various authors of this period[23] see Ocean not as a geographic entity, but

[21] Quoted in the *De Facie in Orbe Lunae* 938d (= Crates fr. 33 Mette); see the note by Harold Cherniss ad loc. in the Loeb edition (*Plutarch's Moralia*, vol. 12 [Harvard 1957] 164–65), and Mette (1936) 60–61.

[22] The addition, moreover, gives a new thrust to the original line which helps adapt it to Crates' purposes: Here Ocean becomes the "begetter" of life by wafting warm, moisture-bearing winds toward the *oikoumenē*, confirming the *anathumiaseis* of the Stoic geographic system. This is how Plutarch's narrator, at any rate, interprets the passage, in his attempt to support Crates' reading (*De Facie* 938d12-e6).

[23] Passages collected by Frederick Williams in an appendix to his commentary on *Callimachus: Hymn to Apollo* (Oxford 1978) 98–99; further discussion in note to lines 105–13, pp. 85–89. Williams believes that the *topos* goes back to Hellenistic times and underlies Callimachus's comparison of Homer to the Assyrian river (88–89), but it cannot be denied that most of the extant instances date from the first and second centuries A.D.

as an analogue for Homer himself. On one level this analogy embodies the idea that all subsequent poetry has derived from Homer in the same way that all rivers and streams were thought to derive from Ocean (cp. *Iliad* 21.196–97); hence Quintilian:[24]

> For just as Ocean, according to Homer himself, gives rise to the current of all rivers and fountains, so Homer supplies a model and a starting point for every branch of eloquence. No one has surpassed him in lofty portrayal of great matters or in judicious treatment of small ones. He is at once fecund and restrained, cheerful and solemn; equally wondrous in his fulsomeness and his economy, and preeminent not only in poetic but also in rhetorical prowess. (*Inst. Orat.* 10.1.46)[25]

Beyond this, however, Ocean also formed an analogue for epic poetry because of its grandeur and immense scope. Thus the author of the treatise *On the Sublime*,[26] discussing the stature of great art, remarks that "we are naturally led to wonder not, by Zeus, at small streams, even though these be clear and useful, but at the Nile and the Ister and the Rhine, and far beyond these at Ocean" (35.4).[27]

[24] The idea of Ocean as "father" of all waters on earth is also expressed by Hesiod (*Theogony* 337–70) and Sophocles (fr. 270 Pearson 1–2). Williams also compares Xenophanes fr. 30 Diels-Kranz (*Hymn to Apollo* 88).

[25] It is worth noting that Quintilian's use of this metaphor imports into a new, literary-critical context the qualities of Ocean we explored in the first chapter of this study: its infinitude, temporal primacy, and above all its ability to fuse elemental opposites into a single medium. Thus the Pythean vision of an Ocean in which solid, liquid, and gas are fused together (Strabo 2.4.1) here translates into an all-embracing literary medium that combines great matters with humble; lush with spare styles; poetry with rhetoric. We might compare our own phrase "Ocean of story," which similarly uses the sea to exemplify the infinite range and diversity of fictional narratives.

[26] A work which should probably be assigned to the period in which the Homer/Ocean analogy seems to have flourished, the late first or second centuries A.D. The most reliable evidence for the date of the treatise derives from the range of literature with which its author is familiar, including works from the first half of the first century A.D., but none later.

[27] Arieti Crossetti (*Longinus: On the Sublime* [Texts and Studies in Religion 21, N.Y. and Toronto 1985] 178) astutely links this passage with the Alexan-

In a different section of *On the Sublime*, moreover, the treatise's author—whom we may by convention call Longinus—uses Ocean in an even more complex and suggestive metaphoric formulation. The metaphor to which I refer occurs in the following famous passage, where Longinus compares the *Odyssey* with the *Iliad*, to the detriment of the former:

> As regards the *Odyssey* one might liken Homer to the setting sun, whose greatness endures even without its intensity. For he no longer retains his pitch at the same level as the *Iliad*'s poetry, nor the polish of the sublimities which never descend into bathos, nor the same outpouring of incidents one after another, nor the rapid variations which are both public in scope and packed with realistic inventions. Rather it is as if Ocean had withdrawn into itself and (become tamed?) within its own bounds; henceforth the ebb tide of his greatness reveals itself, and a wandering among the fabulous and unreal. (9.13)

This passage presents difficulties because of the extraordinary density of its imagery (and because of at least one corruption in the text):[28] Longinus moves in quick succession from the metaphor of the setting sun, to that of Ocean, and finally (in a sentence not quoted above, 9.14) to a suggestion that the *Odyssey*'s more exotic episodes can be considered the "dreams of a Zeus." The complexity of this sequence renders the precise meaning of the Ocean metaphor unclear. On a primary level it refers to Homer's temperament and mood, which with advancing age have become calm rather than tempestuous and inspired; but when juxtaposed with the discussion of Odyssean "wanderings" which follows, it also seems to refer to the content of his

drian conceit (cp. Callimachus, *Hymn to Apollo* 108–13) by which poems were configured as rivers; Longinus has here turned this conceit on its head by preferring vast rivers to tiny streams. In addition Longinus's use of *chrēsima*, "useful," in the description of the small streams may be intended as a response to Stoic approaches to literature.

[28] See the commentaries by D. A. Russell, *Longinus on the Sublime* (Oxford 1964) 97–98, and Crossetti 239–41. The principal textual problem concerns *erēmoumenou*, for which I have tentatively accepted Ruhnken's emendation *hēmeroumenou* or "tamed."

work, or at least to that of the Phaeacian tales of Books 9–12. That is to say, Ocean here embodies the qualities of both poet and poem, the former in that the poet's art requires a floodlike "outpouring" of matter (cf. *prochusin* or "flood" in the description of the *Iliad*), the latter in that the *Odyssey*'s most fabulous episodes are actually located in Ocean.[29]

Longinus's elaboration of this second level of the Ocean/Homer analogy, that which centers on the fabulous character of the Phaeacian tales, points us toward an idea that will become central in what lies ahead. Oftentimes narratives become so closely linked to the venues in which they take place that the venues themselves come to represent the narratives; and since Ocean, as Herodotus had recognized, was largely an invented place to begin with, it came to stand for a class of tales which were mostly or entirely invented. Thus, ancient critics recognized a certain kind of story as "Oceanic" in the same way that other kinds were designated Milesian, Arcadian, and the like. Let us look in the next two sections at some ways in which ancient critics elaborated this correlation of place and genre in their attempts to interpret the Phaeacian tales of the *Odyssey* and other exotic travelogues.

The Voyage of Odysseus

The critical task of validating a single geographic entity, like Ocean, becomes vastly more complex when it is extended to the scope of an entire narrative. Now the geographer-critic is faced not only with a wide range of topographic data but also with a narrator, whose character must be assessed before his account can be believed. Indeed, the very first explorer-narrator in the literary record, Odysseus, underwent such an assessment at the hands of his first auditor, the Phaeacian king Alcinous. In the so-called intermezzo of *Odyssey* 11 Alcinous interrupts Odys-

[29] The Ocean figure takes on still other dimensions when we move to the next chapter of *On the Sublime* (10.4–5) and find Longinus comparing various sea storms—including one from the *Odyssey*—as measures of poetic vividness and emotional charge.

seus in order to raise the question of whether his tales ought to be believed (363–67):

> Odysseus, we who behold you do not at all judge you to be a cheat or a swindler, like those many whom the black earth nurtures; such men are wide-strewn, weaving lies derived from the place no one can see. But you have a fine grace in speaking, in you dwells a noble mind.

Fortunately the credibility problem raised here is quickly dismissed, since Odysseus's noble rank in itself suffices to dispel Alcinous's doubts. Nevertheless, the fact that such doubts are raised at all demonstrates the complex critical issues surrounding what Alcinous describes as "the region no one can see" (*hothen ke tis oude idoito*; compare Herodotus's *aphanes*, 2.23). Once a story enters this realm its audience assumes a guarded and skeptical posture, recognizing that nothing in it can be empirically verified; and its narrator must, as a result, employ various schemes either to win belief or to deflect the scorn that accrues to liars.

A more troublesome issue than whether Odysseus had invented the Phaeacian tales, moreover, was whether *Homer* had invented them; and it is a remarkable fact of ancient criticism that this question was consistently answered in the negative, thanks once again to the predominant influence of the Stoics. A scheme of correspondences between Homeric locales in the *Odyssey* and real places in the western Mediterranean, principally in the neighborhood of Sicily, evolved at an early stage[30] in the poem's reception and remained current thereafter. Thus, the Straits of Messina were identified with Homer's Charybdis,

[30] Exactly how early is difficult to say, but at least some elements go back as far as Thucydides (6.2), and the use of Homeric poetry in general as a source for geographic and ethnographic data is already evident in Hecataeus (see Pearson, *Early Ionian Historians* 69). However, the refinement and codification of the system seems to have been a Hellenistic undertaking, associated initially with the historians Timaeus and Timagetus. A brief history of the debate is recounted by Germaine Aujac in the introduction to the Budé edition of Strabo, 1.13–19, and by Ramin 121–37; for more detail see Bunbury 1.49–71.

because of the fierce eddies of the currents there; the Cyclops episode was located in the vicinity of Mt. Aetna, probably because a tribe of Cyclopes (though in fact different Cyclopes) was thought to labor at this "forge of Hephaestus"; and the name "Thrinacia" was corrected to "Trinacria" or "three-cornered," making it a plausible description of triangularly shaped Sicily. With three such impressive correlates as a foundation, moreover, the rest of the interpretive edifice was completed in kind, so that virtually every episode of the wanderings was given a western Mediterranean locale.

The validity of this geographic approach was accepted as an article of faith by the Stoics, whose readings of Homer always focused on the veracity and utility of his epics; but there were also some who questioned it, especially among the learned and exacting Homerists at the library of Alexandria. The most prominent and outspoken of these dissenters was Eratosthenes of Cyrene, head of the library during the late third century B.C.[31] Eratosthenes, as we have seen elsewhere, saw himself standing at the threshold of a new era in geography ushered in by Alexander's conquests, and thus felt obliged, like Herodotus before him, to exorcise the shade of Homer from the geographic record. To this task Eratosthenes applied himself with zeal and with devastating wit; for example, in a now-famous pronouncement on the wanderings of Odysseus, he claimed that "one can find the route of Odysseus if one can find the cobbler who sewed the bag of the winds" (Strabo 1.2.15 = I A 16 Berger). This reductio ad absurdum is clearly an attempt to blacken the eye of the Stoics, who received it in kind, as we shall see below.

Nor did Eratosthenes attempt to narrow the distance between text and map by way of a system of recondite allegories, like that posited in the Homeric criticism of Plato, Aristotle, and others. For Eratosthenes, as for only one or two other an-

[31] See the analysis of his Homeric criticism by Berger (1880) 19–40, (1903) 386–87, 535; Aujac (1966), chap. 3; K. Pfeiffer, *A History of Classical Scholarship*, vol. 1 (Oxford 1968) 164–68; and A. Thalamas, *La Géographie d'Eratosthène* (Versailles 1921) 195–201.

cient critics,[32] poetry was aimed principally at *psuchagōgia*, a species of aesthetic pleasure (perhaps "entertainment"),[33] rather than at instruction (Strabo 1.1.10, 1.2.3 = I A 20, 21). If Homer had used Ocean as the backdrop for Odysseus's wanderings, this could be explained in purely literary rather than cosmologic or geographic terms:

> Eratosthenes says that one might suppose Homer had wanted to place the wanderings of Odysseus in the western Mediterranean region, but held off from this plan, both because he did not know the area in any detail, and because he preferred to push his episodes outward (*exagein*) toward the more striking and the more fabulous (*to deinoteron kai to teratōdesteron*). (Strabo 1.2.19 = I A 14)

The terms *deinoteron* and *teratōdesteron* here, like Herodotus's *thaumasiōterē*, describe the purely emotional and static experience conferred by mysterious and strange phenomena—an experience which counted for little among the Stoics (who held it a mark of moral virtue to marvel at nothing), but which Eratosthenes treats as a legitimate goal of literary endeavor. This validation of the *thauma* relieved readers of any need to find hidden meanings behind poetry's veils; if a poem provided *psuchagōgia*, that was enough to make the experience of reading it worthwhile.

Eratosthenes' indictment of attempts to "map" the *Odyssey* in strictly geographic terms went on to become a kind of credo among his fellow Alexandrian scholars. For example, his description above of Homer's tendency to "export" (*exagein*) the *Odyssey* narrative is echoed by another of the Alexandrian library's directors, the great Homeric critic Aristarchus.[34] Aris-

[32] A similar doctrine has been ascribed to Philodemus (who also used the word *psuchagōgia*, Book 5, col. xiii) in his dispute with Neoptolemus; see the speculative reconstruction by A. Rostagni, "Filodemo contra l'estetica classica," *Rivista di Filologia* n.s. 2 (1924): 1–28, and Pfeiffer 1.166–67.

[33] So Pfeiffer 1.166. The word *psuchagōgia* seems to have taken on this second meaning in later antiquity, beyond its original sense of "persuasion (via rhetorical argument)."

[34] See Pfeiffer 1.213–20; K. Lehrs, *De Aristarchi Studiis Homericis* (Leipzig 1882); and (on a somewhat different topic) D. M. Schenkeveld, "Aristarchus

tarchus's grammatical study of Homer led him to the same conclusion Eratosthenes reached by way of geography, namely that the voyage of Odysseus had been removed into the fabulous realm of Ocean for purely aesthetic purposes; thus for example Homer had situated the island of Calypso in "indefinite and outward-removed places" (*ektetopismenois topois aoristois*) rather than in real-world locales.[35] What is striking in this concept of an *ektopismos* or "out-placement" of episodes is that Aristarchus, like Eratosthenes, seems to have charted the *Odyssey* on a literary rather than a geographic "map," gauging its veracity according to how far from *terra cognita* its narrative progresses.[36] At the furthest remove from the *oikoumenē* the poem is assumed to become utterly fabulous, so that it must be approached on entirely different terms than a factual or utilitarian treatise.

This anti-geographic analysis of Homeric poetry was further elaborated by Aristarchus's pupil Apollodorus, a critic whose work we know in somewhat better detail than that of his predecessors.[37] In the prologue to the second book of his treatise *On the Catalogue of Ships*, Apollodorus, perhaps quoting Eratosthenes,[38] described the Phaeacian tales as an *exōkeanismos* or "removal into Ocean" of a journey that originally took place in more familiar waters. Thus, Apollodorus claimed, attempts by scholars like Callimachus to find Mediterranean correlates for the *Odyssey* were "inconsistent with the *exōkeanismos* of the lo-

---

and *Homēros philotechnos*: Some Fundamental Ideas of Aristarchus on Homer as Poet," *Mnemosyne* 23 (1970): 162–78.

[35] Schol. ad *Od.* 5.55; cf. Lehrs 244 and n. 155. The term *aoristos*, here, suggests that Aristarchus, again like Eratosthenes, saw the distancing of the *Odyssey*'s setting as an authorial strategy designed to circumvent questions of credibility; however the extant fragments of Aristarchus's work are too scanty to allow for much interpretation along these lines.

[36] The same scheme, we note, is implied in the English adjective "outlandish," originally meaning "derived from distant lands."

[37] See Pfeiffer 1.257–60, and B. Niese, "Apollodors Commentar zum Schiffskatalog," *Rh. Mus.* 32 (1877): 267–307.

[38] So thinks Pfeiffer 1.259; Berger (1880) also claims the term *exōkeanismos* for Eratosthenes (fr. I A 3, pp. 26–28), but see Thalamas (above, n. 31, p. 199 n.1) for the opposite view. The wording of Strabo's secondhand account leaves the question open.

cations in which Homer sets Odysseus's wanderings" (fr. 157 = Strabo 1.2.37). The poet's tendency to "ocean out" (*exōkeanizein*) his story, moreover—like the technique described by Eratosthenes with the verb *exagein* and by Aristarchus with *ektopizein*—aims at a particular narratological goal, that is "for the sake of mythologizing" (*muthologias charin*, Strabo 7.3.6; cp. Eratosthenes' reference to *to teratōdesteron* above). Like the other Alexandrians, then, Apollodorus placed the *Odyssey* in the outermost zone of a concentric scheme of narrative fictions, a zone here specifically identified with Ocean and therefore with absolute poetic license.

The strong reaction of the Stoic school against such views reveals how fundamentally they challenged the existing critical order, predicated as it was on Homer's stature as master teacher and sage. It will be instructive to look at the arguments mounted against the Alexandrian readings of the *Odyssey* by three prominent Stoic geographer-critics: Crates of Mallos, Polybius, and Strabo. All three sought to uphold Homer's greatness by restoring the historicity and paideutic content of the fabulous wanderings, and by refuting the idea of the *Odyssey* as a fictional *exōkeanismos*.

As we saw earlier in section 2, it is Crates of Mallos who adopts the most extreme fundamentalist position on the question of Homeric poetry's geographic content. In the case of the *Odyssey* this rigid stance led Crates into an interpretive showdown with his contemporary and rival Aristarchus. Crates asserted that Odysseus had indeed sailed outside the Mediterranean; that Homer knew this accurately, just as he knew the true structure of the four-part world; and that therefore Books 9–12 of the *Odyssey* should be read quite literally as the record of a voyage into Ocean.[39] Unfortunately, we know very little about the route which Crates laid out for this voyage; but if it

[39] Geminus 16.22, 28–30 = Crates fr. 34a Mette, 236–39; Strabo 34.4 = Crates fr. 30. Discussion by Mette (1936) 59–60, 68–74; Berger (1903) 441–49; Wachsmuth, *De Cratete Mallota* 24–26, 42–47; and most recently James Porter in a paper entitled "Hermeneutic Lines and Circles: Aristarchus and Crates on Homeric Exegesis," soon to be published by Princeton University Press in *Homer's Readers* (ed. R. Lamberton).

was at all similar to the one Crates assigned to a different *Odyssey* hero, Menelaus, then it may have taken Odysseus into the southern hemisphere or even around the world at the equator.[40] In any case it seems certain that in tracing both voyages, as in his other critical endeavors,[41] Crates sought to "map" the Homeric poems on the enormous globe he devised to illustrate Stoic geographical theory. In order to do so he had to invalidate Aristarchus's theory of the "exportation" of the *Odyssey* narrative into Ocean, and the debate between the two men over whether Odysseus had sailed the "inner" or "outer" seas went on to become famous as a crux of Homeric criticism.[42]

Polybius, for his part, adopted a middle ground between these positions, agreeing with Crates on the essential historicity of the fabulous wanderings, but seeing them nevertheless as having been "exported" from their original Mediterranean setting.[43] In support of the latter point Polybius computed the sailing distance between the start of Odysseus's journey and the Pillars of Heracles, arguing that the "nine days' blow" that had initially driven him off course (*Od.* 12.82) could never have taken him so far—especially since the winds in question were "stormy" and did not blow consistently westward (34.4 =

[40] Crates, according to Strabo, defined Menelaus's voyage as a *periplous* from the Pillars of Heracles to India (1.2.31), which probably means a coasting voyage around the south of the *oikoumenē* but may conceivably imply a circumnavigation of the globe (following the calculations made by Lübbert, "Zur Charakteristik des Krates von Mallos," *Rh. Mus.* 11 [1857]: 434–39, and endorsed by Kretschmer 69; but see the objections raised by Berger [1903] 442–43).

[41] Other examples of this process include the emendation of a verse describing the Ethiopians, perhaps making it more likely that they dwelt on both sides of the equatorial Ocean (Geminus 16.26 [= Crates fr. 34a], Strabo 1.2.24–25 [= Crates fr. 34c]); and the interpretation of two verses describing Odysseus's return from the underworld (*Od.* 12.1–2) as a reference to the meridional branch of Ocean (Strabo 1.1.7 [= Crates fr. 35a]).

[42] Aulus Gellius 14.6.3 (= Crates fr. 31 Mette); Seneca *Ep.* 88.7, Plutarch *De facie* 983d.

[43] For Polybius's Homeric criticism see F. W. Walbank, "The Geography of Polybius," *Classica et Mediaevalia* 9 (1948): 168–73, and *Polybius* (Sather Classical Lectures 42, Berkeley, Los Angeles, London 1972) 125–27; Paul Pédech, "Polybe et la science de son temps," in *Polybe* (Entretiens Hardt, vol. 20, Geneva 1974) 54–59.

Strabo 1.2.17). This sort of painstaking calculation, we note, is typical of the geographic studiousness which Stoic critics brought to bear on the poem. Also typical is Polybius's identification of the *Odyssey*'s Scylla with the predatory swordfish found in and around the Straits of Messina (34.2–3 = Strabo 1.2.15–16). Having observed these swordfish preying on tunas that became trapped in the treacherous currents of the straits, Polybius was quite naturally put in mind of *Odyssey* 12, where Odysseus's ship is exposed to Scylla's ravages while passing through a narrow channel.[44] With such arguments Polybius was able to place most of the wanderings within the western Mediterranean and, as Strabo puts it, "dismantle the *exōkeanismos*" of the Alexandrians (1.2.18); although he must have also found that some episodes could not be made to "fit" his reading, since he conceded, according to Strabo, that "small elements of myth had been added" to the wanderings (34.2.9).

Strabo himself,[45] while accepting the system of intra-Mediterranean correlates devised by Polybius and others, directs most of his energies toward closing the loopholes formed by these "mythic elements." As Strabo notes in his response to Polybius (1.2.18), even the most exact mapping of the wanderings would still be open to attack so long as some episodes remained unaccounted for. Homer's direct references to Ocean, to Ogygia as the "navel of the sea," and to the isolation of the Phaeacians, for example, cannot possibly be made to fit the Sicilian scheme; as a result a more sophisticated model is needed

[44] The contradiction between this parallel and a second which Strabo goes on to describe—comparing Scylla not to the swordfish but to the fishermen who spear them—is difficult to resolve; perhaps Strabo has misunderstood Polybius in the second instance, and it is the ferocity of the swordfish as they are speared that forms the point of comparison.

[45] For Strabo's criticism of Homer, a vastly underexplored topic in literary history, see Berger (1903) 533–38; Aujac (1966) 31–34; K. J. Neumann, "Strabons Gesammturtheil über die homerische Geographie," *Hermes* 21 (1886): 134–41; D.M. Schenkeveld, "Strabo on Homer," *Mnemosyne* 29 (1976): 52–64; and most recently Anna Maria Biraschi, "Strabone e la difesa di Omero nei Prolegomena," in *Strabone: Contributi allo studio della personalità e dell'opera*, vol. 1, ed. F. Prontera (Perugia 1984). I am also indebted to Jack Winkler for sharing with me an unpublished manuscript on the topic.

which will accommodate these *muthoi* while still upholding the *Odyssey*'s overall factuality. The model which Strabo goes on to develop is in fact exceptionally complex, incorporating several different types of maneuver in an effort to cover every possible contingency. In some cases Strabo uses the poem's internal requirements to account for apparent errors; thus in explaining why the whirlpool Charybdis reverses its flow three times a day, instead of twice as one would expect of true tidal phenomena, Strabo looks to the context in which this "error" occurs, Circe's sailing instructions to Odysseus:

> If Homer said "thrice" even though the returning tide comes *twice* each day and night, he may be allowed to say it this way. We must not assume that this was said in ignorance of the real situation (*tēs historias*), but for the sake of fear and tragic emotion; for Circe adds a lot of these into her speech in order to scare Odysseus away [from making the journey], and therefore mixes in a portion of falsehood. (1.2.36)

In other cases, such as that of the famous "Ethiopians sundered in two," Strabo resorts instead to a very different type of solution, claiming in this instance that geologic changes taking place since Homer's time have rendered his data obsolete (1.2.32).

By far the most important of Strabo's interpretive dodges, however, is the notion that Homer deliberately included a few "myths" in his narrative of the wanderings simply to make the whole story more appealing to his audience. Strabo explains this technique at length in a crucial chapter of Book 1 (1.2.9):

> Since Homer devoted his stories to the principle of education, he largely occupied his mind with facts; "but he set therein" fiction (*pseudos*) as well, using the latter to win popularity and marshall the masses while still giving sanction to the former. "And just as when some workman pours gold overlay onto silver," so the poet set a mythical element into his true events, sweetening and ornamenting his style.

The technique outlined in this passage is illustrated by its own use of Homeric quotations as a "sweetener" to enliven a matter-of-fact text. The enticements that Strabo here calls *pseudos*, lies or inventions, were used by Homer to grab the attention of a wide audience, the better to impart the pragmatic truths which were his primary concern. With this versatile solution, we note, Strabo could account for any apparent error not covered by other explanations, and still retain Homer's reputation as a master scientist and teacher: *Pseudos*-filled passages could be understood purely as a vehicle for delivery of the *Odyssey*'s geographic lessons (2.1.11).

In framing this solution to the problem of the wanderings Strabo adopted as his "straw man" Eratosthenes of Cyrene, the greatest of the Alexandrian geographer-critics. Eratosthenes, as we have seen, treated the wanderings as an exemplary case of *psuchagōgia*, the capacity to entertain or to impart pleasure which he saw as poetry's objective. Strabo, by conceding that Homer had indeed had recourse to *psuchagōgia* as an embellishment to the wanderings, was in danger of lending support to Eratosthenes' position, as he no doubt realized. Hence Strabo begins his discussion by drawing a sharp ideological distinction between himself and his rival: Whereas Eratosthenes had claimed *psuchagōgia* as poetry's *sole* function, Strabo considers it only a *part*, and a subsidiary part at that (1.2.3). He then parodies Eratosthenes' approach by claiming that it makes poetry into "an old woman giving out fairy tales" (*graōdē mythologian apophainōn*, 1.2.3) and demotes the Phaeacian tales to the status of "idle nonsense" (*phluaria*, 1.2.19). In the vehemence of Strabo's attacks on Eratosthenes we can perceive how vital an issue the interpretation of the wanderings had become: In these four books of the *Odyssey* lay the primary line of attack against the utilitarian basis of poetry and of all mythic narratives, a line which Strabo, as a devoted Stoic (cf. 1.2.34), was determined to defend at all costs.[46]

Strabo further underscores his differences with the Alexandrians by appropriating one of their favorite critical terms, *exōkeanismos*. In Strabo's usage this becomes a positive attribute

[46] Strabo adds weight to his scornful assessment of Eratosthenes by portraying him as a lapsed Stoic (1.2.2).

rather than a shortcoming, denoting a "mythic embellishment of factual narrative" rather than a capitulation to out-and-out fantasy.[47] Unable to follow Polybius in denying that the *Odyssey* uses *exōkeanismos*, that is, Strabo instead shifts the word's emphasis so as to foreground Homer's intention (*proairesis*, 1.1.7) rather than the apparent qualities of the text. Despite this shift, however, the term *exōkeanismos* still implies for Strabo, as it had for his Alexandrian forebears, a movement toward the outer edges of a taxonomic "map," that is, toward the seat of literary *pseudos*. In fact we recall that Strabo uses a similarly spatial approach in his attacks on the Indian wonders authors, accusing Megasthenes, for example, of having "gone beyond the bounds" (*huperekpiptōn*) of legitimate writing in allowing his narrative to cross the river Hyphasis.

It is significant for our purposes that Strabo could apply the term *exōkeanismos* to a text which was actually, as he believed, situated not in Ocean but in the western Mediterranean. Just as Longinus adopts Ocean as a metaphor for the Homer of the *Odyssey*, we here see Ocean's name attached to the Phaeacian tales, the portion of the *Odyssey* most dominated by elements of *pseudos*. In fact Longinus, though seemingly unaware of the term *exōkeanismos*, evokes a similar link between the fabulous content of the *Odyssey* and its maritime setting: He refers to Homer's technique as a "wandering (*planos*) in the midst of the fabulous and unbelievable" (9.13), deliberately using a variant of a word (*planē*) which had become a virtual subtitle for Books 9–12 of the poem.[48] The result is a rather complex metatextual

[47] See Berger (1880) 27–28, (1903) 536. At 1.2.19 Strabo concedes that he agrees with Eratosthenes on Homer's removal of Mediterranean episodes into Ocean, but disagrees with him as to the intent of that strategy.

[48] So used frequently by Strabo. The episodes which Longinus goes on to cite as examples of *planos* derive almost entirely from the Phaeacian tales: Circe's transformation of Odysseus's crewmen into swine, Odysseus's survival of a ten-day voyage without food, and Aeolus's notorious bag of winds (which had also been singled out by Eratosthenes, as we have seen). Of all the episodes mentioned here only the slaying of the suitors comes from outside the Phaeacian tales; in addition, "the raising of Zeus by doves, like a nestling" refers to a myth which, properly speaking, takes place outside the tales, but is mentioned by Homer only within their boundaries (12.63).

pun similar in spirit to that of *exōkeanismos*: Homer's narrative rambles all over the map along with the ship it describes; both bard and hero are, in parallel senses, at sea.

Nor were Longinus and Strabo the only critics to play on this fusion of nautical and narratological levels of meaning. Among the ancient lexicographers who explained the proverbial phrase *Alkinou apologos* or "Phaeacian tales,"[49] all of whom list such equivalents as "babbling," "long-winded," and the like, we find one who gives the synonym *anermatistos* or "unballasted"[50]—envisioning the rambling course of a story as a listing and unmanageable vessel. The Antonine orator Aelius Aristides, in a speech we shall look at in the next section, jokingly tells a lying explorer: "Your mind (*noun*) has gone out beyond the Pillars" (*Orat.* 48 Dindorf 354.1), perhaps punningly implying that his ship (*naun*) had not gone there.

Among the canniest examples of this metatextual play, though, is contained in the *Argonautica* of Apollonius of Rhodes. Here we are dealing with an epic poem rather than a work of literary criticism, but we should note that the *Argonautica* shares many of the scholarly concerns of the Alexandrian audience for which it was written, including, above all, the question of the location of Odysseus's wanderings. In fact it is now recognized[51] that the route which Apollonius's heroes follow in their return from the Black Sea (*Argonautica* 4) consists

[49] Earliest known use in Plato, *Republic* 614b; for a survey of its usages see K. Tümpel, "*Alkinou apologos*," *Philologus* 52 (1893): 522–33. The phrase occasionally refers to the entire portion of the *Odyssey* set in Phaeacia, not just Books 9–12 (Aristotle *Poetics* 1455a7, *Rhetoric* 1417a13; Aelian *Varia Historia* 13.14).

[50] Pollux 2.6.120 Bekker. The definition is presented among a group of meanings all having to do with verbosity, and hence must be understood in a rhetorical context.

[51] Most recently by Charles Beye, *Epic and Romance in the Argonautica of Apollonius* (Carbondale and Edwardsville, Ill. 1982) esp. chap. 4, and Christina Dufner, "The *Odyssey* in the *Argonautica*: Reminiscence, Revision, Reconstruction" (diss. Princeton 1988; I am grateful to the author for supplying me with a copy of her work). See also Emile Delage, *La Géographie dans les Argonautiques d'Apollonius de Rhodes* (Paris 1930), and Lionel Pearson, "Apollonius of Rhodes and the Old Geographers," *AJP* 59 (1938): 443–59.

mainly of a reprise of those wanderings, in which Apollonius implicitly points out to his readers various places where Odysseus's adventures occurred. For example, in following the *Argo*'s course around Sicily, Apollonius is careful to note the locations of the Sirens (890–92), Aia (660–61), Clashing Rocks (922–23), and other Odyssean reference points, sometimes designating these with their Hellenistic toponyms so as to pinpoint their exact locale.

Given that a geographic commentary on *Odyssey* 9–12 underlies much of *Argonautica* 4, then, we note with great interest that in this book Apollonius refuses to let his heroes enter Ocean:

> Here a certain side channel led toward the gulf of Ocean, which they, lacking foresight, were about to enter; from thence they would not have been saved or returned home. But Hera, leaping down from the sky, shouted aloud from atop the Hercynian rock; all shuddered in fear of her, each man alike, and the air rang out harshly afar; backward they turned on account of the goddess, and knew the path (*oimon*) by which a homecoming would be fulfilled for the travellers. (4.637–44)

The willfulness[52] with which Apollonius here dismisses the possibility of entering Ocean is striking, especially since Ocean had been a viable enough route in previous *Argo* stories. Is the author here highlighting his refusal to include an *Odyssey*-style *exōkeanismos*?[53] This interpretation is made more likely by Apollonius's conspicuous use of *oimon* in the final line above, a word which can refer to the course of a poem as well as to a course of travel (as in Pindar's *oimon aoidēs*, *Ol.* 9.72); in fact Apollo-

[52] Delage (193–94, 219) comments on the abruptness of this and other transitions in the *Argonautica*. Beye sees this as an essential feature of Apollonius's narrative persona, which everywhere exhibits a consciousness of its own control over the story (13–15).

[53] A similar impulse seems to stand behind Apollonius's two references to the Hyperboreans (2.674–76, 4.611–17), both of which imply the existence of the race but rather pointedly keep them off the narrative stage. Apollonius seems not to have been interested in debunking such mythic entities so much as excluding them from his text. On the restriction of the Book 4 journey to mysterious but known parts of the *oikoumenē*, see Beye 147–48.

nius had used a variant form of the word, *oimē*, earlier in Book 4 to mean simply "song" (4.150). The *Argo*'s route is also, in a larger sense, the route of the poem itself, so that the ship's sudden retreat from the bourne of Ocean inevitably carries implications concerning the author's intentions for his work.

In saying this I do not mean to reduce the *Argo* to a "ship of narrative" which sends out metatextual signals at every port of call. However, the metaphor of the poem as sea voyage is well established in Greek literature from as early as the time of Hesiod (as a recent article has demonstrated).[54] When the poem in question actually *portrays* a sea voyage, as does the *Argonautica* or the *Odyssey*, that metaphor takes on added dimensions, encompassing the content of the work as well as its aesthetic pitch. Apollonius seems to have been aware of these added dimensions and to have used them as a way of taking part in the contemporary *exōkeanismos* debate. His deus ex machina introduction of Hera at this crucial moment, in fact, can be seen as a reimposition of Hellenistic critical norms, which demanded that epic narratives be kept within well-defined historical and geographic boundaries.

Pytheas, Euhemerus, and Others

The *Odyssey* was not the only *periplous* to undergo the kind of fact-finding critique we have been examining above; explorer's logs and travel tales of all kinds were similarly scrutinized by ancient geographer-critics. Such investigations are usually not considered under the heading of "literary criticism" when they are directed at sub-literary texts, but this distinction, as we have already noted, is an arbitrary one. In fact the terminology employed in geographic criticism consistently reveals its literary orientation: For instance a standard term applied to lying travel writers, "Bergaean," places such writers into the same generic

[54] Ralph M. Rosen, "Poetry and Sailing in Hesiod's *Works and Days*," *Classical Antiquity* 9 (1990): 99–113. For a prominent occurrence of the *topos* in Horace see Gregson Davis, "*Ingenii Cumba*? Literary Aporia and the Rhetoric of Horace's *O navis referent*," *Rh. Mus*. 132 (1989): 331–45.

category as Antiphanes of Berga, a Hellenistic fabulist.[55] Since the mendacity of Antiphanes' travelogue—which included an account of regions so cold that one's words froze in mid-air (Plutarch, *De profect. in virtute* 79a)—was obvious to all, the term "Bergaean" can virtually be translated as "purely fictional," establishing a domain of narrative in which the inventions otherwise scorned as *muthoi* or *pseudea* could be tolerated and even encouraged.

That the boundaries of this literary category were a source of continuing dispute, however, is clear from Strabo's *Geographies*, which here as elsewhere serves as a treasure-trove of the fragments of Hellenistic critical debate. In discussing Euhemerus of Messene, for example, the self-proclaimed discoverer of the island of Panchaea in the Indian Ocean, Strabo records that Eratosthenes had labeled Euhemerus a Bergaean.[56] But Polybius later contested this characterization and asserted that more credence should be given to Euhemerus than to Pytheas of Massilia, the discoverer of Thule (see chap. 4, pp. 157–58, above). Whereas Pytheas was alleged to have visited many lands and "explored as far as the end of the world," Euhemerus claimed only one discovery, and a nearer one at that. And in addition Pytheas, a poor man who (according to Polybius) lacked state funding, could scarcely have afforded to undertake the expedition he describes (34.5.7 = Strabo 2.4.2).[57] Polybius then capped off this critique by turning the "Bergaean" attack back on Eratosthenes, who, because he had reversed the

[55] On Antiphanes and his legacy see Otto Weinreich, "Antiphanes und Münchhausen: Das antike Lügenmärlein von den gefrornen Worten und sein Fortleben im Abendland," *Sitzungsberichte der Akademie der Wissenschaft in Wien* 220 (1942): 5–122; also G. Knaack, "Antiphanes von Berge," *Rh.Mus.* 61 (1906): 135–38.

[56] Strabo 1.3.1 (= I B 6 Berger), 2.4.2 (= I B 7). Eratosthenes here seems to have been carrying forward the project begun in his Odyssean criticism: the attempt to purge the geographic record of fables and inaccuracies.

[57] Walbank sees this argument as the product of Polybius's contempt for merchants (see "Geography of Polybius" [above, n. 43] 160–62, *Polybius* 126–27), but the passage in question seems to address only the issue of finance. Pytheas was "an *idiōtēs* and beyond that a poor man," so that his expedition could not have been funded by either public or private resources.

poles of truth and fiction—believing Pytheas while rejecting Euhemerus—had himself "gone beyond and out-babbled Antiphanes of Berga, leaving behind no further extreme of nonsense for his successors to attempt" (34.5.15).

If the categories of Bergaean fiction and truthful *periploi* were already becoming confused in Polybius's time, moreover, things get considerably murkier when we come to Strabo. Strabo, for his part, puts stock neither in Pytheas, whose accounts of Thule branded him as "the very worst of liars" (1.4.3),[58] nor in Euhemerus. Furthermore, he attacks as another Bergaean Eudoxus of Cyzicus (2.3.4–5), an explorer of the late second century B.C. who claimed to have attempted a circumnavigation of Africa.[59] Poseidonius had quoted Eudoxus's log as a truthful account of southerly latitudes,[60] but Strabo mounts a long and bitter challenge to Poseidonius on this point, barraging his predecessor with endless questions regarding the inconsistencies in Eudoxus's story. At length Strabo concludes by contemptuously lumping both Eudoxus *and* Poseidonius together with other notorious Bergaeans:

> All this comes close to the fictions of Pytheas, Euhemerus, and Antiphanes. But since lies are what they strive for we can forgive those men, as we forgive performing magicians (*thaumatopoiois*); but who could forgive a philosopher and an interpreter [i.e., Poseidonius], who is very nearly in first place among his competitors? No indeed, this was not well handled. (2.3.5)

As in Polybius's attack on Eratosthenes it is here the undiscriminating critic, Poseidonius, whom Strabo tars with the Ber-

[58] Strabo's extremely harsh treatment of Pytheas is in part explained by his polemics over the size of the *oikoumenē* in Book 2: Pytheas, by extending the *oikoumenē* as far north as Thule, had given support to the dimensions espoused by Strabo's rivals Eratosthenes and Hipparchus. The same motivation applies to his attack on Euthymenes, who had enlarged the boundaries of the *oikoumenē* in the other direction.

[59] For his story see Hennig (1936) 219–25, Cary and Warmington 123–28, Casson 118–20.

[60] Poseidonius fr. 49 in *Posidonius* (Part I: The Fragments), ed. L. Edelstein and I. G. Kidd (Cambridge Classical Texts and Commentaries 13, Cambridge 1972).

gaean brush for putting too much trust in dubious travelogues. But Strabo himself, we note, was hardly innocent on this score; indeed modern critics have turned his own words here back against him, in response to his stalwart attempts to map the events of Homer's *Odyssey*.[61]

Nor is this paradox the strangest twist in Strabo's zealous attempt to establish a firm boundary between truthful and Bergaean narratives. Directly after his attack on Eudoxus, Strabo suddenly changes tack and introduces a tale he seems inclined to believe, Plato's myth of Atlantis. Supporting Poseidonius now, Strabo argues that Plato's assertion of the factuality of his story, "the island of Atlantis is not an invention,"[62] should be accepted in preference to an unnamed critic's statement to the contrary—which had compared Plato's all-too convenient sinking of Atlantis to Homer's obliteration of the Achaean wall at the beginning of *Iliad* 12 (2.3.6).[63] Strabo's vehement opposition to such an approach probably has as much to do with his reverence for Homer as with his interpretation of Plato; indeed he seems to be once again wrestling with the shade of Eratosthenes here, since this anonymous critique of the Atlantis legend strongly recalls the Eratosthenic theory that the *Odyssey* adopted a distant setting *dia to eukatapseuston*, "because it was easy to lie about." For Strabo such cowardly concealments were the hallmark of third-rate authors;[64] it was unthinkable that writers of Homer's or Plato's gravity would make use of them (except, on occasion, for the sake of adding spice).

Strabo's deeply stratified and hierarchical approach to travel texts—allowing him to place acknowledged masters like

[61] E.g., Thomson 321, Bunbury 1.66.

[62] Probably recalling the statement of Socrates at *Timaeus* 26e, as noted by H. L. Jones in the Loeb edition of Strabo (vol. 1, Cambridge, Mass. 1917) 390 n. 1. The historicity of the Atlantis myth was an article of faith among the Neoplatonists; see, for example, Proclus, *Commentaire sur le Timée* (ed. A. J. Festugière, Paris 1966) 1:234–38. Marsilio Ficino would later refer to the story as *valde mirabilis, sed omnino verus*.

[63] See the note by Jones ad loc., who incorrectly assumes that the *ho plasas* under attack in this statement is Solon rather than Plato.

[64] As we have seen earlier, in his handling of the Indian wonders texts; cp. 11.6.4, for example (chap. 3, pp. 96–98, above).

Homer and Plato beyond the possibility of *pseudos*—also helps explain his characterization of Bergaean writers as *thaumatopoioi*, "wonder-workers," in the passage quoted above. The word has here been translated "magicians" but seems to have referred to various types of professional performers, including the famous shadow-players who entertain the residents of Plato's cave (*Republic* 514b; cf. 602d). Such artists can be "forgiven" by their audiences because all are aware of their intent to deceive; similarly the meaningless marvels of the Bergaeans are permissible so long as they are accepted as such and not allowed to intrude on the serious business of understanding the earth. What Poseidonius did in elevating Eudoxus above the Bergaean stratum, however, was a crime against the literary scale of value, mirroring Eratosthenes' sin of demoting the *Odyssey* to the stature of "an old woman spreading fairy tales." In both cases the geographer's inability to distinguish truth from fiction results in a conflation of high and low forms of literature, and a collapse of the critical canon.

One other Greek author and critic, the second-century A.D. rhetorician Aelius Aristides, helps illustrate how much was at stake in this distinction between the *Odyssey* and other, less substantive *periploi*. In his oration about the source of the Nile (no. 48 Dindorf), Aristides conducts an examination of a *periplous* attributed to Euthymenes, an explorer who claimed to have rounded southern Africa and to have located the Nile's source in a huge freshwater sea. Aristides refutes Euthymenes' account at great length, even to the point of surveying the entire *oikoumenē* to show that no such freshwater sea can possibly exist. Having completed this hydrographic tour Aristides pauses to ask his audience: "But what's the relevance of all this? For I'm not idly spinning an *Alkinou apologos*" (354.20).[65] The conspicuous reference to the Phaeacian tales situates the entire discussion within the context we have examined above: the problems created by ambiguous texts which derived from "the realm no

[65] Tümpel ("*Alkinou apologos*," above, n. 49) notes the ironic jab at Euthymenes contained in Aristides' use of this phrase (513).

one can see," and the need to pin down the truth status of such texts once and for all.

Indeed, the vehemence with which Aristides attacks Euthymenes' efforts to cloak his fictions in the guise of fact reveals that he, like Strabo, regards this as a literary sin of the first magnitude. Debunking Euthymenes for filling his false sea with crocodiles and hippopotamuses, in an effort to make it seem more plausible as the source of the Nile, Aristides retorts:

> The fictional nature [of the dubious log] has been exposed mostly by this, and Euthymenes has been shown a braggart. For he did not see the crocodiles and hippopotamuses, and then describe them, but, in order that his other narratives might seem more like the truth, he added them in, taking refuge in familiar things and trying to win belief for his fictions with the help of another fiction tailored close to the truth. But as for me, I feel that it is better to hand over these kinds of stories and fables to wet-nurses, for them to read to little children when they need to go to sleep; since fresh-water seas, hippopotamuses, and a sea which flows into a river, and such things, are the very charms of sleep. (356.15–357.2)

Interestingly enough, Aristides sees nothing particularly objectionable in the fictions themselves, which, when understood as such, can be treated as harmless "old wives' tales" (compare Strabo's *thaumatopoioi*). But when such fictions begin to intrude into the realm of factual narrative, Aristides must intervene to redraw the boundary line.

However Aristides, again like Strabo, could not allow the process of distinguishing truth from fiction to challenge the essential framework of the literary canon, and thus while he scoffs at Euthymenes here for having created a mythical sea he will not permit the same critique to be mounted against Homer. In his *Roman Oration* Aristides instead scoffs at the scoffer—in this case Herodotus—and comes valiantly to the rescue of the Homeric conception of Ocean:

> And as for Ocean, which some early prose-writers claimed did not at all exist, and did not surround the globe, but that poets had invented its name and included it in their verse in order to impress,

> you [Romans] have so thoroughly explored this element that not even the island in it has eluded you. (*Orat.* 26 Dindorf, 28)

With the conquest of Britain, Aristides claims, the Romans had at last confirmed the poets' vision of Ocean, and had given the lie to those who had impudently called it into question. Herodotus's daring act of critical fission, which first split Greek poetry into separate spheres of truth and invention, became a badge of shame when it was seen to undermine the authority of a Homer.

The Fictions of Exploration

In all the material we have examined thus far we have seen struggles over ambiguous explorer texts, those which could be categorized either as factual or fictional narratives. Different critics attempted to situate these texts in one category or the other; Strabo and his Stoic brethren resolutely dragged the *Odyssey* into the historical camp and banished the logs of Pytheas and Eudoxus, while Eratosthenes and Aristarchus did just the reverse. In no case, however, were any such texts allowed to remain in middle ground, except insofar as Strabo and Polybius admitted that Homer had made use of a few inventions to enliven the wanderings of Odysseus. In fact the very idea of a text which could not be securely placed in either camp, or which disguised itself in order to move from one to the other, caused deep distress among many of these critics, and led to strident efforts at reimposing a firm boundary between truth and fiction.

However, there were others in later antiquity who perceived the intermediate nature of these texts not as a problem needing to be resolved but as an opportunity waiting to be exploited. It is no coincidence, for example, that several of the most innovative works of prose fiction in the second century A.D. took the form of explorer's logs. I refer in particular to Lucian's *True Histories* and Antonius Diogenes' *Wonders beyond Thule*, both of which consist of long "voyages" into a realm which has been variously designated as Menippean satire, comic fiction, or even science fiction.[66] It is as if the authors of these two texts were taking advantage of the license Strabo had granted to Bergaean writings, the right to invent *thaumata* candidly without incurring critical disdain. At the same time, however, both seem aware that the explorer text cannot ever be wholly relegated to the ranks of fiction, and that the very act of composing a fabulous *periplous* works to undermine the rigid *historia/muthos* distinctions on which much of ancient criticism was based.

Before turning to these two fictions of exploration, however, let us look briefly at another text which similarly plays off of the ambiguous status of the *periplous*. Plutarch's *On the Face of the Moon* is not a work of fiction per se but a philosophic dialogue, the ostensible purpose of which is to explain in scientific terms the seemingly anthropomorphic markings on the lunar surface. However, Plutarch ends this work by abandoning both his dialogue format and the scientific approaches it contains, and instead introduces an exotic traveler's tale (in imitation of the structure of Platonic dialogues like the *Phaedo* and *Republic*).[67] In fact this finale diverges so widely from the discussion that precedes it that Plutarch attributes it to a nameless "stranger," rather than to any of the more sober-minded participants in the dialogue; and that stranger is further described as a "poet" (*poiētēs*), who launches into his mysterious tale by way of a quotation from the *Odyssey* (7.244):[68]

> "*An island, Ogygia, lies far away in the sea*, a five days' run off from Britain for a ship sailing west; and there are three other islands sep-

[66] Of course sea voyages were also a standard feature of the so-called erotic romances (those dealing principally with the separation of a pair of lovers), but function there chiefly as a plot vehicle rather than as the governing model of the literary form. The voyages of the erotic romances also confine themselves to the known world instead of venturing into the unknown, a distinction noted by Cary and Warmington (244).

[67] The connections with Plato have been explored by W. Hamilton, "The Myth in Plutarch's *De Facie*," *CQ* 28 (1934): 24–30. See also the introduction to the work by A. O. Prickard, *Plutarch on the Face of the Moon* (London 1911), and the painstakingly thorough notes by Harold Cherniss in the Loeb edition (*Plutarch's Moralia*, vol. 12 [Cambridge, Mass. 1957]).

[68] On the text of this sentence see Harold Cherniss, "Notes on Plutarch's *De Facie in Orbe Lunae*," *CP* 46 (1951): 148–49 and n. 79.

arated as far from it as they are from each other, situated near the place of the summer sunset." (941a)

The story which follows describes the stranger's sojourn on the island of Cronus, where he learned occult truths about the nature of the moon from a sect of semidivine priests. But what chiefly concerns us is the *Odyssey* quotation that introduces this story, by means of which Plutarch compares his "poet" narrator to Odysseus first broaching the story of his wanderings while among the Phaeacians. However this brief evocation of the *Odyssey* then takes an abrupt and un-Homeric turn, as Plutarch gives a numerically exact set of coordinates for the Odyssean Ogygia and other lands beyond it.[69] It is as if one were to quote Shakespeare's descriptions of Prospero's island in *The Tempest*—and then offhandedly supply the precise latitude and longitude of the place. Plutarch deliberately fuses the language of poetry and science, emphasizing perhaps the permeability of the boundary between the two: If on the one hand the *Odyssey* can be read as straightforward geography, then on the other there is nothing to stop a *poiētēs* from illuminating the nature of the moon.[70]

More could be said regarding the ending of *On the Face of the Moon*, but since we are here concerned with narrative literature rather than dialogue I shall pass on to a text that belongs more properly to that category. The late Greek novel *Wonders beyond Thule* now deserves our attention, even though its text has been

[69] In fact, the directions he here supplies are suspiciously similar to those Pytheas had given for Thule, an island situated at "a *six* days' sail from Britain, toward the North" (Strabo 1.4.2 = fr. 6a Mette, my emphasis). Whether the author intends to put us in mind of Pytheas in particular is open to question, but the larger point lies in his juxtaposition of this precise, *periplous*-style language with the *Odyssey* quote that precedes it.

[70] If Plutarch's intent in thus mixing *periploi* was to confuse the boundaries of science and fiction, he succeeded better than he could have hoped. In one of the more bizarre episodes in the annals of interpretation the astronomer Johannes Kepler, after translating and annotating the *Face of the Moon* as part of his own selenological studies, became convinced that Plutarch's Ogygia corresponded to Greenland and the island of Cronus to Hispaniola. See my "Lucian and Plutarch as Sources for Kepler's *Somnium*," *Classical and Modern Literature* 9 (1989): 97–107.

almost entirely lost, and even though its author, Antonius Diogenes, remains unknown to all but the most specialized of classical scholars. This is to be regretted, since the remains of the lost work—which consist principally of a plot summary set down by the Byzantine Patriarch Photius in the ninth century A.D.[71]—reveal it to have been one of the most daring and inventive literary efforts of all Greco-Roman antiquity. Fortunately though, the notes Photius took on his reading of the *Wonders beyond Thule* are extensive enough to convey a fairly clear picture of what we are missing, and to allow us to discuss the work in some depth. It is clear from these notes that Diogenes, like Plutarch in *On the Face of the Moon*, used the explorer's log as a way of mediating between the poles of geography and fiction, or perhaps as a way of questioning whether any real distinction could be drawn between the two categories.

The first feature of the *Apista huper Thoulēn*, or *Wonders beyond Thule*, that Photius presents us with is one of the most telling: its title. This novel was defined not by its central pair of lovers, as are most of the erotic romances—*Chaereas and Callirhoe*, *Leucippe and Clitophon*—but instead by the teratological "wonders" or *apista* that dangled like exotic beads from every thread of its plot line.[72] In fact this unique title brings the work more into the tradition of paradoxograpy, the genre which specialized in collecting pseudoscientific exotica, than that of the novel; it is worth noting that one such paradoxographical col-

[71] Cod. 166, pp. 140–49 in vol. 2 of R. Henry's Budé edition of the *Bibliothèkè* (Paris 1960); translation and commentary forthcoming shortly in *Fragments of the Ancient Greek Novels*, J. J. Winkler and Susan Stephens (I am indebted to these authors for showing me a preliminary version of their work). Other analyses by Rohde (1914) 250–87; O. Schissel von Fleschenberg, *Novellenkränze Lukians* (Halle 1912) 101–9; L. Di Gregorio, "Sugli *Apista Hyper Thoulēn* di Antonio Diogene," *Aevum* 42 (1968): 199–211; Klaus Reyhl, *Antonios Diogenes* (diss. Tübingen 1969); and J. R. Morgan, "Lucian's *True Histories* and the *Wonders beyond Thule* of Antonius Diogenes," *CQ* 35 (1985): 475–90.

[72] See Thomas Hägg, *The Novel in Antiquity* (Berkeley and Los Angeles 1983) 120: "*The Marvels beyond Thule* could never have been titled *Deinias and Dercyllis*."

lection, compiled by Isigonus of Nicaea in the first century B.C., was similarly entitled *Apista*.[73]

Of course the second element of Diogenes' title, *beyond Thule*, might seem more typical of an erotic romance in that it situates the narrative in a particular place—just as Heliodorus's *Theagenes and Charicleia* was also known in antiquity as the *Ethiopica* or *Ethiopian Tale*, and other romances like Xenophon's *Ephesiaca* and Iamblichus's *Babyloniaca* were named for the central locale of their action. But this superficial similarity also helps highlight ways in which Diogenes' novel was different. For his title does not evoke the grand, ages-old cities of the East but the raw oceanic frontier of the West—a realm associated not with the pageant of history but with the future-directed progress of navigation and scientific inquiry. To venture beyond Thule, as both Vergil and Seneca had speculated in contemplating the westward march of empire, would constitute a final, climactic step in human social evolution (see chap. 4, pp. 158–60, 170–71).[74] For a *novel* to venture beyond Thule, moreover, would break the frame of the cartographic scheme of literary criticism examined above: Diogenes seems to have promised his readers the ultimate *exōkeanismos*, a journey into as-yet uncharted realms of fictional invention.[75]

The program implied in this title is confirmed when we discover that the novel indeed had an exploring scientist, one Deinias of Arcadia, as its central character. The very first event recounted in Photius's plot summary (109a13–14) is the embarkation of Deinias in pursuit of scientific knowledge, *kata zētēsin historias*, accompanied by his son (or perhaps slave) Demochares. This research expedition evidently took Deinias through the Black Sea and north to Scythia, where his progress was impeded by Arctic cold; then around the southern edge of

[73] See A. Giannini, "Studi sulla paradossografia Greca," Part II, *Acme* 17 (1964): 124–25 and n. 150.

[74] The link between Vergil's *ultima Thule* and Diogenes' novel is provided by Servius, who refers to the *Wonders beyond Thule* in his note to *Georgics* 1.30.

[75] The significance of the title is assessed somewhat differently by Winkler and Stephens, who see the name "Thule" as inextricably linked to Pytheas of Massilia; hence *Apista huper Thoulēn* could be paraphrased as "Wonders surpassing those of Pytheas."

the world to Thule in the far West.[76] The latter part of his journey, we note, would have overlapped to a large degree with that of Pytheas of Massilia, the controversial figure who claimed to have discovered Thule—a circumstance that we shall return to shortly.

While stopping over on Thule (that is, while using it as a *stathmon*, 109a24, on the way to places beyond), Deinias meets Dercyllis, a noblewoman from Tyre, who has arrived there with her brother Mantinias after fleeing from an evil Egyptian sorcerer named Paapis. At this point the *Wonders beyond Thule* takes a hiatus from its exploratory theme and seems about to become a more traditional romance, as Deinias begins to court Dercyllis "in the time-honored way of love" (109a26). However, the courtship of hero and heroine proves to be only a frame for further explorations of exotic locales, as Dercyllis recounts to Deinias her travels throughout the *oikoumenê* and the marvels that she, or her brother, or their traveling companions, have seen along the way (a long flashback which apparently occupied almost all the rest of the novel). I shall not attempt to summarize these inset tales here, since that task would require quoting in full the already lengthy summary provided by Photius; but it should be said that each one involves some bit of pseudoscientific lore, allowing the Tyrian characters to encounter fabulous animals, monstrous races of men, and bizarre properties of springs, rivers, winds, and weather.[77] (Dercyllis's tales also brought various mystical and semidivine figures into the *Wonders beyond Thule*, including the philosopher Pythagoras, but this element goes outside our present concerns.)[78]

[76] Such, at least, seems to be the implication of Photius's summary description, *kuklôi tên ektos perielthontes thalassan*, "rounding the outer sea in a circle" (see Rohde 259–60 n.4); although the same words could easily describe a voyage around the globe from east to west, the opposite *periplous* to that which Crates attributed to Menelaus in *Odyssey* 4.

[77] Indeed, some episodes seem to have been set up in such a way as to focus on these wonders rather than on the experiences and development of the central human characters. The episode of Dercyllis's visit to the Acutanoi, accompanied by her brothers' friends Ceryllus and Astraeus, provides a good example of how Diogenes has used *paradoxa* as the nuclei of his plot.

[78] The Pythagorean element of the *Wonders beyond Thule* has been overemphasized by critics, especially Reitzenstein (*Hellenistische Wundererzählungen*

Eventually Dercyllis, still narrating the tales of her adventures to explorer-turned-suitor Deinias, reaches a point at which all of her entourage has arrived on Thule, including—unfortunately—the evil sorcerer Paapis. At this point the action moves rapidly toward resolution: Paapis is assassinated after he puts a spell on Dercyllis and her brother, turning them into zombies who live by night and fall into a deathlike trance by day; the pair then undergo further misadventures in their trance state before being freed by Azoulis, a member of Deinias's crew (who conveniently discovers a counterspell among the dead sorcerer's effects). Dercyllis and her party all return happily to Tyre, where they are reconciled with the family they left behind and prepare to live happily ever after. However, Deinias does not, as we might have expected, accompany the cast back to Tyre—though he does get there in the novel's final scene, as we shall see. But first he separates from the Tyrians in order to resume the quest for "knowledge" that had begun back in Book 1, a quest in which Thule, we recall, had formed only a "stopover." Here at last (as Photius impatiently observes, 110b16–19) Diogenes makes good on the promise of his title, *Wonders beyond Thule*; up to this point all his material, though exotic in the extreme, had derived from within the *oikoumenē*.

The purpose of this final, other-world voyage has been one of the principal cruxes in modern interpretations of the *Wonders beyond Thule*, in particular because the episode had accidentally gotten tangled with a similar voyage described in Lucian's *True Histories*.[79] Now that the two works have been effectively

[Leipzig 1906] 17–18, 31) and Reinhold Merkelbach (*Roman und Mysterientum* 225–33); that it is better seen as a single theme among many, rather than as the raison d'être of the novel, has been demonstrated by Wolfgang Fauth in "Astraios und Zamolxis über Spuren pythagoreischer Aretalogie im Thule-Roman des Antonius Diogenes," *Hermes* 106 (1978): 220–41.

[79] The suggestion that the *Wonders beyond Thule* was a principal target of the parody of the *True Histories* goes back to Photius (111b32–34) and to a Byzantine scholium on *True Histories* 2.12 (Marcianus 840, fol. 47a; see the Testimonia section of the Winkler-Stephens *Fragments*). It has attained a kind of reductio ad absurdum in the work of K. Reyhl (above n. 71), who attempts to reconstruct much of the lost novel based on supposed Lucianic parodies of its episodes.

disengaged, however,[80] we can begin to consider this voyage beyond Thule as an integral part of the *Wonders beyond Thule*, perhaps even as its raison d'être. As Photius describes this episode,

> Deinias claimed here to have seen what the devotees of astronomy speculate about, for instance that there are some men who live beneath the great bear, and that the night can be a month long, or more or less, or even six months, or even a year. . . . And he reports having seen other things of that sort, tribes of men and other curiosities, which he says no one had seen, nor heard of, nor even imagined before. And, most incredible of all, he claims that in his voyage north he approached the moon, as if towards some exceedingly pure version of Earth,[81] and there saw the kinds of things you might expect from such a fictionalizer of outlandish fables. Then the Sybil recovered her power of prophecy from Carmanes [one of Deinias's men]; and after that each man wished his own wishes, and while all the others got what they wished for, Deinias said that *he* awoke to find himself in Tyre, at the Temple of Heracles, and that arising from there he met Dercyllis and her brother. (110b39–111a11)

What is immediately striking about these adventures is the way they progress from science to out-and-out fantasy as Deinias moves further from the shores of Thule. Initially his experiences closely parallel those of his predecessor in Arctic exploration, Pytheas of Massilia: His observations about the extended length of Arctic nights, for example, or the inhabitation of the septentrional zone, only recapitulate the discoveries published in Pytheas's *Concerning the Ocean*[82] (which partly ex-

[80] Thanks to John Morgan's superb article (above, n. 71).

[81] I have given the most literal sense of Photius's phrase *gēn katharotatēn*, for which several possible meanings have been proposed: "bright," "bare," "genuine." My translation also preserves the ambiguity in Photius's sentence as to whether Deinias actually landed *on* the moon, or only reached a point on earth from which the moon seemed closer. The run of the sentence easily admits either interpretation.

[82] Strabo reports Pytheas as the source for "men living under the Great Bear" (2.5.8), a notion that was otherwise deemed impossible due to extreme cold (cf. Herodotus 5.9). The astronomic phenomena described by Deinias were also uniquely Pythean: Apparently Pytheas had been credited (though proba-

plains Photius's remark that Deinias had here confirmed the suppositions of the astronomers). After Deinias's ship carries him beyond the ambit of Pytheas his reports seem to have become more fantastic, though still remaining within credible bounds: At least, Photius quotes him as describing "things never seen, nor heard of, nor fashioned by the imagination," without implying that they also surpassed belief. At the final stage, however, when Deinias lands on or near the moon—the epitome's language allows for either interpretation—a pitch of strangeness is attained which causes Photius to throw up his hands in despair and refuse to summarize further. According to the critical terms we looked at earlier, that is, the narrative has first approached the threshold of *exōkeanismos* (by way of Pytheas's log, itself an ambiguous and much-debated text), then attained it, and finally plunged without reserve into the realm of fabulous invention.

Diogenes' intentions in thus plotting the *Wonders beyond Thule* along a parabolic course are further revealed by an epistle that concluded the novel,[83] in which, according to Photius, the author candidly explained his creation to a friend named Faustinus. Here Diogenes reportedly identified himself as a *poiētēs kōmōidias palaias*, "a poet of the Old Comedy;"[84] yet he claimed that "even if he wrote wonders and lies (*apista kai pseudē*), he nevertheless had support for most of his fables from ancient authors" (111a35–38), and to prove the point cited the names

bly inaccurately) with reports of nights lasting six months (Pliny *Hist. Nat.* 2.71.187, 4.16.104; Geminus, *El. Astr.* 6.9.22) and even, by one source at least, year-long nights (Cosmas Indicopleustes 116d; see Berger [1903] 343–44 and n. 1). The further fact that Pytheas seems to have discovered the true cause of tides (cf. Plutarch, *De plac. phil.* 3.17 [987b]) places him quite prominently in the background of earlier episodes of the *Wonders beyond Thule*, such as one in which Astraeus's eyes are said to wax and wane with the phases of the moon (Photius 109b25–33).

[83] At least, Photius places it after the conclusion of the narrative in his summary; but some scholars would prefer to situate it at the beginning of the novel.

[84] There has been some dispute over the meaning of this term; Rohde (251 n. 2) sees it as a periphrasis for "free invention in prose," but there is no parallel for the use of *palaias kōmōidias* to mean anything but what it seems to mean. See di Gregorio 199–200 n. 1.

of the sources for each book alongside the narrative itself. The resulting formulation of the novel's relationship to the truth—in which an author who claims to be a comic poet cites a battery of scientific authorities for his fictional creations—appears to have been fraught with paradox; and that paradox is redoubled when we later discover, thanks to an offhand remark made by Photius, that the "bibliography" of sources included none other than Antiphanes of Berga (112a5–6). Diogenes seems to have pressed home the range of possibilities inherent in the explorer text, forcing the reader to hold in counterpoise both the Pythean and Bergaean ends of the spectrum—much as Plutarch, as we have seen, did in the finale of the dialogue *On the Face of the Moon*.

In both the *Wonders beyond Thule* and *On the Face of the Moon*, that is, the story's departure from the realm of fact takes the form of an actual *exōkeanismos*, a merging of nautical and narratological voyages of the kind that we looked at earlier in connection with the *Odyssey*'s Phaeacian tales. By adopting the form of the explorer's log, both Plutarch and Diogenes situate their texts in the very middle ground between truth and fiction that Strabo and other critics had worked so hard to eliminate.

To this pair of late Greek forays into the "Ocean of story," moreover, we may add a third, the *True Histories* of Lucian of Samosata. Let us conclude with a brief look at this celebrated and influential text, in which the explorer's log can be said to have achieved its grandest literary apotheosis.

Lucian begins his *True Histories*[85] much as Diogenes had ended *Wonders beyond Thule*, by openly discussing his intentions for his work and by telling his audience how to receive it.

[85] The most useful scholarship on the *True Histories* includes some interesting new approaches: S. C. Fredericks, "Lucian's *True History* as SF," *Science Fiction Studies* 3 (1973): 49–60; Roy Arthur Swanson, "The True, the False, and the Truly False: Lucian's Philosophical Science Fiction," ibid. 3 (1976): 228–39; and Massimo Fusillo, "Le Miroir de la Lune: *L'Histoire vraie* de Lucien de la satire à l'utopie," *Poétique* 73 (1988): 109–35. For more traditional approaches see also the article by Morgan cited above (n. 71); and the discussions by J. Bompaire: "Comment lire les *Histoires Vraies* de Lucien?" *Hommages à Henri le Bonniec*, ed. D. Porte and J.-P. Néraudau (Collection Latomus, vol. 201, Brussels 1988); and chap. 3 of *Lucien écrivain* (Paris 1958).

In a prologue addressed to his readers he advises that his text should be used only as a refreshing interlude between their encounters with serious literature, so that it will provide "mere entertainment" (*psilēn psuchagōgian*, 1.2). And if such "light reading" should seem too trivial for his well-educated audience, Lucian promises to sprinkle in learned parodies of familiar classics so as to provide a minimal educative function at the same time. Above all, the reader must not look for any record of the truth, for this will not be found: Lucian confesses that every word he is about to say is a lie, and that he will describe things he has neither seen nor heard of, which do not and cannot exist (1.4; cp. Photius's report of the wonders beyond Thule, "things no one had seen, nor heard of, nor imagined before").

In this way Lucian begins by demoting himself to the stature of Strabo's *thaumatopoioi*, the entertainers who escape censure because they openly admit their use of fictions. But this seemingly unprepossessing message takes a different turn when Lucian, concerned over the unorthodoxy of his decision to compose *pseudea*, begins discussing his literary models (1.3):[86]

> Ctesias the Cnidian wrote about the land of the Indians and the regions near there, compiling things he neither saw himself nor heard from anyone's report. And Iambulus, too, recorded many marvels regarding places in the great sea; he's recognized by everyone as an inventor of lies, yet nevertheless the weave of his composition is not unpleasing. . . . But the captain of these men and chief preceptor of such foolish nonsense is Homer's Odysseus, who re-

[86] That this list contains a series of literary models, and *not* the authors Lucian intends to spoof in his learned parodies, becomes clear as soon as one removes the *hoion* or *hōn* which have improperly been inserted by most editors prior to the name Ctesias. The textual problem which led to this emendation is much better handled in Jerram's text (Oxford 1879, recently reprinted), which deletes the relative pronoun *hos* after *Knidios* (treating it as a dittography of the last syllable). If the figures mentioned here were indeed examples of the parodic targets Lucian had been discussing just prior, he would be ruining the sport of his own game; he tells us that he will not give away the names of his targets but that we must guess them ourselves. See Joseph Dane, *Parody: Critical Concepts Versus Literary Practice, Aristophanes to Sterne* (Norman, Okla., and London 1988) 76.

> lated to Alcinous's people the episodes of the enslavement of the winds, and the one-eyed men, and the savages, and various wild men. . . . With many similar things that hero enchanted (*eterateusato*) the provincial Phaeacians.

Here Lucian has sided more with Eratosthenes than with Strabo, blithely tossing the Phaeacian tales of the *Odyssey* into the category of Bergaean or self-evident fictions. Far from reinforcing the traditional literary hierarchy now, he instead pulls its most revered figure down to his own level of "foolish nonsense" (though he judiciously assigns the blame for that nonsense to Odysseus rather than to Homer). In suggesting that the Phaeacian tales were only so much *terateia* Lucian effectively pulls the rug out from under the Stoics and their precious distinction between *historia* and *muthos*. At the same time he clears some running room for his own fictional endeavor, which now has a respectable tradition behind it rather than a collection of worthless Bergaeans.

With his audience thus attuned to the complex ambiguities of the explorer text, Lucian enters into the narrative portion of the *True Histories*, the story of a voyage outside the Pillars of Heracles and across the Atlantic. Like Deinias's expedition in the *Wonders beyond Thule* this voyage has purely scientific goals, and ambitious ones at that: "The cause and purpose of my departure," declares Lucian's narrator, "was my restless search for understanding and my eagerness for new experiences, and my desire to know what the end of Ocean is and what people dwell on the other side" (1.5). These questions were not idly chosen but, as we have seen in chapter 4, represent the most puzzling and insoluble mysteries of Roman-era geography; in fact the speculative nature of such questions had caused Strabo, Pliny, and other empiricists to exclude them from serious discussion (see chap. 4, pp. 131–32). In framing his fabulous voyage as a quest for the answers to these questions, Lucian again calls attention to the region of overlap between exploration and fiction. At a certain point, he suggests, any version of what the world is like beyond the *oikoumenē* amounts to an imaginative construct, as Herodotus had initially pointed out in connection with Ocean; the *True Histories* differs only in degree, not in kind, from other accounts of the "invisible" realm, even from those which pretended to strict scientific authority.

The ship which carries Lucian's narrator into this invisible realm lands him in a vast array of places, including the one locale which would later become an obligatory landfall for fabulous voyages: the new world in the moon.[87] We need not however follow his progress through these various lands, since once his narrative has passed into the realm of *exōkeanismos* its essential importance, from the perspective of this study, is already clear enough. In sending his narrative out beyond the *oikoumenē* Lucian magnifies to immense proportions the ambiguities inherent in the explorer's log, revealing how easily it allows truth and fiction to change places with one another. Only in a fluid and fungible medium of this type could he find a safe haven for pure, imaginative prose fiction, a genre which was otherwise neither recognized nor condoned by ancient literary critics.

[87] For the increasing importance of the moon as an objective of ancient and early modern fabulous voyages, see the two surveys by Marjorie Nicolson, *A World in the Moon* (Smith College Studies in Language and Literature 17.2, 1936); and *Voyages to the Moon* (N.Y. 1948).

Epilogue

After Columbus

THE ANCIENT CONCEPTION of the world and of the place of the *oikoumenē* within it changed irrevocably after 1492, a change whose scope and implications still inspire awe exactly half a millennium later. The history of this change has recently been documented by Edmundo O'Gorman[1] and others; it is not my intention to contribute materially to it here, since to do so would go well beyond the scope of the current study. Still there is one aspect of the Renaissance geographic revolution which demands comment in a book devoted to antiquity: the degree to which ancient geographic myths and fictions, the narratives we have looked at in the previous five chapters, attained new life when read against the background of the voyages of exploration.

Indeed, nearly every one of the texts examined in the foregoing study could be traced through sixteenth-century metamorphoses, which saw them transformed into sources of insight about the new American world. Three legends in particular—Plato's myth of Atlantis, the pseudo-Aristotelian story of a Carthaginian landfall in the West, and Seneca's "pro-

[1] Edmundo O'Gorman, *The Invention of America: An Inquiry Into the Historical Interpretation of the New World and the Meaning of its History* (Bloomington, Ind. 1961), and *La Idea del Descubrimento de América: Historia de esa interpretacion y crítica de sus fundamentos*[2] (Mexico City 1976). See also Thomas Goldstein, "Florentine Humanism and the Vision of the New World," *Congresso Internacional de História dos Descobrimentos* 4 (Lisbon 1961): 195–207; in the same volume (347–86), W.G.L. Randles, "Le Nouveau Monde, l'Autre Monde, et la pluralité des mondes"; W. H. Tillinghast, "The Geographical Knowledge of the Ancients considered in relation to the Discovery of America," in *Narrative and Critical History of America*, vol. 1, ed. J. Winsor (Cambridge, Mass. 1889) 1–58; and the authoritative volume by Konrad Kretschmer, *Die Entdeckung Amerikas in Ihrer Bedeutung für die Geschichte des Weltbildes* (Berlin 1892).

phetic" lines in the *Medea* (375–79) about the discovery of *novos orbes*—certainly played the biggest part in Renaissance attempts to understand the meaning of the new discoveries.[2] But in addition Homer's *Odyssey*, Vergil's *Aeneid* and *Georgics*, Plutarch's *On the Face of the Moon*, Cicero's Dream of Scipio, Theopompus' legend of Meropis, and many other texts were carefully reexamined during this period, in an effort to situate Columbus's New World within the venerable framework of ancient geography.[3] In fact the central questions that Renaissance readers asked of these texts often centered on their geographical rather than literary or historical significance, to a degree that we now find surprising.

We can isolate at least three major ways in which ancient literature was reconciled to the newly expanded *mappa mundi* of the Renaissance. One school of thought held that the ancients had known nothing of the New World; the Americas constituted *regiones extra Ptolemaeum*, as Glareanus identified them in his *Geographia* of 1527, or a *quarta pars orbis* wholly outside the three-part *oikoumenē* of antiquity.[4] In opposition to this view,

[2] It is these three, for example, that are cited by Lopez de Gómara as the prevalent theories advanced at the moment Columbus first returned from the New World; see the *Historia General de las Indias*, chap. 17. Of the three the Atlantis myth received by far the most attention, as described in the works cited in chap. 4 above (n. 8). For a survey of the uses of the Senecan text in the Renaissance see my "New World and *novos orbes*: Seneca in the Renaissance Debate over Ancient Knowledge of the Americas," forthcoming in vol. 1 of *The Classical Tradition in the Americas*, ed. Meyer Reinhold (due 1992). The pseudo-Aristotelian report of a Carthaginian discovery (*De mirab. auscult.*, chap. 84; cf. Diodorus Siculus 5.19–20) figured prominently in Oviedo's *Historia General y Natural de las Indias* (2.3), where it was used to support an elaborate Spanish claim to ownership of the New World.

[3] A detailed survey of these and other supposed antecedents of the discovery can be found in the first two volumes of Alexander von Humboldt's magnificent *Examen critique de la géographie du nouveau continent* (5 vols., Paris 1836–39); also Paul Gaffarel, *Etude sur les rapports de l'Amérique et de l'ancien continent avant Christophe Colomb* (Paris 1869). The Bible also provided fuel for the ancient-discovery debate, as indeed it still does today.

[4] For some prominent articulations of this view see Antonio de Herrera, *Historia General de los Hechos de los Castellanos*, Decade 1, chap. 1; Joseph de Acosta, *De Natura Novi Orbis* 1.11; Abraham Ortelius, *Theatrum Orbis Terra-*

however, stood the hypothesis that the New World had indeed been known to, or even visited by, ancient scientists and navigators.[5] Naturally these two opposing positions led to radically different readings of classical texts: Adherents of the first were obliged to invalidate all seeming evidence of ancient discoveries, and therefore treated texts like Plato's tale of Atlantis as out-and-out inventions; while those who sought support for the latter position looked to such material for confirmation of ancient knowledge of the New World. Often the same text could be made to serve either argument, as I have demonstrated elsewhere in the case of the second chorus of Seneca's *Medea*.[6]

A third major position on ancient geographic literature can be described as occupying a middle ground between these two. According to this last view the ancients had never glimpsed the Americas clearly, but had somehow imagined or guessed at their existence; texts like Seneca's *Medea* and Plato's tale of Atlantis should therefore be read as myths or as oracular prophecies, giving vague expression to truths which their authors had half-consciously perceived—*quasi per nebulam et caliginem*, "as if through a mist and fog," as one scholar expressed it.[7] This intermediate position, of course, presented a greater challenge and demanded more intellectual subtlety than the other two. If ancient texts could be said to contain a certain truth, but couched in distorted or mythicized form, then where exactly

---

rum fol. 6, s.v. "Novus Orbis"; Gian Battista Ramusio, *Delle Navigationi et Viaggi* fol. 3 *r.*

[5] The staunchest supporters of this position include the astronomer Johannes Kepler, as demonstrated in the notes to the *Somnium* and to the translation of the *De Facie*; see my article "Lucian and Kepler as Sources for Kepler's *Somnium*," *Classical and Modern Literature* 9 (1989): 97–108, esp. 103 and n. 13. Also Erasmus Schmid, "De America," appended to the end of the 1616 edition of his *Pindarou Periodos*.

[6] See my "New World and *novos orbes*," esp. pt. 3. Seneca's prediction of new worlds lying beyond *ultima Thule* was taken by some to point toward the North, rather than the West, suggesting that the philosopher had in fact been talking out of his hat.

[7] Perizonius on Strabo 7.3.6, as quoted by Tillinghast (above, n. 1) 22 n. 2. It was along these lines that the classical scholar Lipsius answered his own question, *Americam noruntne veteres: nosse non dicam proprie, sed scivisse* (*Physiologiae Stoicorum Libri Tres* [Antwerp 1604] 122).

was one to situate the boundary between truth and fiction? Might not even something as outlandish as Lucian's *True Histories* contain, as the seventeenth-century German astronomer Johannes Kepler believed it did, "some information concerning the nature of the entire cosmos"?[8] At the same time, how were the obviously fabulous elements of such texts to be understood—as true errors, or as deliberate mystifications added in for effect? And, perhaps most intriguingly, if there were *some* references in classical geography that had been borne out by the discovery of the Americas, might there not be *others* that pointed the way toward new worlds as yet undiscovered and unguessed at?

This spectrum of opinions over the factuality of ancient voyage accounts, it will be noted, parallels quite closely the Hellenistic *periplous* debates we examined in the previous chapter. There too we saw a polemical opposition between Alexandrian critics like Eratosthenes, who chose to see the *Odyssey* as a purely fictional *exōkeanismos*, and the "hardline" Stoics like Crates who tenaciously defended its veracity. Other critics like Strabo can be situated somewhere in the middle, in that they sought to explain away certain elements of the *Odyssey* as *muthoi* or *pseudea* even while upholding the overall factuality of the poem. In this as in other ways the critical climate of later antiquity was very much like that of the Renaissance; both eras wrestled with the problem that the oldest, and most highly revered, texts in the literary canon seemed out of line with the image of the world that had subsequently been brought to light. And, as we saw in later antiquity, so again in the Renaissance, this misalignment of text and world helped engender the first tentative attempts to articulate a poetics of fiction: Just as Eratosthenes had explained Homer's use of Ocean as *dia to eukatapseuston*, "because it was easy to lie about," so Renaissance critics like Tasso and Lopez Pinciano advised aspiring romancers to use distant geography to "cover" their inventions.[9]

[8] So expressed in note 2 to his *Somnium sive de astronomia lunari*; see the English translation by Edward Rosen, *Kepler's Somnium* (Madison, Wis. 1967) 30–32, and my "Sources of Kepler's *Somnium*" (above, n. 5).

[9] Lopez Pinciano, *Philosophia Antigua Poetica*, epistle 11; Tasso, *Del Poema*

In accordance with this strategy many of the most ambitious experiments in prose fiction in the sixteenth century, again as in the second century A.D., took the explorer's log as both model and point of departure. Thomas More's *Utopia*, to cite one prominent example, opens with a reference to the letters of Amerigo Vespucci, which are said to be "in everyone's hands" at the time of the book's composition. In the next moment we are introduced to a character portrayed in those letters: Raphael Hythlodaeus, allegedly one of the contingent of men which Vespucci had left in a coastal garrison in the course of a voyage to the Americas. The tale which Hythlodaeus goes on to tell, then, is constructed by More as an extension of Vespucci's narrative—as if the first reports returned from the New World, with their seemingly fantastical contents, had perforated the barrier between truth and fiction and opened up vast new possibilities for literature.[10] In fact the very title *Utopia*, as has long been recognized, promises to exploit these possibilities, situating itself midway between Greek *outopia* ("noplace") and *eutopia* ("good place").

Much the same analysis might be applied to the fourth and fifth books of Rabelais's Pantagrueline fictions, another fabulous voyage narrative which takes its impetus from New-World explorations—in this case those of Jacques Cartier, a contemporary and personal friend of the author.[11] The ship *Thalamège* which bears Rabelais's heroes toward Lanternland—a location,

Eroico 2.63. See William Nelson, "The Boundaries of Fiction in the Renaissance: A Treaty between Truth and Falsehood," *English Literary History* 16 (1969), esp. 54–55. Heliodorus's *Ethiopica* was often held up as a narrative model by Renaissance critics, since it had used exotic locations and distant travels to preserve credibility; see pt. 1 of Alban Forcione's *Cervantes, Aristotle, and the Persiles* (Princeton, N.J. 1970).

[10] See George B. Parks, "More's *Utopia* and Geography," *Journal of English and Germanic Philology* 37 (1938): 224–36.

[11] The relationship between Pantagruel's voyages and those of Cartier have been elaborated in great detail by Abel Lefranc, *Les Navigations de Pantagruel* (Paris 1905); and while Lefranc may sometimes carry these parallels too far, there can be no doubt as to their general validity. See also Arthur Tilley, "Rabelais and Geographic Discovery," in two parts: *Modern Language Review* 2 (1907): 316–26, and 3 (1908): 209–17.

we note, borrowed directly from Lucian's *True Histories*—gets underway from the same harbor as that used by Cartier's expeditions; and the pilot who steers the vessel, a shadowy figure named Jamet Brayer, has been identified by some critics with Cartier himself.[12] Not surprisingly, the *Thalamège*'s first port of call is made to evoke Cartier's discoveries, by the author's remark that it was an island "bigger than Canada"; though the name given to this new world, following a strategy borrowed from Thomas More, is *Medamothi* or "Nowhere."

Of course, the parallel I am here suggesting, between ancient and Renaissance appropriations of the explorer text as a model for pure prose fiction, must not be pressed too far; it may be objected, for example, that the Renaissance's foremost exploration of the possibilities of fictional prose, Cervantes' *Don Quixote*, reveals little awareness of either ancient or contemporary navigational texts. Yet in his other writings Cervantes too shows that he has read such texts and has thought deeply about their intermediate position between *historia* and *muthos*. In his little-known romance *Persiles and Sigismunda*, he allows his hero and heroine to crisscross the North Atlantic in search of one another, visiting, among other places, the mystical island of Thule. In fact the resemblances are so close between this novel and Antonius Diogenes' lost *Wonders beyond Thule* that it has been thought Cervantes may have seen, or heard about, Photius's summary of the earlier work.[13] However that may be, the two works are very much alike in their use of exotic *periplous*

[12] First suggested by Margry in *Les Navigations Françaises* (Paris 1866) 338–40; endorsed by LeFranc.

[13] E.g., by Thomas Hägg, *The Ancient Novel* (Berkeley and Los Angeles 1988) 203. I have developed the parallels further (though without claiming any direct connection between the two texts) in "Novels beyond Thule: Antonius Diogenes, Rabelais, Cervantes," forthcoming in the published proceedings of the International Conference on the Ancient Novel (ed. James Tatum; Baltimore, due 1993). For Cervantes' use of paradoxographic and pseudogeographic material in the *Persiles*, including the fictional *periplous* of the brothers Zeno, see the recent article by Diana de Armas Wilson, "Cervantes on Cannibals," in *Revista de Estudios Hispánicos* 22 (1988): 1–25. I am grateful to the author, and to Mary Gaylord and Alban Forcione, for their advice on matters connected with the *Persiles*.

material—borrowed in Diogenes' case from Pytheas and Antiphanes of Berga, in Cervantes' from Olaf Magnusson and the now-discredited voyage account of the brothers Zeno.

Perhaps the most illustrative example of the link between ancient discovery literature and Renaissance prose fiction, however, can be found in Bishop Hall's *Mundus Alter et Idem*, a Neolatin fabulous voyage published in England in 1605.[14] The tale begins with a dialogue in which various interlocutors debate the ancient-exploration question: Were Plato, Seneca, and other ancient sources really informed about the New World? After much discussion the conclusion is reached that Seneca's *novos orbes* did not in fact refer to the Americas, but to some other place lying even farther off; the company then resolves to set sail for this new horizon, and thus begins the journey which occupies the rest of the book. As we saw earlier in the case of Plutarch's *On the Face of the Moon*, fiction here steps into the vacuum created when a "mappable" text suddenly loses its cartographic coordinates. The irresolution of the opening debate, with its shifting perspectives on the geographic content of ancient literature and the problems of interpretation, serves to propel the voyage which follows; the ambiguous status of the ancient explorer text gives sanction to the Renaissance writer attempting even more far-reaching flights of fancy.

In such instances, then, did Renaissance prose fiction take its impetus from explorer's logs, in much the same way as Greek prose fiction had done before; only now, that impetus had become much stronger, to the degree that those logs were growing more numerous and more impressive than at any period of antiquity. Indeed, the impression one gets from reading the sixteenth century's responses to New-World voyage accounts is of an age in which, due to the magnitude of the new discoveries, the very boundary between fact and fiction had very nearly collapsed. One sentiment in particular echoes over and over throughout this era: "The golden age, a fiction of the Old

[14] Text and translation by John Miller Wands, *Another World and Yet the Same* (Yale Studies in English 190, New Haven 1981).

World, is realized in the New."[15] Whether or not antiquity had actually known of the Americas, it could hardly be denied that the most exotic and idyllic of ancient distant-world myths had there been translated into reality. Never before had ancient geography seemed so potent, nor had fictional literature seemed so pregnant with truth.

[15] Quoted by Harry Levin in *The Myth of the Golden Age in the Renaissance* (Oxford and N.Y. 1969) 68. Levin adds a similar comment of his own at p. 93: "Much of the Renaissance is the record of truths outdistancing fictions."

Index

Abii, 53
Achilles, 52
Aelius Aristides, 13n, 194, 200–202
Aeschylus, 25, 30, 60
Aesop, 77
Africa, 82–83; circumnavigation of, 16, 35, 122, 132n; explored by Hanno, 19–20; wonders of, 88–90, 91–92. *See also* Ethiopians
Agathemerus, 14n, 42
Agricola, 148
Alcaeus, 63–64
Alcinous, 183–84. *See also* Phaeacian tales
Alexander: and Augustus, 138; contemplates crossing Ocean, 25–26, 137–39; as explorer, 112, 151–52, 166; halts at Hyphasis, 100–101, 109–10; and Heracles, 110, 115, 121, 138; Indian expedition of, 83, 93–94; and Julius Caesar, 154–55; paired with Aristotle, 107–9, 112–15, 139–40
Alexander Romance, 108, 116
Alexander's Letter to Aristotle, 112–16, 139
Alexandrian criticism, 185–88, 218
allegorization, 68–69, 119, 177–79
Americas, 94, 161, 215–18
Anacharsis, 74–76, 81. *See also* Scythians
Anaximander, 27; and *apeiron*, 11, 22–23; map of, 10, 34
animal fable, 77, 78
Antichthones, 131–32, 149–50. *See also* Antipodes; other worlds
Antiphanes of Berga, 196–97, 211
Antipodes, 129–31, 142; inaccessibility of, 131–33; Roman designs on, 133–39. *See also* Antichthones; other worlds
Antonius Diogenes, 202, 204–11, 220–21
"ants" in Indian desert, 70, 97–98, 101
apeiron or Boundless, 10–12, 16, 22–24, 171
Apollo, 60, 62–64
Apollodorus of Athens, 187–88
Apollonius of Tyana, 116–19
Apollonius Rhodius, 31, 194–96
Arabians, 70
Aratus, 5
Archilochus, 77
Arimaspeia. *See* Aristeas of Proconnesus
Arimaspians, 40, 66, 68, 69–74, 78
Aristarchus, 186–87, 189
Aristeas of Proconnesus, 66, 71–74, 85
Aristophanes, 4
Aristotle: on antipodal continent, 129; on early maps, 14n, 27–28, 42; on fiction, 173; in Indian wonders tradition, 84, 88, 107–8; on Ocean, 178; paired with Alexander, 107–9, 112–15, 139–40, 151
[Aristotle], 126–27, 139, 215
Arrian, 31, 103
Artemon, 26
Asia, extent of, 83. *See also* India; Indian wonders
Atlantic: as "outer sea," 32; as Roman objective, 151–71, 213. *See also* Ocean
Atlantic Islands, 157n, 162n. *See also* Thule

Atlas, 160–61
Augustus, 103, 136–37, 158–59
Aulus Gellius, 103–4
Avienus, 21, 31

barbarians, idealization of, 48n, 50–52, 60–61, 70, 72, 79–81. *See also* golden age; primitivism
Bergren, Ann, 12
Biondi, Giuseppe, 168–69
Black Sea, 16n
Boeo, 61
boundary. See *apeiron; peirar*
Britain, 136, 140–41, 148, 156, 202. *See also* Thule

Callisthenes, 151
[Callisthenes]. See *Alexander Romance*
Calypso, 187
Cambyses, 54–59, 153
cartography. *See* maps
Caspian Sea, 34, 42, 98
catalogue, 91–93, 103, 104–6. *See also* Indian wonders
Caucasus, 98
Celts, 144
Cervantes, Miguel de, 220–21
Charybdis, 184, 191
China, 112
Cicero, 3–4, 130, 134–35, 139–40, 216
Cimbri, 144
Claudius, 141
Cleomedes, 131
climate, 64–66. *See also* zones
Craterus, 109–10
Crates: on equatorial Ocean, 129–30, 180; on four-part earth, 130–31; as Homeric critic, 179–80, 188–89, 218; on shield of Achilles, 14–15. *See also* literary criticism; Stoics
credulity of ancient geographers, 87, 93, 95, 100–104
Ctesias, 27, 146, 212; Dog-heads described by, 78–80; *Indika* of, 86–88, 92, 117, 120. *See also* Indian wonders
Cynicism, 76, 77–78, 81

Deimachus, 96
Delos, 61–62
Delphi, 61–63
Democritus, 27, 42
Dicaearchus, 30–31, 42. *See also* maps
Diodorus Siculus, 90, 149
Diogenes Laertius, 74
Dionysius Periegetes, 5, 29n, 31
distance as literary strategy, 98, 173–74, 218. *See also* literary criticism
Dog-heads, 77–81, 87. *See also* Ctesias, Indian wonders
Donatus, 160
dragons, 118–19
Drusus, 147–48

Egypt, 16, 55–56, 59, 78, 90, 92, 151–52. *See also* Nile
empiricism, 32–33, 184; in Herodotus, 35–38, 172–73; in Strabo and Pliny, 132, 213
Ephorus, 45, 72, 144
epic poetry, 10, 21, 24; geography in, 33, 34
Eratosthenes, 42–43, 128–29, 135; encyclopedism of, 31; literary criticism of, 173, 185–87, 192, 197–98, 212, 218
eschatiai or outermost parts, 38–41, 40n
Ethiopians, 30, 191; in Herodotus, 54–60, 75; in Homer, 49–54; in Pliny, 106. *See also* Africa
ethnocentrism, 46–48, 54–55
Eudoxus of Cnidus, 30–31, 150, 153
Eudoxus of Cyzicus, 105, 198
Euhemerus, 48, 197–98

Euripides, 168
Europe, boundaries of, 34, 40
Euthymenes, 10, 200–201
exōkeanismos, 195, 206, 210–11, 218; discussed by Alexandrian critics, 187–88, 190; by Stoics, 192. *See also* literary criticism
expansion of known world, 32–33, 41, 83–84, 99; under Romans, 134–35. *See also* empiricism

fictional invention, 172; in Homer, 191–93; in Indian wonders, 95–96. *See also* literary criticism
Fish-eaters, 55–58
Florus, 141
Fortunate Isles, 157. *See also* Isles of the Blessed

Geminus, 14n, 42
geography: early sources of, 9–11; as literary tradition, 3–6; and myth, 9, 18–19, 82, 124–27; origin of word, 9–10; survival of, 20, 41, 94n, 161–62, 215–16; of whole earth, 26–28, 30–31, 41–44, 121–22, 170. *See also* Herodotus; literary criticism; Pliny the Elder; Strabo
Germanicus, 139, 142–45
Glycon, 26
golden age, 50–51, 60–61, 74, 125–27, 162–64, 167, 171, 271–72. *See also* noble savage; primitivism
gorillas, 20
griffins, 69–70, 118

Hall, Bishop, 221
Hanno, 19–20, 122
Hecataeus, 5, 10, 172; map of, 34; *Periodos Gēs* of, 27–29
Hellanicus, 95–96
Hemikunes, 30, 78. *See also* Dog-heads
Heracles, 62–63; as primitive, 68–69; as voyager, 18
Heraclitus, 24
Heraclitus, author of *Homeric Allegories*, 179
Herodorus, 133
Herodotus, 5, 16–17, 69–70, 71, 77, 78, 84; on Africa, 91–92; on Anacharsis, 76; on *eschatiai*, 38–41; on Ethiopians, 54–60, 75; and mythic geography, 33–38, 172–73, 176, 202; as mythographer, 95–96. *See also* empiricism; geography; literary criticism
Hesiod, 10, 24; primitivism in, 51, 65, 68. *See also* epic poetry
[Hesiod], author of *Periodos Gēs*, 27, 29–30, 85, 128; author of *Shield*, 13–14
Hesperides, 69
Himilco, 20–22, 148
Hipparchus, 43, 133, 150
Hippocrates, 65
Homer, 10, 15, 46, 77; Ethiopians in, 49–54, 130; *Iliad* of, 13, 14, 23, 25n, 26, 72, 199; Ocean in, 179–83, 201–2; *Odyssey* of, 12, 57, 65, 74, 143; Phaeacian tales of, treated by ancient critics, 173, 175, 183, 192–94, 211. *See also* epic poetry; literary criticism
Homeric hymns, 13, 63
Horace, 5, 162–64
hybrid wildlife, 89, 90–91, 115. *See also* Indian wonders
Hyperboreans, 30, 60–67
hypertrophic landscapes, 88, 93, 105
Hyphasis River, as boundary of East, 100–102, 109–10, 121, 137

Iamblichus, 206
Iambulus, 48, 212
Ichthyophagoi. *See* Fish-eaters
India, 36; exploration of, 83–84

Indian wonders, 82–83, 85, 147; in Alexander literature, 110, 115–20; described by Ctesias, 87–91; described by Pliny, 105–8; described by Strabo, 95–103. *See also* Ctesias; Dog-heads
Indians, 70, 78
Indus River, 152
Ionia, 64, 77
Isle of Cronus, 204
Isles of the Blessed, 15n, 65, 156. *See also* Fortunate Isles
Issedones, 66, 71–73

journey, 28, 29n
Julius Caesar, 135–36, 141, 152–55, 165

Kunokephaloi. *See* Dog-heads

Libya. *See* Africa; Ethiopians
literary criticism: in Alexandrians, 185–88, 192, 218; in Aristotle, 178–79; and explorer's log, 172–75, 196–204, 216–18; in Herodotus, 172–73, 176, 184; and Homer, 176–82, 184–96, 200–204, 213; in Longinus, 181–83, 193–94; and Ocean, 176–83; in Plato, 177–78; in Stoics, 179–80, 184–85, 188–93, 218
longevity of foreign races, 54, 80
[Longinus], 72–73, 181–83
Lopez Pinciano, 218
Lucan, 138, 152–55
Lucian, 202, 208–14, 218, 220

Macrobius, 130
Manilius, 5, 137n, 165, 167
maps, 9, 14, 82; and *periodoi*, 27–28; revisions of, 33–36, 41–44. *See also* Aristotle; Dicaearchus; Geminus; Herodotus
martichora, 87, 119
Maximus of Tyre, 152
Medea, 163–64, 168–71
Megasthenes, 96, 98, 101–3, 105, 193
Mela, 29n, 122, 133, 150–51
Menelaus, 189
Meropis, 67
Messalla Corvinus, 136
monstrosities, 85, 116, 146. *See also* Indian wonders
moon, 209, 214
More, Thomas, 6, 48, 219
Mountains of the Moon, 151
muthos, 10, 95, 174, 188
Mysians, 53

nature vs. culture, 57–58, 69–70, 75–76, 79–80. *See also* golden age; primitivism
Nearchus, 96–97
Nero, 155–56
Neuri, 36
Nicolet, Claude, 6–7, 123
Nile, 83, 149–56, 200. *See also* Egypt
noble savage, 48, 70, 75–76. *See also* golden age; primitivism
North Sea, 141–49

Ocean: antiquity of, 23–25, 24n; as boundary of earth, 12–17; etymology of, 13n; as foe, 144–45; as marvel, 176; monsters in, 21, 24–26, 143; as origin of cosmos, 23, 177–79; rejection of by Herodotus, 33–35; terrors of, 16–17, 20–26; torpidity of, 21–23, 148. *See also* geography; Homer; literary criticism
Odysseus, 74, 142, 183–84. *See also* Homer
Odyssey. *See* Homer
Ogygia, 203–4
oikoumenē, meaning of, 37–38, 130n. *See also* other worlds
Olympus, 50, 65

Onesicritus, 96, 100, 103
Orphic hymns, 23, 177
other worlds, 15, 36, 121, 123–24, 129–33, 141–42, 150–51; conquest of, 133–34, 140–41, 148–49. *See also* Alexander; Antipodes; Atlantis; Thule
Ovid, 121–22

paradoxography, 92, 205
Parthia, 99
Patrocles, 42, 97–99, 103
Pausanias, 61
Peary, Robert, 175
Pedo, 142–44
peirar or boundary, 10–15, 36, 40n. See also *apeiron*
periēgēsis or guided tour, 29
periodos gēs, as literary genre, 29–31; meaning of, 26–29
Periplous. *See* Hanno
Persians, 33, 54–59
Phaeacian tales. *See* Homer; literary criticism
Pherecydes, 25
Philostratus, 116–20
Phoenicians, 18–22, 126–27. *See also* Hanno; Himilco
phoenix, 119
Photius, 86, 88, 205, 212
Pillars of Heracles, 17–19, 147–49, 213
Pindar, 195; on Hyperboreans, 63; on Pillars of Heracles, 17–18, 149
Plato, 81, 118, 200, 221; Atlantis myth of, 124–28, 199, 215, 217; Ocean in, 24, 177–78
Pliny the Elder, 4, 156; Aristotle in, 107–8; on Indian wonders, 82, 104–8; on seafaring, 164; on Taprobane, 133
Plutarch, 77, 203–4, 211, 216, 221
Plution, 26
Polybius, 22, 43, 189–90, 193, 197
Pompey, 135–36
pontos or sea, 16n, 21
Poseidonius, 198–99
primitivism, 23n, 47, 59, 67–69, 74. *See also* golden age; nature vs. culture; noble savage
Prometheus, 25, 98
psuchagōgia or entertainment, 186, 192, 212. *See also* literary criticism
Ptolemy, 5, 43–44, 151
Pygmies, 96–97, 102
Pythagoras, 207
Pythagoreans, 10n, 124, 131
Pytheas, 22, 148, 197–98, 207. *See also* Thule

Quintilian, 138, 181
Quintus Curtius, 121, 144

Rabelais, François, 6, 219–20
Ramayana, 87
Renaissance geography, 6, 161–62, 215–22. *See also* geography, survival of
Rhetorica ad Herennium, 137
Rhine River, 147
Rhipaean Mountains, 65
Rohde, Erwin, 175
Rosenmeyer, Thomas, 168

Sataspes, 16
satire, 48–49, 59, 67, 76–77, 81
satyrs, 105
scientific approaches to geography, 91, 107–8. *See also* empiricism
Scylax, 10, 35, 84–85, 94
[Scylax], 31, 84n
Scylla, 190
Scymnus, 31
Scythians, 30, 36, 45–47, 66. *See also* Anacharsis
seafaring, 16n; dread of, 16–17; as metaphor for narrative, 196; and moral decline, 73–75, 163–67. *See also* Ocean

sea monsters, 21, 24, 110, 143. *See also* Ocean
Seneca the Elder, 25–26, 138–39
Seneca the Younger, 5, 138–39, 206, 215, 217; on Nile exploration, 155–56; on seafaring, 165–71
Servius, 160
Sesostris, 153
Shadow-feet or *Skiapodes*, 85–86, 119
Simmias, 31, 64n
Socrates, 127–28, 178. *See also* Plato
Stoics, 14, 168–70, 179, 185. *See also* Crates; literary criticism; Strabo
Strabo, 122, 144, 197; as critic of Greek culture, 46–47; encyclopedism of, 30; on Homer, 190–93; on Indian wonders, 95–103, 173; as source for early geography, 5, 28–29, 43; on veracity of explorer's logs, 198–200. *See also* geography; literary criticism
symmetry of world structure, 34, 60–61, 66, 129–31, 140, 150

Table of the Sun, 56, 58–59. *See also* Ethiopians
Tacitus, 4, 141–42, 144–46
Taprobane, 133. *See also* India; other worlds
Tasso, Torquato, 218
Tethys, 170
Theopompus, 67, 95–96, 216
Thrace, 36, 53
Thule, 148, 157–58; in Antonius Diogenes, 206–7, 209–11; in Vergil, 158–60. *See also* other worlds
Tiamat, 24n
Tiberianus, 133
[Tibullus], 136
Tin Islands, 40
Tiphys, 169–71. *See also* seafaring

Vergil: *Aeneid* of, 136, 159, 161; *Eclogues* of, 141, 160; *Georgics* of, 4, 158–59; in Renaissance, 161, 216; Thule in, 158–60, 206
Vernant, Jean-Pierre, 14–15
Vespucci, Amerigo, 219

wine, 57–58

Xenocles, 97–98
Xenophanes, 12n, 71
Xenophon, 68

Zeno, 179–80. *See also* Stoics
Zeus, 24, 51, 53
zones, 128–30, 134–35. *See also* climate

CPSIA information can be obtained at www.ICGtesting.com
Printed in the USA
BVOW05s2101270514

354524BV00001B/113/P

9 780691 037882